Popular Music and Automobiles

Popular Music and Automobiles

Edited by Mark Duffett and Beate Peter

BLOOMSBURY ACADEMIC
NEW YORK • LONDON • OXFORD • NEW DELHI • SYDNEY

BLOOMSBURY ACADEMIC
Bloomsbury Publishing Inc
1385 Broadway, New York, NY 10018, USA
50 Bedford Square, London, WC1B 3DP, UK
29 Earlsfort Terrace, Dublin 2, Ireland

BLOOMSBURY, BLOOMSBURY ACADEMIC and the Diana logo
are trademarks of Bloomsbury Publishing Plc

First published in the United States of America 2020
Paperback edition first published 2021

Volume Editors' Part of the Work © Mark Duffett and Beate Peter, 2020

Each chapter © of Contributor

For legal purposes the Acknowledgments on p. ix constitute
an extension of this copyright page.

Cover design: Louise Dugdale
Cover image © Johner Images / Getty images

All rights reserved. No part of this publication may be reproduced or
transmitted in any form or by any means, electronic or mechanical,
including photocopying, recording, or any information storage or retrieval
system, without prior permission in writing from the publishers.

Bloomsbury Publishing Inc does not have any control over, or responsibility for,
any third-party websites referred to or in this book. All internet addresses given
in this book were correct at the time of going to press. The author and publisher
regret any inconvenience caused if addresses have changed or sites have
ceased to exist, but can accept no responsibility for any such changes.

Library of Congress Cataloging-in-Publication Data
Names: Duffett, Mark, editor. | Peter, Beate, editor.
Title: Popular music and automobiles / edited by Mark Duffett and Beate Peter.
Description: New York: Bloomsbury Academic, 2020. |
Includes bibliographical references and index. |
Summary: "Explores the multi-facetted relationship between automobiles
and popular music through both broad analysis and specific
case studies."–Provided by publisher.
Identifiers: LCCN 2019027517 (print) | LCCN 2019027518 (ebook) |
ISBN 9781501352300 (hardback) | ISBN 9781501352317 (epub) |
ISBN 9781501352324 (pdf)
Subjects: LCSH: Popular music–History and criticism. | Automobiles–Songs and
music–History and criticism. | Automobiles–Social aspects.
Classification: LCC ML3470.P667 2020 (print) | LCC ML3470 (ebook) |
DDC 781.6409/04–dc23
LC record available at https://lccn.loc.gov/2019027517
LC ebook record available at https://lccn.loc.gov/2019027518

ISBN: HB: 978-1-5013-5230-0
PB: 978-1-5013-8464-6
ePDF: 978-1-5013-5232-4
eBook: 978-1-5013-5231-7

Typeset by Deanta Global Publishing Services, Chennai, India

To find out more about our authors and books visit
www.bloomsbury.com and sign up for our newsletters.

Contents

Notes on contributors	vi
Acknowledgements	ix
Introduction *Mark Duffett*	1
1 Rock 'n' roll: Cars, convergence, and culture *Tim Wall and Nick Webber*	15
2 "She's my little Deuce Coupe": Freudian transformation in the car songs of the Beach Boys *Georgina Gregory*	33
3 Music is the vehicle: Queen's "Don't Stop Me Now," *Top Gear*, and the driving anthem *Roddy Hawkins*	51
4 The passenger? Gender, cars, mobility, and dance music *Katie Milestone*	71
5 Rave journeys: Intimacy, liminality, and the changing notion of home *Beate Peter*	83
6 Driving on the A470: Cars and roads in Welsh-language popular music *Craig Owen Jones*	97
7 "Ich will Spaß, ich geb Gas": German pop between fun and subversion *Barbara Hornberger*	111
8 *Las chivas*: Fiesta in motion *Santiago Niño Morales*	119
9 Listening to music in cars while black: Popular music, automobility, and the murder of Jordan Davis *Amanda Nell Edgar*	137
10 Crash! Music press coverage of performers in automobile accidents *Mark Duffett*	155
Notes	169
References	172
Index	194

Notes on contributors

Dr Mark Duffett is an Oxford-educated scholar and Gales-listed author who currently works as Reader in Media and Cultural Studies at the University of Chester, where he has published widely on popular music, Elvis Presley, and music fandom. Dr Duffett is known for his monographs *Understanding Fandom* (Bloomsbury, 2013) and *Counting Down Elvis* (Rowman & Littlefield, 2018). He has also edited several books and journal special editions, written many articles and book chapters, and been an invited or keynote speaker at international conferences in Moscow, Rotterdam, London, Cardiff, and Seinäjoki (Finland). Dr Duffett is currently working on an edited volume, *Rethinking Elvis* (Oxford University Press, forthcoming).

Dr Amanda Nell Edgar is Assistant Professor in the Department of Communication at the University of Memphis. She studies the politics of sound in popular culture. Dr Edgar is co-author of *The Struggle over Black Lives Matter and All Lives Matter* (Lexington Books, 2018) and the author of *Culturally Speaking: The Rhetoric of Voice and Identity in a Mediated Culture* (Ohio State UP, forthcoming). She has also authored numerous articles in journals including *Communication, Culture & Critique*, *Critical Studies in Media Communication*, and *Quarterly Journal of Speech*.

Dr Roddy Hawkins is a musicologist and lecturer in music at the University of Manchester, where he teaches courses in contemporary music studies and popular music. His current research is focused around the production and consumption of avant-garde music in Britain during the 1980s, part of wider interests in performance, reception, and the cultural politics of music in Britain since the 1970s. Central to all his research is the contested, gendered, and constructed nature of marginality as it relates to the categories of sound and listening.

Georgina Gregory teaches media and film studies as Senior Lecturer in the School of Humanities and Social Sciences at the University of Central Lancashire. She has given international conference papers and published on a range of subjects, including fashion and popular music, tribute entertainment, boy bands and masculinity in pop, grieving and loss, gender and performance, and popular music and automobile culture. She is also known for her book *Send in the Clones: A Cultural Study of the Tribute Band* (Equinox, 2011).

Professor Barbara Hornberger read cultural studies and aesthetic and applied arts at the University of Hildesheim, Germany, and specialized on popular culture, especially popular music. Her PhD was an exploration of the topic 'New German Wave' (Neue Deutsche Welle). Currently, she is Professor of Popular Music Didactics at the University of Applied Sciences, Osnabrück. Her research focuses on popular culture and music, on popular culture history, and on popular music and education.

Dr Craig Owen Jones is Honorary Research Associate of the School of Music and Media at Bangor University. He has published over two dozen articles on aspects of cultural and social history, including popular music, television, and sports. He is currently co-writing a book called *Regenerating Doctor Who: Fan Reception and Evaluation* (Bloomsbury, forthcoming) with Paul Booth of DePaul University, Chicago.

Dr Katie Milestone is Senior Lecturer in Sociology at the Manchester Metropolitan University. Her research interests are focused on gender and popular culture, creative industries, place and identity, and popular music. She began her research career at the Manchester Institute for Popular Culture where she undertook a PhD on music and the regeneration of Manchester's Northern Quarter. Dr Milestone is currently completing a second edition of *Gender and Popular Culture* (Polity Press, 2012), a book jointly authored with Anneke Meyer. She has published a number of works on popular music on themes including 'Madchester,' northern soul, 'northernness,' and pop music culture in mid-1960s Manchester.

Dr Santiago Niño Morales has a PhD in music from the University of Edinburgh. He was former Dean of the Arts Faculty at Universidad Distrital Francisco José de Caldas (Colombia), plus former director of the Master in Art Studies, and research coordinator of the Music Program, among other academic roles at the same institution. Dr Morales holds a master's degree in Cultural Management from the Universitat de Barcelona (Spain) and pursued postgraduate studies in Arts and Cultural Management at the Universidad del Rosario (Colombia). He is a member of the research group CuestionArte and has written books, articles, book chapters, and papers in the field of cultural policy, cultural economics, and the sociocultural aspects of music. He has presented lectures at universities and institutions in Colombia, Spain, England, Italy, Mexico, Brazil, Cuba, Slovenia, and the United States. Dr Morales is a member of the Popular Culture Association (PCA), the American Culture Association (ACA), the International Association for the Study of Popular Music (IASPM), and the founder member of the Colombian Association of Researchers in Music Psychology and Music Education (PSICMUSE).

Dr Beate Peter currently teaches at Manchester Metropolitan University and has been researching club culture on and off the dance floor for more than twenty years. For the past five years, Beate has focused on a history of electronic music in Greater Manchester called *The Lapsed Clubber Project*. She engaged the original raving community through exhibitions, public events, workshops, discussion panels, and the Lapsed Clubber Audio Map—an open source live archive—to which lapsed (and so much lapsed) clubbers can contribute by leaving audio memories (https://www.mdmarchive.co.uk/map/the-lapsed-clubber-audio-map). Her contribution in this edition is the result of interviews for the Lapsed Clubber Project.

Professor Tim Wall works at the Birmingham Centre for Media and Cultural Studies at Birmingham City University, where he is Professor of Radio and Popular Music Studies. He researches the production and consumption cultures around radio and popular music. Professor Wall is author of *Studying Popular Music Culture* (Sage, 2003/2013) and co-editor, with Sarah Raine and Nicola Smith, of *The Northern Soul Scene* (Equinox, 2019). His publications include articles on online music radio, the transistor radio, personal music listening, popular music on television, jazz collectives, jazz on radio, *The X Factor*, and radio sound. He is currently writing a history of jazz on BBC radio from 1922 to 1972 and co-editing *Rethinking Miles Davis*.

Dr Nick Webber is Associate Professor in Media at Birmingham Centre for Media and Cultural Studies, Birmingham City University. His research focuses on cultural history, historiography, and identity, with particular attention to games of all kinds. Dr Webber's current projects explore public history in virtual worlds, the national cultural dimensions of video games, and commemorative practices around the First World War.

Acknowledgements

This book would not exist if we had not held a one-day symposium on popular music and automobile culture at the University of Chester in June 2012. We would like to thank staff in the Faculty of Arts and Media for their assistance at that event. The same goes for all participants, especially the speakers, and for other contributors who have come on board since then.

There are also specific acknowledgements for particular chapters:

Beate Peter's chapter was made possible by the Heritage Lottery Fund (OH-16-02562), which funded the project upon which it is based.

Craig Owen Jones would like to thank both Dafydd Iwan of Recordiau Sain and his doctoral student Deian ap Rhisiart for their kindness in permitting reproduction of the images in his chapter. He would also like to thank Emyr Williams, who runs the publishing arm of Ankst, for permission to use the lyrics from "Mynwent" and "Cân I Gymru" by Datblygu.

We would like to thank Kerstin Bueschges for translating a version of Professor Barbara Hornberger's chapter from its original German.

In relation to his chapter, Santiago Niño Morales would like to thank several people for their dialogues and inspiring ideas: Professor Skip McGoun (from Bucknell University), Professor Gloria Patricia Zapata Restrepo (Universidad Juan N. Corpas), and the documentary producer and filmmaker Juan Mario Rubiano Durán. Thanks also to Juan Mario Rubiano Durán for the photographs that accompany the chapter.

Mark Duffett would like to dedicate his part of this project to his father, whose fascination with car design has taken them to motor shows and car museums.

Finally, as editors, we would like to thank the staff at Bloomsbury for their considerable patience and faith in this project.

Introduction

Mark Duffett

For anyone who has seen it, the moment in the heavy metal comedy *Wayne's World* (Spheeris, 1992) is not hard to recall. Rock fan Wayne Campbell, played by Mike Myers, says, "I think we'll go with a little 'Bohemian Rhapsody,' gentlemen." He loads a tape into the cassette player of his friend Garth's car. The two enthusiastically sing in operatic style while two more buddies add backing. Everyone rocks to the music as they cruise the streets of Aurora, Illinois. Wayne and Garth's friendship is reflected in the way that they sit together, grin from ear to ear, and sing along in harmony. Their sociability is not just signified through a shared admiration for Wayne's choice of song, or by their mutual karaoke prowess. The fact that we see a choir of singing heads, a bit like Queen in the "Bohemian Rhapsody" video, only adds to the moment's mirth. Any recognition of communal emotion is enhanced by the fact that the scene is encapsulated within a motor vehicle. Wayne and Garth are not just moving in their car. They are enjoying an experience that connects their love of Queen to the pleasure of riding in Garth's light blue 1976 AMC Pacer Burton, a model made more individual by its mismatched wheels and tacky 'go-faster' stripes. The head bangers' geographic and musical journey forms a unified experience. It signifies their adolescent masculinities. They understand that the two spheres, cars and music, are the connected ways of traversing the world.

With its light-hearted communality, the *Wayne's World* ritual seems strangely familiar—not just because it has been regularly resurrected by comedian James Corden with different music celebrities for the 'carpool karaoke' segment of his version of the CBS series, *The Late Late Show*. One way or another, part of us is, somehow, a bit like Wayne and Garth. We live, and move, in cars. We drive, we ride, we listen, we sing. We participate in popular music. The head bangers' experience reminds us that we understand motor vehicles as intimate spaces. It demonstrates how motor cars and commercial music have become closely associated as *symbiotic commodities*.

This volume has its origins in an international symposium called *Popular Music and Automobile Culture*, organized at the University of Chester in June 2012 with the help of my co-editor, Dr Beate Peter. In what follows, most chapters are contributions from delegates who attended that event. We argued in our call for papers that automobiles and popular music have long been intertwined. It almost goes without saying that the match is widely understood as a natural one, even though it remains relatively unexamined by researchers. In 2001 Michael Berger wrote:

> Aside from articles in periodicals there is very little of the automobile's influence on and portrayal in music. There is no book length, scholarly treatment of the subject. In fact, only three volumes devote any attention to it, and one of those is a reference work. . . . This paucity of material is somewhat surprising given the long association between motoring and musical composition. (p. 220)

More scholarship has emerged since Berger's reference guide was published. With some notable exceptions, much of it has, however, been piecemeal. One might ask, then: Why should we put music and automobiles together? Is it just a vague theme—little more than a kind of common sense connection?

Not only has popular music formed a soundtrack to the age of the automobile; its driving beat has constantly provided a playlist that *reflects* the era of the combustion engine. As Widmer (2002) suggests, cars have long exerted a hypnotic hold on the imaginations of commercial songwriters. Not only do people love to sing about motor vehicles; when we look at their efforts in context, they also form stages in a regular movement between consumerism and customization, margins and mainstream. In 1941, for example, Memphis Minnie's "Me and My Chauffer Blues" reflected African American aspirations. "Rocket 88" spoke of the pleasures of using a shiny new Oldsmobile as a means to secure bragging rights in games of courtship. Gene Vincent starred in the juvenile delinquency flick *Hot Rod Gang* (Landers, 1958). The Beach Boys' 1963 "Little Deuce Coup" expressed an owner's affectionate relationship with his reliable and trusted vehicle. Who, too, could forget Rose Royce's later hit "Car Wash"? In the 1970s, "Chevrolet" by ZZ Top and "Low Rider" by War offered different, but equally cinematic, perspectives on the experience of driving. In complete contrast, in 1978 and 1979, "Warm Leatherette" by the Normal and "Cars" by Gary Numan imagined futuristic worlds in which motor vehicles reflected human alienation. In the 1990s, hip-hop took over the steering wheel with songs like "Two Dope Boyz (in a Cadillac)" by Outkast and "Let Me Ride" by Dr Dre. In the early

YouTube era, South African rap-ravers Die Antwoord flaunted their 'Zef style': a self-conscious tackiness centred on the idea of driving the Ford Zephyr. Die Antwoord formed its own label in 2011 called Zef Recordz. These are just a few flashpoints in the ongoing connection between popular music and automobiles, a cultural intersection that has frequent and regular traffic.

For the rest of this introduction, I will outline eight dimensions of a relationship between commercial sounds and motor transport.

My first point is that as parallel commodities, cars and popular music became instrumental in *catalysing America's shift into an era of high modernity*. It is just not the case that cars were in one cultural place and music in another. They were, instead, two elements that were more closely connected when the United States underwent a monumental process of social transformation. Rock 'n' roll, for instance, indicated changing times, but not only as an expression of sexual liberation or generational rebellion. The music was practised as part of what was literally a change of landscape designed to promote the increased use of automotive transport. It was hardly surprising, therefore, that the first episode of BBC4's recent three-part documentary *Rock 'n' roll America* (O'Casey, 2015) began not with Elvis but with a newsreel about Levittown, New Jersey: "a city that was completely planned before the first house was built." The federal government secured America's economic boom, in part, by guaranteeing mortgages and passing the 1956 Interstate Highway Act. A series of new residential communities reflected collective settlement of Americans in neatly regimented single-family homes. Between 1945 and 1960, rapidly fabricated suburbs attracted 30 million inhabitants. In this new environment, mass consumption began to blur hierarchies established in the workplace and contributed to new expressions of social identity (Gartman, 1994, p. 139).

Motor vehicles became the key mode of transport used to navigate miles of neatly kept streets and move to and from the workplace, but they were not simply a means of transportation. Car manufacturing and popular music were inspired by the shared practice of motoring—commuting, cruising, or escaping. As car sales increased, styling came to the forefront of the automobile industry, to the extent that by the middle of the 1950s the most popular product lines were updated every two years. Under the creative leadership of Harley Earl, General Motors opened at $125 million Technical Centre in Michigan (Gartman, 1994, p. 148). Cars became desired as spaces for living in—dream machines. They developed more powerful engines and sleek forms with chromium, fins, and fenders. Motor vehicles began morphing into space rockets. Aided and abetted by portable and in-car transistor radio technology, 1950s drivers enjoyed popular music as their chosen soundtrack (see Wall and Webber in this volume). It was the sonic supplement for a widely shared experience.

Secondly, musical attention to car travel has *reflected upon the landscape*. From highways to suburbs, the use of automobiles brought whole new localities into being. Popular music often accompanied the experience of surveying the world of 'carchitecture.' Such was the link between contemporary music and cars that the emergent mid-century freeways hosted what became known as 'doo-wop' architecture. Referencing dual determinants from the same taste category—a music genre and automotive geography—'doo-wop' locates a style characterized by motels, highways, gas stations, diners, drive-ins, and miles of unhindered freeway. Such places have now become monuments reflecting not only *how* the mass adoption of automobiles reshaped physical infrastructure and geography, but how far they transformed the experience of living in the modern, Western world (see Foster, 2003). Although 'doo-wop' now looks as kitsch as Bakelite, it remains in need of heritage preservation as a style that defined a playful era of modernity. Driving has its own, distinctly modern rhythm: passing crossroads, waiting at crossings, taking the fast lane, stuck in a jam. Car travel makes vistas of the city visible both by day and at night. Popular music explores that territory.

Thirdly, in the 1950s cars were, more so than ever before, sold and used not simply as transportation tools or means to an end. Instead they became *branded*: imbued with symbolic meaning and linked to personal fantasies. As commuting confined conformist drivers to the quotidian rhythm of moving between suburban life and daily labour, new visions of escape fired the motoring imagination. Cars became instruments of freedom and individuality. American culture developed a fascination with speed and escape. James Dean's lethal crash near Paso Robles at the end of September 1955 sent shockwaves through teen circles across the country. While the probability that Dean was speeding when his Porsche 550 Spyder hit a Ford Custom has been contested, the fact that he called his car 'little bastard' indicates that defiance expressed through reckless driving had already become part of his celebrity image. In a time when the tempo of generational change was rapidly increasing, Elvis saw James Dean as an emblem of the youth market and its changing concerns. Though Dean did not leave a direct *musical* legacy, his 'live fast, die young' image (see final chapter, this volume) became associated with rock 'n' roll stereotyped as the choice of reprobates, hot rod racers, greasers, and hoods. Dean's passing also helped to start a decade-long fascination with the car crash as a moment of tragedy or veiled suicide that resulted in a spate of 'death discs' and 'splatter platters' (Plopper and Ness, 1993). Automation and speed became driving forces in the emergent rhythm of modern society and consumer culture. Rock 'n' roll was designed to suit commercial radio formats, encapsulated in three-minute symphonies, and pressed on to mass-produced vinyl singles; the music was placed alongside buzzing neon signs, flash clothes, fast food, and other short order delights of the era.

Notions of 'the road' defined cars as steel horses of a new frontier, suggesting a greater sense of personal freedom. Scholars such as André Nóvoa (2012) have examined the argument that musicians actually *depended* on transportation for their 'cool' identities. On tour, they are perceived as figures *of mobility*. Expressing the notion that freedom can be found by taking off on the highway, Bobby Troup's "Route 66"—which was first performed by the Nat King Cole trio in 1946—has been covered by many artists, from Chuck Berry and the Stones to Manhattan Transfer and Depeche Mode. Ten short years after Levitt and Sons announced their first residential community, Viking Press published Jack Kerouac's *On the Road*, a beat novel championing the emancipating benefits of enjoying life on a trip. At least for those who were able to share in the dream, life out on the highway became emblematic of the possibilities of personal freedom. Touring musicians were seen as *freewheelin'*: socially rebellious and sexually liberated.

Fourthly, allied to a broad gendering of driving practice, cars have become *mobile sites of heterosexual courtship and display*. Drive-in theatres, which boomed in the early 1950s, allowed young people to escape domestic spaces. Away from the watchful eyes of their parents, teens had greater control over their personal conduct and social lives. Other activities like dining rapidly went mobile too (Marsh and Collett, 1986, p. 194). Automobiles functioned as domains controlled by adolescents that could always be relocated if they wanted more privacy. Brookesmith (1983, p. 100) summarizes at least some of the ways in which car ownership, drive-ins, and popular music came together to facilitate a new and more liberated dating environment for 1950s teens:

> What happened at the drive-in, however, remained beyond parental control, and was nothing that adjusting one's dress before leaving the theatre could disguise. American cars were like American teenagers: over comfortable, over-powered. But cars brought young people together—as couples, as individuals, in groups—and the constant rambling on the car radio of the Saturday night DJs and their frenetic, suggestive music bound them all together in what felt like a nation within a nation.

Nostalgically celebrated in the film *American Graffiti* (Lucas, 1973), the hedonistic and newly mobile 'nation within a nation' kept its motor running on a diet of rock 'n' roll.

One of the numbers that have been forwarded as a candidate for the first record in the new genre was Jackie Brenston and his Delta Cats' tune "Rocket 88"—a song which many 1950s music fans know was written in celebration of the pulling power of the Oldsmobile 88. The new models were rapidly equipped with Rocket V8 engines, push-button starters, and automatic transmission systems. Such powerful cars epitomized the enticing prospect of carefree driving. No wonder, then, that the "88" stayed in Oldsmobile's catalogue until the organization was shut down by General Motors at the dawn of the new millennium. Back in the 1950s, the vehicle's popular slogan had been "Make a date with the Oldsmobile 88." For a time—to use the parlance of John Travolta's single from the blockbuster musical *Grease* (Kleiser, 1978)—the car was as smooth, and seductive, as "greased lightnin'." Discussing Jackie Brenston's recording, in their history of Sam Phillips' Memphis Recording Service, Escott and Hawkins (1980, p. 18) explain, "It was not the first eulogy to the automobile but this slab of unsolicited advertising for Olds' latest product predated Chuck Berry by almost five years and was a rollicking example of contemporary commercial R&B." Brenston's "Rocket 88" song was released on Chess in 1951. A few months after the Chess release, Bill Haley, accompanied by his western swing outfit Saddlemen, delivered his own cover. In Haley's hands, "Rocket 88" began with the sound of beeping horns and screeching breaks, as if inadequate motoring could be effortlessly surpassed by the superior pleasure of a ride in an Oldsmobile. His Holiday Record's single resonated with a demand made long before by Luigi Russolo in a Futurist manifesto called *The Art of Noise*:

> We must break at all cost from this restrictive circle of pure sounds and conquer the infinite variety of noise-sounds . . . [as] we get infinitely more pleasure imagining combinations of the sounds of trolleys, autos and other vehicles, and loud crowds, than listening once more, for instance, to the heroic or pastoral symphonies. (1913/2004, p. 6)

It was almost as if Haley's cover of "Rocket 88" formed a missing link between Russolo's manifesto and the Art of Noise—a British avant-garde pop group that featured a sample of a stalling Volkswagen Golf on its 1984 single "Close (to the Edit)."

Fifthly, car ownership became linked to *racial and class-bound aspirations*. Possibilities of social advancement through material abundance enabled the American dream to be formulated not just in personal terms—as a kind of individual escapism—but also in collective ones. On the one hand, there were those who were left out of the automotive revolution. Poor folk were immobile and had to make do with their own localities. Street corners therefore became mythologized locations where public singing depended intricately on the limitations of wealth, race, and class (see Goldblatt, 2013). Cars were expensive items. They were sold in a variety of types produced for a socially stratified marketplace. Thus they became a key way to express material desires and the possibility of 'moving on up.' Elvis's early car purchases were often Lincolns; he said in 1956 to Wink Martindale, "My daddy's got Presley's Used Car Lot out on Audubon Drive! . . . I'll tell you the reason I bought those cars. Maybe I'll go broke one day and sell one of 'em" (Osborne, 2000, p. 37). In other words, Elvis initially collected cars as potential collateral and recognized the possibility that his fame was fleeting. History associates him, however, with an important symbol of having 'arrived' in 1950s America; Elvis will always be remembered as the man who bought Cadillacs.

In his portrait of the 1950s, David Halberstam (1994, p. 118) suggested that the Cadillac was for "the top executive or owner of the local factory." It was not marketed to the very pinnacle of the luxury market, but positioned somewhere just below as a car that reflected *well-deserved* comfort. The idea was to appeal to a Calvinist mentality that said affluent buyers deserved glittering prizes that could be justified as a result of material success *through hard work*. Elvis's connection to pink Cadillacs dates back to April 1955, when Sun released his rockabilly version of Arthur Gunter's "Baby Let's Play House." In the middle of the song, its new singer customized the lyrics to reflect 1950s car culture by portraying a girl driving her own luxury vehicle. As music critic Mike Eder (2013, p. 20) noted, Elvis's version of the song "has the bonus of adding the pink Cadillac to the list of 1950s iconography, once a flip religious reference was replaced by one adding the grandiose vehicle." Elvis bought his first actual pink Cadillac early in 1955. While his band was touring Arkansas that summer, it was destroyed in a fire. In July, when "Baby, Let's Play House" stormed the *Billboard* country chart, he purchased a replacement which he donated to his non-driving mother and then used himself. Elvis bought a pink suit too, which he proudly wore on stage until excited fans ripped it apart. The following January, Presley explained to interviewer Don Davis, "I kinda thought that would be a gimmick and really, it drew a lot of attention from the trade papers, about the pink suit and pink car" (Osborne, 2000, p. 8). Elvis was not the only 'poor boy' aiming to 'make good' in the land of the free. Musicians from non-white ethnic groups have frequently bought into more universally shared car cultures and found niche spaces to express their own version of material success. George Lipsitz (1989, p. 277) observed:

> The car culture's quest for fun and good times expressed a desire for the good life and material success, but it also provided a means for satirizing and subverting ruling icons of consumer society. Just as Chicano car customizers 'improved' upon the mass-produced vehicles from Detroit, Chicano rock songs like "Whittier Boulevard" celebrated Mexican-American appropriations of automobiles as part of a community ritual.

Sixthly, when identity became associated with consumption and collecting, cars were used as the ultimate *markers of personal style*. Of course, automobiles are, for some, simply a convenient means of transportation. Yet, although cars represent an interest long shared by many, some lines have never quite been mass commodities—demographically segmented, expressing cultural capital—they are understood as reflecting something personal. Many prize them as chromium-plated materializations of ego. In other words, as public vehicles of self-expression, cars have become used as a way to boost personal and collective self-esteem. As the media technology theorist Marshall McLuhan put it, back in 1964, the car has become a kind of automotive prosthetic, "an article of dress without which we feel uncertain, unclad and incomplete" (1994, p. 217). Car owners frequently use their vehicles to attract wider attention. Jonathan Bell (2001, p. 115) explained, "Car stereo culture offers not only another means of self-expression but also allows the driver to control their surroundings, producing sounds so intense that the bystander is literally physically moved." I once saw one antisocial motorist receive odd stares for playing Gloria Gaynor's "I Will Survive" at full volume as he casually cruised downtown Vancouver. It made me think about how city walkers expect to hear dub bass or other particular sounds when they notice drivers who have installed huge speakers and cranked up their stereos.

Cars are not simply boom boxes. The connection between driving, music, and self-esteem can work in quieter ways. As Derber (2000, p. 64) explains:

> The automobile is another possession that symbolizes social worth and is 'displayed' to bring attention to the self. By driving such luxury cars as Cadillacs, Continentals, Mercedes, and Rolls Royces, wealthy individuals attract attention

in the streets and in public places. One millionaire's "outsize white Cadillac with a gold plated dashboard" has been described by C. Wright Mills as a lavish example from an earlier era. Nowadays, the acquisition of expensive but less blatantly garish vehicles, including sports cars, antique automobiles, and chauffeured limousines, remains a means by which dominant groups indirectly 'purchase' attention.

While artists from many different genres are known for collecting cars—in Britain some notable examples include Jay Kay of Jamiroquai and Brian Johnson from AC/DC—it is hip-hop that has, perhaps, been most associated with the public process of 'purchasing' attention through the acquisition and display of spectacular material possessions.

The popular website CarThrottle.com has listed "40 Rapper Stars and Their Performance Cars" (Ebrahim, 2009). The article reveals that 50 Cent drives a Rolls Royce Phantom and a Lamborghini Murciélago Roadster. Eminem and Dr Dre prefer their Hummer H2s. Snoop Dogg, meanwhile, loves his 1969 Buick Riviera, and Pharrell Williams owns a Mercedes-Benz SLR McLaren Roadster. Missy Elliot drives a Lamborghini Gallardo and Jay-Z, a Maybach 62S. Such cars are, of course, elite reflections of a materialist lifestyle that defines social status as something *bought into* through acts of conspicuous consumption. Not only do they signify that their owners have achieved their aims, risen out of poverty and become small corporations. They also act as endorsements for car manufacturers and spread brand names to far corners of the market place. That stars collect cars is no accident; we might think twice if we saw Snoop in a Ford Fiesta or Pharrell driving a Skoda.

Seventhly, given that cars have been so intimately associated with the masculine ego, they have also become *a barometer for the rising tide of female independence*. Car advertising in the 1950s, for example, positioned women as decorative objects (Walsh, 2006, p. 7). Sexist ideologies located female autonomy as a potential threat. Widespread adoption of the pill allowed women to demand more enfranchisement in the labour market, and in the 1960s they gradually became more independent. Songwriters used male fascination with cars as beautiful machines to raise the parallel questions about male control and objectification of women. Since cars had primarily been claimed as male spaces, anxieties about masculine authority could be expressed through portrayals of women assuming the driver's seat.

The Beatles played on the era's rapidly shifting cultural landscape in their racy pop tunes "Day Tripper" and "Drive My Car" which were both recorded at the

1965 *Rubber Soul* sessions. Literary scholar James Decker offers an interesting analysis. After saying that earlier material like "Ticket to Ride" focused on a male narrator's love, or frustration, he continues:

> "Drive My Car," by contrast, establishes a dialogue in which the female announces her dreams and desires—desires that include thinly veiled sexual urges ("you can drive my car"; "I can show you a better time"), but not necessarily love ("maybe I love you"). No longer the central attraction, the male narrator functions now as a way station of sorts: "You can do something in between." Love, while still present as an idealized state that the female may withhold, fades to the background, as the lover expresses her true design "to be famous, a star of the screen." The cosmopolitan narrator, far from put off by this cynical attitude, fully participates in this transaction, pledging not, as in "Love Me Do," to be true, but that his prospects are good and he could start right away. The lack of a car, rather than a male companion—whether the narrator or not—is the impetus behind the materialistic 'girl's' heartbreak. The male cares little that his paramour wants to call the shots or that she lacks the symbol of her would-be superiority—so long as his sexual appetites are satisfied, and the repeated lines that close the song suggest that they are. (Decker, 2009, p. 78)

Exploring the ways in which sexual desire—plus its connection to love and marriage—has been used to renegotiate gender roles, Decker considers the way that cars can function as metaphors for the shifting battle of the sexes. During rapid changes which heralded the permissive society era, notions of the 'lady driver' as a woman who took charge were used to explore changing attitudes towards female independence.

Eighthly, to bring things back to Levittown, cars and music have long been united as *they both reflect the social and industrial rhythms of the contemporary era*. Car travel, after all, can be seen as a sensory and, for some, sensual experience, even one generating 'automotive emotions' (Sheller, 2004). Think of cars and music and you might also think about Berry Gordy's Motown, the 'hit factory' label that reflected the mechanized bustle of automotive construction in Detroit, the motor city (see Quispel, 2005). Another seamlessly *automated* variant of the experiential connection between motoring and music can be found in the demand for 'drive time' formats to fill daily slots on commercial radio. Songs like the 1984 number "Drive" by the Cars offer a sense of expansiveness which, for many, best reflects the desire to escape rush-hour traffic jams and experience unfettered driving.

Europeans have offered a more minimalist but no less pleasurable take. Krautrock's focus on the droning motoric beat reached its aesthetic conclusion in the disinterested and yet compelling music of Kraftwerk. The group's fourth album, *Autobahn*, was released late in 1974 with a title track, which made *Billboard's* Top 30 singles chart when it was reduced to a length accepted by commercial radio. Ralf Hutter, a key member of the group, explained to Pascal Bussy (2000, p. 56) that anyone driving on the motorway soon realizes that their car itself is a musical instrument. "Autobahn" actually had its roots in the Regents' 1958 doo-wop hit, "Barbara Ann," a song made a surf music classic in 1965 by the Beach Boys. Kraftwerk re-imagined their own version of "Barbara Ann" while giving impression of smoothly sailing down one of Germany's federal motorways. In Kraftwerk's version, traces of the original disappear in an almost celestial electronic symphony calculated to express the carefree feel of approaching the national speed limit. Creating robotically automated, minimalist music, playing upon notions of German efficiency, and adding an edge of nostalgic futurism, the group attempted to capture "the experience of modernity through music" (Bracewell, 2002, p. 289). Motorway driving became emblematic here of a whole way of life.

As Paul Virilio points out in his extended essay "Speed and Politics" (2006), as society has embraced its technological destiny, public life has come to be measured on the basis of its increasing velocity. A recent report for Scotiabank notes that international car sales have almost doubled since 1990, to a figure of 73 million units per annum, with China growing the most rapidly and now accounting for a quarter of all sales (Gomes, 2015, p. 2). Despite warnings about the limits of fossil fuel consumption and global climate change, late modern society shows very few signs of relinquishing the automobile.

In the context of a car-driven society, what does popular music now mean? For many decades, consumer demands have been served by a silent partnership based on ergonomic imperatives. Not only have vehicle designers worked to improve the experience of popular music listening; as Justin Williams's (2010a and 2014) interesting studies of hip-hop have shown, music producers also carefully mix their tracks, adjusting sub-bass frequencies and other tones for in-car audio environments. Sound studies is likely to continue its significant contribution to our understanding of music and automobile culture in future years.

With a $250,000 grant, in recognition of a long-running association, the Ford motor corporation financed the creation of the Rock & Roll Hall of Fame in Cleveland (Berger, 2001, p. 220). Their grant indicates that cars and popular music are closely hitched. Together they represent the triumph of the idea of consumer choice in segmenting the market, reflecting the nostalgia, and heralding the future.

In a post-Kraftwerkian world, where automobility, retro-futurology, and popular music form a complex nexus, one writer who manages to balance this set of concerns is Paul Morley. His book *Words and Music* (2004) was subtitled *A History of Pop in the Shape of a City*. Reviewing Morley's playful volume for the *Guardian*, journalist Steven Poole (2003) said that its "main structural conceit concerns a robot [pop star] Kylie [Minogue] driving in a fast car towards a virtual city, which is of course the city of pop." He continues:

> Tattooed at the nape of this cyber-Kylie's neck is a microscopic prehistory of music. The author himself tries to persuade Kylie that he is qualified to ghost write her autobiography. And throughout the book various other characters appear in the passenger seat next to cyber-Kylie in order to conduct bizarre conversations with her: from Philip Glass to Ludwig Wittgenstein. . . . Kylie's story is told in a language of acid-fuelled science-fiction euphoria. "She has her flesh-covered hand on the stupendously suggestive gear stick of her golden speedmobile as it slices through the landscape of a robot's imagination towards a city where she is queen," Morley assures us. Alternatively: "Somewhere in some universe down some wormhole on the edge of some supernova, Tangerine Dream were a time-travelling science-fiction boy band, and Kylie, as a coltish, bare-cheeked Barbarella, guested on their biggest hit, a song that went on for centuries and whose lyrics consisted simply of the sounds 'la la la la la la la la.'" Such reveries are regularly punctuated by pitch-perfect drollery—"Kylie in a car crash might be a very commercial event."

Music functions, in Morley's fantasy world, not optionally, but alchemically—anchoring moments of a turbulent social journey which encapsulate conflicting tendencies that include male *and* female, global *and* local, future *and* past. Various performers and genres act as a form of social shorthand used to explore possibilities that are as political as they are cultural. Beyond them all, there is a futurological sense that we can measure the emotional charge of human relationships most accurately in their technological and ergonomic contexts in cars. Morley's discussion works not only because matters of taste can bring people together or push them apart, or because automobile lines, like pop songs, have become markers of social change and objects of nostalgia. His book acknowledges cars as automotive machines that function as part of pop's material grounding and cultural heritage. In *Words and Music*, cars epitomize a future-tech environment within which musical choice happens. As *vehicles*, they enable us to move forward *in cultural space*. Transportation affords an answer to the question of where we might go from here. In the new millennium, pop is taking us to destinations that we could, once, only dream of going. For Morley, it is women who are in the driving seat.

The ongoing, socially charged collision between transport technology and sonic pleasure now seems overfamiliar yet under-examined. As the chapters in this volume demonstrate, academic interest in the association between cars and popular music shows no signs of running out of gas.

1

Rock 'n' roll: Cars, convergence, and culture

Tim Wall and Nick Webber

In traditional narratives of American cultural history, the period from 1955 to 1965 is represented as one of 'newness'. Depictions of this period, in both academic and popular form, draw attention to phenomena seen to result from post-war social, economic, and cultural change: the so-called rise of the teenager, the creation of rock 'n' roll, the advent of the transistor radio, and the central importance of the car. In association, ideas of technology, mobility, and teen culture are combined to give us the presentations of the period in films such as *American Graffiti* (Lucas, 1973), in which we see teenagers in custom cars—so-called hot rods—cruising around town, with music pouring from the radio. This 'rock 'n' roll moment', captured for California, 1962, by *American Graffiti*, is one of display and consumption, and of music and culture.

None of these practices and technologies were genuinely new. The association of car customization and teenagers had a longer history, the radio and the car had been linked from at least the 1920s, and, musically, cars had been the subject of songs since the nineteenth century. Indeed, when we examine the practices and technologies more closely, the continuities appear more important than the idea that this was a period of time in which a major disruption in culture occurred. In what follows, therefore, we will explore the relationship between cars, radio, and music in the decade between 1955 and 1965 in the United States. We will present these objects, and the cultural practices which connect them, as the end result of a gradual convergence of mobility and entertainment in the United States during the first half of the twentieth century. We will suggest that the particular importance accorded to this moment of rock 'n' roll results not from 'newness' but from the way in which the visual and auditory 'image' of these disparate activities of cars, radios, and music form a coherent set of meanings over the decade after 1955. Most importantly, we will explore how new culture was made out of the elements of US commercial culture, and the way that the commercial culture took them back into mass production in the early 1960s.

As we have already indicated, there is a rich variety of representations of this era within later media texts and popular culture. There are, in addition, several very useful academic and popular historical investigations of the precursors to the cultural practices on which we focus here. Intriguingly, though, there are attempts to understand how they come together in what anthropologist Claude Lévi-Strauss (1966) termed 'bricolage'—the reuse of materials and practices for the solution of new cultural dilemmas. In this chapter, then, we use some of the eulogizing scenes woven throughout *American Graffiti* to stimulate our investigation, and explore existing scholarship on the history of the individual strands of this culture in order to draw together the sophisticated ways in which cars, radio, and mobile music converged to create a meaningful culture.

Cars

George Lucas's *American Graffiti* opens, to the soundtrack of Bill Hayley's "Rock around the Clock," with the arrival of three of the central characters at Mel's Drive-In restaurant by different modes of transport. The cool of the '58 Impala is evident, set against the utility of the motor scooter and Citroen CV. Cars, therefore, feature centrally in the narrative of the film, not as modes of functional transport, but as symbols of youth, mobility, and competition. The car is presented as the means through which the other aspects of youth culture are articulated: music, relationships, coming of age. This connection of cars to youth culture, however, is much older than the 1950s or 1960s. In fact, even as early as the late 1920s, cars had become the technological innovation most identified with young people in films, songs, and novels (Ides, 2009, p. 110), and US manufacturers were advertising cars "that might appeal to younger drivers" from the mid-1930s (Best, 2006, p. 11).

Following the introduction of the Model T Ford in 1908, the ownership and widespread use of cars by the young resulted, primarily, from the massive increase in automobile production and decrease in price. Adjusted for inflation, between 1909 and 1925, the price of a new Model T fell in real terms by 82 per cent (Ides, 2009, p. 122), creating both the broad distribution of *new* cars and a burgeoning market in *used* cars. It was this latter market that was the principal source of youth car ownership, and by the mid-1930s, in Los Angeles at least, middle-class high school students were driving to school (Ides, 2009, p. 102 and 123). Ford's mass production model also incorporated consistent and widely available car parts, and these factors were vital to the increasingly popular practice of car modification: or hot rodding, as it came to be known.

Southern California, and particularly Los Angeles, was central to the development of hot rodding practices (Luckso, 2008, pp. 65-66 and 69), in part due to the increasingly distributed nature of the urban environment of Los Angeles both driving and being driven by huge growth in car usage. While the population of Los Angeles roughly doubled between 1919 and 1920, car registration in the area more than quintupled (Shackleford, 2004, pp. 31-32). By the end of the 1920s, the practice of altering a production car for speed was well established throughout the United States. In Southern California, competitive racing took place along dry lakebeds, a practice which rapidly grew in perceived legitimacy and formal organization. Car clubs, first appearing in the area in the 1920s, were initially focused on adult hobbyists, but these became more youth focused during the 1930s, and in many cases were amalgamated into sanctioned racing and timing associations (Ides 2009, pp. 102, 123-24; Moorhouse, 1986, p. 84). Although the lakes were commandeered by the military during the Second World War, lakebed racing resumed after the war, with the timing associations continuing to lend the practice an air of credibility and, increasingly, respectability. However, there is more to this picture.

The 'hot rod' problem

American Graffiti, significantly, does not show us a hot rod involved in a lakebed race; rather, the race presented in the film takes place on a road. The trend of increasing access to cars continued throughout the 1930s, as production volumes grew, but increasing in parallel to the ownership of cars were some car-related problems familiar from our contemporary experience: those of high-speed road driving in general and, as we see in the film, street racing. While marking a departure from the intentions of many of those who might have considered themselves 'genuine' hot rodders, by the 1960s street racing was not only a well-established phenomenon but something seen as a serious problem, strongly associated with youthful delinquency. As early as 1913, records show that 115 juveniles were arrested in LA in one year for joyriding (Moorhouse, 1991, p. 29), and it is clear that speeding was an issue throughout the 1920s and 1930s. In the 1940s, teen drivers—"wild-eyed kids in hopped-up jalopies"—were seen as a major social problem across the United States, and a new term, 'teenicide,' was coined to describe the perceived proclivity of teens to die in car accidents (Moorhouse, 1991, pp. 29, 31, 35). Many street races took place at night, after sanctioned club meetings, leading one Los Angeles police captain to refer to them as "suicide clubs of midnight owls" (Ides, 2009, pp. 135–36).

In actual fact, there were few accidents (although figures from California for 1949 suggest the vehicle accident rate was well above average among people under eighteen), but the discourse of delinquency remained strong, meaning that accidents which did occur were sensationalized (Moorhouse, 1991, pp. 29, 35; Ides, 2009, p. 136). In some cases, any and every car driven by a teenager was labelled as a hot rod (Ides, 2009, p. 138). Ben Shackleford (2004, p. 37) draws our attention to an indicative November 1949 article in *Life* magazine, which decries "The 'Hot-Rod' Problem" with the subheading "Teenagers organize to experiment with mechanized suicide." By the late 1940s, 'hot rod' was used to refer to "a highly visible, relatively affluent, teenage lifestyle which seemed to turn on drive-ins, noise, jalopies held together with chewing gum and dangerous driving on public highways" (Moorhouse, 1991, p. 33). These negative associations created consternation among self-proclaimed genuine hot rodders, the (by this point often older) devotees of lakebed racing, and motivated them to try and coax street racers back to the relative safety of sanctioned speed events. In addition, a threat of state legislation that would affect all hot rodding and racing activity in California drove a vigorous attempt to present lakebed races as a sober, respectable, and self-regulating sport, distinctly at odds with the practices vilified by the press (Moorhouse, 1991, pp. 32–41).

Fashion

Approaching 1955, then, there was already a well-established association between cars, high-speed driving, and teenagers. So what was actually happening between 1955 and 1965, in the rock 'n' roll moment? In terms of cars, we can start to understand this period through the meaning of the term 'hot rod.' If the practices here were not new, the terminology certainly appears to have been. 'Hot rod' was not an expression in use among lakebed racers of the 1930s, and in 1945 *Life* magazine—which used the term confidently only four years later—felt the need to provide a definition for its readers (Moorhouse, 1986, pp. 83, 86–87). Although it appears to have been employed at first as a belittling contraction of 'hot roadster' (Luckso, 2008, pp. 10, 66–67), by the end of the 1940s 'hot rod' was in wide circulation. Significantly, in 1948, self-identifying usage appeared in the form of *Hot Rod* magazine, launched in January of that year by a group of lake racing enthusiasts (Moorhouse, 1986, p. 84). This magazine was aimed at the 'genuine' hot rodders to whom we have already alluded; those who defined themselves in terms of the hard work and innovative engineering they performed on their cars. The first issue dismissed as 'shot rodders' those who did not espouse this ethic and instead settled simply for the appearance of speed, and the magazine explicitly rejected the construction of hot rodding that had become a media commonplace (Moorhouse, 1986, p. 89). Street racers were labelled as 'squirrels.' Journalists were also castigated when they "presented this 'screwball few' to the mass audience as if they were true hot rodders" (p. 89). The editor of the second issue suggested that 'hot rod' was among "the most misused of words" (Moorhouse, 1991, pp. 40–41). Importantly, such struggles for definition reflected a divide that became increasingly significant into the 1950s: between speed and style, between *being* fast and *looking* fast.

Street racing survived the years of the Second World War through impromptu drag meets and improvised solutions to fuel restrictions (Moorhouse, 1991, pp. 31–32). In the following years, the cars became more varied in their mechanics, creating a diversity which changed the nature of hot rodding practices. Ford's shift to interchangeable parts in the early part of the 1930s, along with the large stock of old cars available and the decreasing cost of cars, had made hot rodding a hobby accessible to a broad range of middle and working-class youth (Ides, 2009, p. 124). Fords of the 1930s, prominent among them the "Little Deuce Coupe" of Beach Boys fame (see the next chapter in this volume), were particularly prized as a basis for hot rod work. In *American Graffiti*, a yellow hot rod version is driven by John Milner, the character in the film who represents eternal youth and who the main characters are reluctantly leaving behind. However, the diverse mechanics of the 1950s meant that in reality, parts were harder to get, and cars of the 1930s were by that point two decades old and becoming costly to purchase and to modify (Ides, 2009, p. 117). So, much as the low-cost cars of the 1930s had democratized what had initially been a middle-class pursuit into something that cut right across society, by the

1950s 'genuine' hot rodding was once again becoming an activity in which only (upper) middle classes could afford to indulge. If, before the 1920s, speed had belonged to the wealthy, the increasing ownership of fast cars by the working classes thereafter contested that privilege. And by the 1950s, 'fast cars' did not have to mean modified cars: it could happily mean new cars.

Perhaps the most significant change apparent in the 1950s is the engagement of mass culture and mass production with hot rod culture. For a start, Detroit manufacturers started to draw on the expertise within the hot rodding community, offer scholarships to the winners of organized races on the Utah salt flats (Shackleford, 2004, pp. 39–40), and use 'horsepower tricks' to offer production cars with more powerful engines, capable of higher speeds (Luckso, 2008, p. 106). Appropriating the cachet of the process itself, they also began to sell 'customized' models of new cars (Shackleford, 2004, p. 43). In 1955, at the start of our rock 'n' roll moment, the Dodge D-500 was launched and controversially described in *Hot Rod* magazine as a "production line hot rod" (Moorhouse, 1986, p. 91). In the years that followed, 'muscle cars' like the Chrysler C-300 and the AMC Rebel became very popular. There were also notable responses to the adornment practices of hot rodders by mainstream auto manufacturers. Most visibly they adopted the contrivance of adding chrome parts to their production cars. Even those who could not afford, or did not want, a road racing car, could reproduce the symbols of speed and rebellion in their showroom purchases. Driven by a determination to differentiate themselves, the hot rodders (and then the more youthful shot rodders) removed the chrome (Shackleford, 2004, p. 50). In the next production generation, car manufacturers followed suit, at which point hot rodders added it once again in an ongoing cycle of "cultural participation and creativity within mass consumerism" (Ides, 2009, p. 145, paraphrasing Balsley 1950/2011). Interestingly, both the black '55 Chevy and the yellow '32 Deuce Coupe that duelled in *American Graffiti*'s road race had the same amount of chrome on their wheels, though the Chevy kept its chromed bumpers.

Between 1955 and 1965, the car was consolidated not only in its long-term role as an aspect of youth culture, then, but as an item of fashion. In the aftermath of the Second World War, cars were increasingly seen as short lived, to be replaced readily by the new. Car *modifiers* led the fashion and car *companies* followed it, but the majority of people consumed the products produced en masse by the Detroit factories; thus, the car was appropriated and re-appropriated in turn.

Radio

If the story of the cars in our imagined rock 'n' roll moment is not as simple as we might imagine, the same holds true for the radios which they carried. In *American Graffiti*, the radio appears as a major signifier and narrative device, almost as immediately in the film as the cars. After the main characters are introduced, Lucas blurs non-diegetic and diegetic music, as the rock 'n' roll title soundtrack morphs into the sound of music on the car radios, and then on to announcements by radio DJ Wolfman Jack. At almost every moment when a car is key to a scene, music (and radio music in particular) is there as well. In the film, the mobility of people and music, therefore, appears central to both the iconography and story.

Following the perfection of the transistor itself at the end of the previous decade, the first transistor radios appeared in the mid-1950s (Braun and Macdonald, 1978, p. 17; Partner, 1999, pp. 193–98). Perhaps as a consequence, there is a tendency to assume that it was the development of the transistor that allowed radios to become portable, making radio listening a mobile phenomenon that was exploited in turn by a new youth culture. Certainly, transistors used less power, were more rugged and smaller than the valves/vacuum tubes that preceded them, and were easier to mass produce (Tilton, 1971, pp. 16–17; Partner, 1999, pp. 203–5)—qualities that contributed to a greater culture of mobility. Although they were not always the highly portable pocket radios of the 1960s, radio receivers had been mobile for most of their history.

Portable listening devices existed long before the 1950s, and cars had radios from the start of auto mass production. Portable radios, and radios in cars, were far from unusual in the mid-1920s, and low power and small valves, and even pocket radios that used them, could be found in the late 1930s (Schiffer, 1991, pp. 161–71). By 1946 nearly 40 per cent of a total of 9 million US cars had radios, by 1955 most radio receivers were sold in cars, and by 1958 half the population was listening in their cars. Five years later, in 1963, 60 per cent of the 50 million cars in circulation had radios (Douglas, 1999/2004, p. 226; Gomery, 2008, p. 144). Before 1955, therefore, radio listening was predominantly static and domestic, not because listening technology was not portable but because radio listening was driven by a domestic, cultural imperative; the main audience was the domestic family unit at leisure.

Up until 1955, domestic listeners enjoyed evening broadcasts of programming we would recognize from contemporary television: dramas, variety, quizzes, and chat shows. From the mid-1930s, radio broadcasting was dominated by oligopolies in the United States, and by state monopolies in most European nations. US American radio was based upon a network system in which entertainment programmes were made in New York and distributed to local broadcasters. There was some daytime broadcasting, mainly targeted at women, and it is from here that we get the term 'soap opera': daytime melodramas sponsored by washing soap manufacturers for those involved in domestic labour. However, in the early 1950s, television took radio's domestic family audience, and the identification and attraction of new audiences became important. Daytime housewife listeners became far more important than they had previously been, and the audience of poor urban blacks and urban whites, who could not afford television, suddenly became extremely attractive (Rothenbuhler and McCourt, 2002; Barlow, 1999).

Radio and new listeners as markets

One particularly important market in the period under consideration was that of commuting workers, who were seen as captive audiences for radio broadcasters. This is the point at which the car converged with radio in its dominant form. It was these commuters who bought the new mass-produced cars and initiated the widespread installation of in-car radios. By 1955, not only were most new radios produced for cars, but the vast majority (83 per cent) of new cars had radios (Gomery, 2008, p. 144). As the large radio networks moved attention and programmes to television, a new generation of independent radio stations looked for a new, cheap form of programming. That form was based around recorded music. Music radio increasingly moved from blocks of programmes to what Todd Stortz, the 'father' of Top 40 radio, called a "total station sound" (Rothenbuhler and McCourt, 2004)—the emphasis here was on branding a station rather than a single programme. Top 40 predated rock 'n' roll radio and any interest in targeting radio programmes at young listeners. At this time, however, it became the dominant way of organizing the new music as a radio form, and ultimately the means through which radio moved from a predominantly domestic to a predominantly mobile medium. Radio station output became a single rolling experience into which listeners were assumed to dip for a fixed, and usually short, period of time; the drive towards reshaping radio was primarily owed to the need to find new audiences and replace those recently taken away by television. Record labels knew that radio was their main channel of promotion, so they provided their products to stations, in the United

States at least, for free. In an environment where traditional fare was expensive to produce, recordings became a way for station programmers to drive down costs. Radio's use of sound as its medium of communication also made music-based programmes the ideal accompaniment for housework and driving (also see Chapter 4 in this volume).

From the mid-1950s, radio was thus structured around a series of 'imagined listeners'. The first was the industrial worker, primarily in their role as the commuter, who determined the breakfast and drive times. The second was the middle-class housewife, seeking entertainment to underwrite her domestic chores, perhaps supplemented by those workers who were allowed radios in the paid workplace. Yet, these audiences are largely forgotten in recreations of the age of rock 'n' roll because primacy is given to the role that radio had in the leisure times of a third group of listeners: the young. This audience was the creation of America's post-war urban prosperity, in which television sets became more affordable and teenagers became viable consumer markets capable of attracting advertisers. In the United States, "the teenage consumer," to use Mark Abrams's seminal 1959 phrase, could take over both the car and the radio in the evening, while the housewife and the commuter came together at home in front of the television. Here, then, the car, radio, and rock 'n' roll converged.

Radio's new industrial organization

At the centre of the new form of music radio programming was the sense of a personal relationship with listeners, primarily articulated through the talk of the DJ. As we have noted, *American Graffiti* celebrates early 1960s DJ Wolfman Jack, but it is his tamer contemporary Alan Freed who has become best known as the link between 1950s radio programming and US American teenagers (Miller, 1999, pp. 57–61; Jackson, 1995). Freed played black music to white audiences and, from 1954, used black slang for sex in the title of his radio show at WINS in New York: *Moon Dog's Rock 'n' Roll Party*. His listeners came to think of the term 'rock 'n' roll' as descriptive of the music. Freed drew on the style of black radio presenters for his audience just as much as he adopted the hits of the black community to play for youngsters. In this, he was a classic bricoleur, making new meanings out of diverse cultural resources. The music to which people listened and the radio stations that played that music became areas where people might express their affiliation and form bonds with like-minded others.

And these developments in music consumption were echoed in the adoption, by white teenagers, of other elements of culture from their segregated black peers: the jukebox, from the black juke joint, and dances which drove the dance fads that followed rock 'n' roll (Wall, 2006).

While it is Freed and Wolfman who generally receive credit for this musical shift, a deeper understanding is available to us through the consideration of two other radio stations: WDIA in Memphis and WJR in Detroit. These were two of the burgeoning independent radio stations in the United States during the remaking of the US radio landscape that occurred between 1945 and 1965. As we have already suggested, independent stations were central to this transformation. During this period, the number of stations grew enormously, from approximately 1,000 at the end of the Second World War to 4,000 by the end of our period of study. Most of the increase was composed of independent stations; while few had existed in 1945, by 1965 there were over 2,700 'indies' (Sterling, 1984, p. 12), demonstrating their increasing significance.

WDIA in Memphis and WJR in Detroit shared similarities with hundreds of other stations in the United States at the time, but represent quite clear examples of polar positions within US radio of the period. Contrasting them reveals something of the important relationship between the car, radio, and mobile music that we have set out in this chapter. WDIA was the first US radio station to consistently play black music, and its focus on a regional black audience grew from single programmes in the late 1940s to a whole station format by the mid-1950s (Cantor, 1992). Although white owned from its inception, the station played a key role in the development of the African American community and the civil rights movement well into the 1970s (Ward, 2004). But WDIA in the mid-1950s also represents a significant moment of cultural exchange between black and white Americans, and in this moment we can understand more clearly that rock 'n' roll owes its origins to US stations like WDIA. It is no coincidence that so many of the future white rock 'n' roll artists grew up in Memphis, including the one they called the 'king of rock 'n' roll': Elvis Presley. Greil Marcus has suggested that Presley's most important characteristic was "not his ability to imitate a black blues singer, but the nerve to cross the borders he had been born to respect" (Marcus, 1975, p. 155). Presley grew up listening to WDIA, and he was therefore one of the first working-class white Americans to hear large amounts of black R&B while staying broadly within his own white community. He was able to imitate black blues singers because he could hear those singers in a land of racist physical separation, but he had the nerve to cross the boundaries of ethnicity because it was meaningful for a young post-war working-class US American to do so. As we discuss in the next section, engaging with black music was an important statement of rebellion.

WDIA has a central place in the development of black music in the states. Known throughout the southern states of the United States as the 'Mother Station of the Negroes' (Guralnick, 1986), WDIA started with mixed programming featuring hillbilly music for white listeners as well as output specifically targeting black listeners. This probably acted as the link to the R&B programming for Presley and his peers. It was also the station that Rufus Thomas and Jim Stewart worked for in different capacities. Thomas was a central character in the development of R&B and 1960s soul in the southern states. He worked as a DJ in WDIA and as MC at the Handy Theatre for the amateur nights where BB King and Bobby Bland got started, and became a recording artist on Stax records along with his daughter Carla. Stewart started off as a fiddle player in hillbilly bands, playing at WDIA before becoming a music entrepreneur and record shop owner, eventually setting up Stax records with his sister Estelle Axton in the early 1960s (Bowman, 1997).

By contrast, WJR in Detroit emerged from a very different political pole. The station had played host to the earliest broadcasts of the populist anti-Semite, Charles Coughlin, and was owned by George A. Richards who, by the mid-1950s, combined attempts at systematic interference in the national democratic process and virulent anti-Semitism with cross promotion of his football club and radio interests (Barnouw, 1968, pp. 44, 223). Equally, though, WJR represented one of the stations actively trying to attract car commuting listeners. As a 1966 promotional film *WJR: One of a Kind* clearly demonstrates, during the decade under consideration here the station presents commuters and housewives as its most important listeners (Quitney, 2012). As recordings of its mid-1950s broadcasts reveal, its sound and audience address could not have been more different from that of WDIA (Vintagetvs, 2008). Like the Memphis station, it increasingly relied on recorded music, but the Detroit station played light orchestrated versions of country forms and showed hits from Doris Day, as well as big band stomps that predominated. The music was punctuated with gentle homilies to drivers to be careful in the rain. WJR, at the centre of the US American auto industry and one of the first suburban commuter systems, is generally credited with the invention of drive-time music programming, interleaving popular music and local traffic information to directly serve that commuter audience segment which was so important.

Music

At the heart of these discussions is, of course, the cultural activity of consuming music. An important aspect of the story of the rock 'n' roll moment is the perception that 1955 was the year in which rock 'n' roll came into existence. Of all elements of the picture, this is perhaps the best known, but is no less mythologized for all that. Certainly, 1955 was a seminal year for rock 'n' roll music releases. It is noteworthy that *American Graffiti*, although set in the early 1960s, opens with Bill Haley's "Rock around the Clock," one of the defining records of rock 'n' roll and a recording widely used to index the birth of teenage culture. Musically, "Rock around the Clock" was ostensibly a hillbilly western swing version of a blues structure, with a lyric that draws upon African American slang about sexual longevity. In a sense, rock 'n' roll itself can be understood as a process of customization within mainstream US American popular music. Both R&B and hillbilly represented cultures of the margins within US American culture, and they were first customized by and then for young, mainstream, white US Americans. It would not be long until music repeated the pattern of car customization and was re-appropriated into mainstream Tin Pan Alley pop. In exactly the same way that the vigour and innovation of WDIA's black programming was appropriated by DJs like Alan Freed, his rock 'n' roll party was soon re-appropriated by independent radio's Top 40 programming.

The way that *American Graffiti* uses music is particularly interesting. It pervades the film; in one scene it is centre stage in a live show, but mostly it is recorded music that predominates, emanating from the radio station and blasting from car radios. In one of the best scenes, record collecting becomes the basis of an impassioned monologue. The soundtrack record (Various Artists, 1973) collected forty-one of the recordings featured in the film, which reproduced the success of the cinematic release by selling over 3 million copies and achieving a Top 10 placement in sales charts for 1973. The earliest recording was "Rock around the Clock," with other tracks covering 1950s R&B and doo-wop, and rock 'n' roll into the pop of the Beach Boys and proto soul instrumentals of Booker T and the MGs. The largest number of tracks comes from the early 1970s retro rock 'n' roll band Flash Cadillac and the Continental Kids. The importance of cars within the mythologized youth culture of the late 1950s and early 1960s is signalled by the name that the latter group took to identify its historical position. The group performed the role of live hop act Herbie and the Heartbeats in the film.

Two artists seem conspicuously absent from the film's musical line-up: Chuck Berry's "Maybellene" was probably as important as "Rock around the Clock" in establishing the sound we usually understand as rock 'n' roll, and there were no records from Elvis Presley at all. Sean Cubitt (1984, p. 209) has described "Maybellene" as a "saga of the eroticized automobile," with its "cinematic car-chase lyric." In a paean to the masculinized chase after sex and speed, Berry tells us the story of how his Ford V8, which was popular among post-war hot rodders (see Luckso, 2008, p. 67), catches-up with Maybellene's Coupe-de-Ville. However, the lyrical theme of capture is somewhat undermined by a musical structure in which the song form is left unresolved, and as the track fades out we are left in a perpetual present of unending movement. If "Maybellene" was ostensibly R&B music with a lyric about white youthful concerns like cars and sex, Haley and Presley represent a white customization of black musical and verbal forms. This cultural miscegenation presages the dominant 1960s popular music that appealed to both black and white US Americans, a form that Brian Ward (1998) has named 'biracial pop.' While rock 'n' roll has its roots in black and white music forms, this fusion also appealed to *both* black and white teenagers. Berry, Presley, and, to a lesser degree, Haley sold across communities to such an extent that the separate R&B and pop music charts were merged in 1963 (Wall 2013, p. 88), and new forms of popular music associated with fad dances emerged in the early 1960s. It is interesting to note that dance fad records like Chubby Checker's "The Twist" from 1960 are completely missing from *American Graffiti*, even though they would have dominated the output of music radio in the year in which the film was set.

Biracial pop was an important cultural and economic phenomenon. African Americans could believe that the cultural and musical fusions represented by records like Presley's "That's All Right" were the precursor to a more integrated future, but they allowed southern whites to love and imitate black music without having to know blacks. Presley spent the first years of his career fully within the separate country and Western music industry of live venues, radio programmes and record companies, distributors, and retailers, but his appeal was far greater than the usual demographics of this market. His first single was successful in both country and black R&B charts, and his appeal was strong among the newly affluent youth, not just locally in Memphis, but across the United States. It was also a music that functioned as the heart of newly emerging youth radio and a Top 40 increasingly dominated by the tastes of young buyers.

It was not only a convergence of musical taste that made this music so universal but also a convergence of themes. As "Maybellene" shows, ideas of cars and racing were there at the outset of rock 'n' roll, but they were also a theme in pre-rock 'n' roll R&B. "Rocket 88," first credited to Jackie Brenston in 1951 and covered in the same year by Bill Haley, celebrates the cruiser Oldsmobile 88. Its musical form owes something to Jimmy Liggins's song "Cadillac Boogie" from 1947, and sits comfortably with the far more obscure 1949 recording "Rocket 88 Boogie" by Pete Johnson. Given that Brenston's number, because of its guitar sound and rhythmic patterns, is often cited as the first rock 'n' roll record (see, for instance, Dahl, n.d.), its role in articulating combined themes that reverberated through rock 'n' roll culture (automotive technology and sexual allure) had been lost, to an extent, in the telling of pop culture's history. Again, though, these pre-occupations were far from new. The automobile had featured in popular music from at least 1899, when the promotional song "The Studebaker March" was released, and as the production and presence of cars increased, music kept pace. Between 1905 and 1908, more than 120 songs about automobiles were released and, while largely centred on romantic themes, music went on to signal the prominence of the Ford in American culture following the release of the Model T. Indeed, more than sixty songs were written about Ford (either the car or Henry Ford himself) between 1908 and 1940 (Heitmann, 2009, pp. 26–27). Songs about cars continued to be produced in various musical genres, but were particularly popular in country music; Arkie Shibley's "Hot Rod Race," recorded in 1950, is sometimes credited with introducing songs about racing to the fold.

It is in the rock 'n' roll moment, then, that these musical threads were drawn together. Rock 'n' roll tracks highlighted cars as part of teenage culture, in their connection with competition through racing, as a locus of romance and as an icon of freedom and self-determination. Yet, these themes were themselves inherited from an earlier music, and in some cases musicians explicitly linked back to earlier work. On the country or hillbilly side, Charlie Ryan's 1955 recording of "Hot Rod Lincoln" is perhaps demonstrative. An answer song to Shibley's "Hot Rod Race," "Hot Rod Lincoln" took and extended the story of the kid in the 'hopped-up Model A,' as a rockabilly number which was to become a chart hit in 1960. Continuity from the R&B perspective appears elsewhere, for example in Chuck Berry's repertoire, where among several songs focused on cars we can find the famous "Route 66." Although perhaps the best known version, Berry's was not the earliest; the track became an R&B standard, but it was written by white jazz pianist and songwriter Bobby Troup, and first recorded by the Nat King Cole trio 1946.

The music-automotive link also established itself strongly in the era of biracial pop, especially in the music of Detroit's Motown records, often presented as an application of the processes of the car production line to music production. A curious representation of this link can be found in a television recording of Motown singing group Martha and the Vandellas, who are presented miming to their hit "Nowhere to Run" while moving through the Mustang production line in Ford's River Rouge Plant. The short film was included in *It's What's Happening, Baby!*, an even more curious attempt to link the biracial youth culture to a CBS-US Office of Economic Opportunity joint production, which sought to sell the key economic plank of Lyndon B. Johnson's 'Great Society' legislation (see Smith, 2001; Coates, 2011).

Conclusion

In the period leading up to the rock 'n' roll moment, cultural objects which composed it had been removed from a mass-produced context, altered, and replaced; consumption, and the associated cultural practices, had thus nuanced mass production. At this moment of convergence, niche cultures became mass cultures, shifting across boundaries of age, class, race, and gender; fast cars became truly mainstream, marking a final step in the democratization of speed; the focus of radio changed, with the combination of youth-focused music and the Top 40 format becoming the dominant form of radio in the United States from 1960 onwards; and black music had, of course, become white music. Due in large part to these shifts, the moment of rock 'n' roll was also a moment of moral panic, followed later by a moment of romanticization. Consistent throughout was the role of commerce: 1955 marked the first time you could go and buy a hot rod, rock 'n' roll music, and an R&R radio, off the shelf. In so doing, young people, and indeed older advocates of the rock 'n' roll lifestyle, were able to express their identities through their consumption activities. Notions of freedom and mobility that had been core drivers within urban culture were given their own teenage version, and the music encultured these romantic dreams. Listening to a particular radio station rapidly became not only a choice but also a statement. And much of this listening took place in and around cars.

We should also take a moment to think further about the history of these icons of the rock 'n' roll moment, as we can perhaps further unpick the mythology of this period. Such as it is, our understanding is distorted not only by a misleading discourse of newness but also by other elements in popular depictions of this moment like those seen in *American Graffiti*. Just as the sense of moral panic which arose from the breaking of boundaries and the behaviour of young people in cars was driven by media representations and not really supported by the evidence at hand, so, too, was the increasingly romantic image of rock 'n' roll. While the shift in cultural practices from niche to mainstream, the popular access to speed and mobility, the (at least partial) de-racialization of music, and the reshaping of radio infrastructure all occurred, they were not things which happened evenly or in order to tell a happy story about 1955 or 1965. It should not be forgotten that our stopping point was the mass consumption (and thus mass provision) of rock 'n' roll, which was shaped by economic imperatives just as much as it responded to cultural ones. Our mythologized view is both affluent (real hot rods were expensive) and white. In closing, then, we must give some further thought to the rock 'n' roll experience of poorer and non-white consumers.

Cars, clearly, were central to white constructions of the rock 'n' roll moment, and mass-produced 'custom cars' and 'hot rods' allowed access to cars which looked fast but were not necessarily significantly so. Certainly, there seems no sense that hot rods built for racing on the lakebeds would be outrun by production equivalents. While the elite's ownership of speed had been contested in the 1930s, it was regained, albeit to a much lesser (and arguably irrelevant) extent in the 1950s. The shift in focus of customization was, as noted, away from modifications for speed and towards modifications for appearance. One of the most significant styles of such modification was low riding, the practice of lowering a car's suspension. Originating in the Mexican-American communities of California, possibly in response to their exclusion from status in post-war hot rod culture on ethnic lines (Ides, 2009, pp. 113–14, 149–50), this form of modification was immensely popular among both poor white and non-white groups. It was seen by some as a form of protest against class and race divisions and was clearly used to indicate separateness from a prevailing idea of white, middle-class hot rodding (Ides, 2009, pp. 149–69); thus, lowriders were driven slowly to enhance their visibility (Best, 2006, p. 31). Within black American culture, the notion of protest was already firmly established, with cars having rapidly become "signs of insubordination, progress and compensatory prestige ... savoured in accordance with an aesthetic code that valued movement over fixity and sometimes prized public style over private comfort and security" (Gilroy, 2001, p. 94). Thus, car consumption in marginalized communities tended, as Ides notes, to emphasize the social aspects of the car (Ides, 2009, p. 150). This was to reject technical modification for aesthetics and to privilege those elements that were context specific and could not be 'designed in.' These practices thus rejected not only the class and racial segregation of the hot rod scene but also those elements of mass production that responded to it.

In terms of radio, we see a mass-market solution which targeted poor and black markets as a result of economic pressures, rather than a desire to create specific tailored services: we must also not forget that the principal business of radio is selling audiences for advertising. It is also notable that, with very few exceptions, radio stations were white-owned and DJs were white. While Freed may have adopted black DJ patter, it is clear that the architecture of rock 'n' roll radio was determined by the same class of affluent whites that could afford to make hot rods in their spare time. Top 40 formats, and aggressive station branding, shifted the focus away from more expensive programming, much of which had gone over to television. Although rock 'n' roll radio was something that many enjoyed, there is a strong sense that it was also produced, in this romanticized moment, as a result of a scattershot approach to music play, something which gave a broad range of listeners a service that was just about good enough to make them listen, but not necessarily the service they wanted or would have chosen for themselves.

Lastly, we must be wary of assuming that just because rock 'n' roll radio offered a mix of black and white music, the music that was offered was the music that black audiences would have chosen to listen to, had they been more self-determining. Certainly, there is ample evidence that black dances in mainstream rock 'n' roll culture were nuanced through white musical practices as new audiences adopted black music. For black audiences, however, there seem to have been competing pressures at work. The mainstreaming of musical styles which black audiences enjoyed was a novel and doubtless welcome; however, again, it is unclear whether or not the amalgamation of musical charts represented a commercial decision to reduce trade in lines of music which had sold in previous years on the basis that rock 'n' roll was, again, just good enough.

A key query here is the extent to which the rock 'n' roll moment, as imagined in film and song, represents an authentic experience, and if so, whose experience that was. Cars in particular were "public ciphers of celebrity" (Gilroy, 2001, p. 94) recognized by black and white musicians alike, and there is doubtless something to be understood about the way in which cars were inflected as status symbols by celebrities and how this related to the consumption cultures in various segments of society. Did the fact that Chuck Berry sang about a 1930s Ford in 1955, for example, make a statement about class (by this point, these were expensive) or about race (a hot rodder's car against a Cadillac, a brand which has been said to have strong associations with black US Americans—see Gilroy, 2001, p. 97), or was it simply a response to the prevailing culture in which Berry found himself? Was Berry another bricoleur, bringing together cultural symbols from either side of race and class boundaries that defined rock 'n' roll culture even as that culture was seen to transgress them?

Indeed, we might suggest that in 1955, at the very point of its imagined 'creation,' rock 'n' roll—by occupying a position at the centre of mainstream culture, production, and consumption—ceased to be transgressive and became inauthentic. Certainly, there was nothing particularly transgressive or authentic about the purchase of a mass-produced rock 'n' roll lifestyle; however, much of this might allow you to imitate your heroes from music or film. Yet, we can see that these practices of consumption were part of a process of youthful re-appropriation of resources that had traditionally been under adult control. Perhaps, then, the notion of appearance that was so significant in cars was representative of a broader situation in rock 'n' roll. The spectacular and strongly visual and audible aspects of rock 'n' roll culture were less directly meaningful than we might imagine—they provided the appearance of youthful excess and transgression which distracted onlookers from a much more serious activity at work. This moment of convergence marked two kinds of appropriation: not only were culturally significant objects created through a cycle of (sub)cultural labour and mass production, but, in the background, resources and power were appropriated by a new generation.

2

"She's my little Deuce Coupe": Freudian transformation in the car songs of the Beach Boys

Georgina Gregory

Whither goest thou, America, in thy shiny car in the night?
On the Road, Jack Kerouac

This quote from Kerouac's beatnik bible, *On the Road*, evokes the centrality of the car within American consciousness in the immediate post-war period, an era in which the importance of the motor vehicle was indisputably acknowledged in the sphere of popular culture. Among others, Jack Kerouac, John Steinbeck, and Scott Fitzgerald depicted cars as symbols of freedom or rebellion. In films, advertising, and television they were presented as sites of consumption, leisure, and romance. Cars also played a significant role in American popular music, with many artists paying homage via the medium of song. In particular, pop harmony group the Beach Boys celebrated car culture through the lens of the young, male owner, at a time when automobile ownership had reached a new zenith. It could be argued that this preoccupation was symptomatic of an era characterized by mass production, cheap fuel, and a lack of concern with environmental issues. However, on deeper reflection, during a period of intense social change where gender roles were subjected to rapid renegotiation, the car in the Beach Boys repertoire can also be viewed as a repository for repressed feelings of anxiety, hostility, and fear regarding women's desire for emancipation.

In historical accounts, the 1950s and early 1960s are portrayed as a time of rising affluence where economic imperatives dictated a move towards suburbanization that coincided with a growth in car ownership. Wider access to cars and new-found geographical and social mobility gave rise to a more individualized, inner-focused nuclear family structure where ties to the extended family and community were weakened. Suburban life presented particular challenges, and although these smaller, self-sufficient families were presented within the media as an ideal unit, conflicts soon arose between the media depiction of the idealized lifestyle and the realities of nuclear living. Further tensions emerged as contemporary gender relations were strained by the advent of the women's liberation movement and the new-found sexual freedom enjoyed by a generation of women who had access to safer contraception. Inevitably, the traditional dynamics of sexual relationships and the hegemony of patriarchy were challenged as women's calls for equality threatened to overturn the status quo.

In selected examples of popular music from the early 1960s, it is possible to detect allusions to these undercurrents and the tensions evoked by the contradictory social messages informing the era. The Beach Boys' car songs offer an especially rich source of encoded communication about contemporary attitudes to women, sex, and hierarchies of power and control. With a view to understanding the depiction of women and contemporary gender relations in the Beach Boys' work, I will draw on Sigmund Freud's writings on the subconscious to illustrate how repressed emotions could be seen to have found a mode of creative expression within the lyrics and narratives of specific car songs. Using Freud's concept of transformation where he suggests that the fetishization of objects and imagery are an outlet for unreconciled feelings, I will show how, at a time of growing female emancipation, men's conflicted desires and thoughts about the women were transferred onto the safer, less emotionally charged repository of the automobile. Through an analysis of lyrics I illustrate how the music's subtext articulates the fears, frustrations, and misogyny of a generation of young men struggling to come to terms with women's sexual and social liberation.

Social context

The 1950s and early 1960s were unequivocally affluent years. During this period, the US Gross National Product increased fivefold as consumer items flooded the market and home ownership rose significantly. According to Leiby (1978, p. 273) returning servicemen were among the first to take advantage of the affluent zeitgeist by setting up home and establishing families. Within the newly expanded economic climate, the nuclear family was presented as a model of stability, particularly after the turbulent years of the Depression and the Second World War, where family life had been badly fractured and fragmented. Alternative styles of living were not sanctioned, and contemporary mores dictated that young people should stay at home before going on to create a nuclear family:

> At mid-century almost 80% of all people lived in households in which there was a married couple. This meant that many adult children lived with their parents until getting married, or only lived on their own for a very short period. This was clearly the cultural standard. Other household forms were either deviant or transitional. (Wright and Rogers, 2010, p. 8)

However, while nuclear living provided a perfect solution to the need for a more self-reliant and mobile workforce, in practice the socially engineered template concealed a far darker reality. The media depiction of nuclear living romanticized the small, tight-knit units, but the restrictive, rigidly proscribed gender roles, isolation, and narrowly internal focus could be frustrating and stifling. It should be taken into account that the pre-eminence of the nuclear family was not a response to the collective desires of individuals, and as a result, the lifestyle it determined was somewhat artificial. Nuclear living was based more upon economic imperatives, and, inevitably, the problems of realizing an artificially constructed mode of living created pressures that were difficult to resolve. In particular, for women whose lives were more circumscribed anyway, the pressures of nuclear life were magnified. Within the parameters of the more traditional extended family, there had been a range of socially acceptable roles for women, and intergenerational living offered a good deal of social and practical support to those at either end of the age spectrum. With the advent of the nuclear unit, marriage and childbearing were the only socially sanctioned lifestyle options, as Harvey (1993, p. 69) explains:

> The institution of marriage had a power and inevitability in the fifties that it has never had since. You simply didn't ask yourself 'if' you wanted marriage and children; the only relevant questions were when and how many? And the answers were, as soon as possible and as many as possible.

Undoubtedly, within the evolving landscape of sexual relations, the obsession with early marriage was a source of great tension. The rules surrounding the sexual behaviour of women were at odds with contradictory messages circulating in the media, creating a recipe for conflict and confusion. Birth control was now more freely available but whereas before the 1950s cultural expectations ensured that men would respect a woman's chastity, increasingly the onus now fell upon women to protect their virginity. This could prove to be difficult, since the pressure to marry as quickly as possible forced women to engage in any form of sexual activity (short of penetration) in order to secure the attentions of a man. Furthermore, as pregnancy outside marriage was not sanctioned, any sexual activity before marriage had to be counterbalanced against fears of unwanted pregnancy. Young people of either sex found themselves under pressure to marry as early as possible because alternative ways of living were yet to be condoned, a point elaborated in a study of contraception by Marks (2001, p. 22):

> The nuclear family was perceived as conforming to certain ideals. Anyone who failed to achieve these ideas was viewed with suspicion. They included those bearing children outside marriage, couples who conceived more children than intended, as well as those who failed to produce children.

In an era when marriage was at the pinnacle of social success, the single life was not a desirable option for women—that is unless they were prepared to face a life of poverty and social abjection. According to O'Brien (1974), spinsters were outlawed during the 1950s because society was unable to countenance their existence. In the wake of a world war where social reconstruction was so dependent on increasing the birth rate, women were expected to embrace motherhood positively and rapidly. In this context, single and childless women posed such a threat that some were even subjected to psychoanalytic and pharmacological interventions on the grounds that child rearing was a natural impulse. In the words of Fink and Holden (1999, p. 237):

> By the 1930s the spread of psychoanalytic ideas focused concern on the dangers of repression, that if an outlet was not found for the childless woman's sexual and maternal instincts they were a potential destructive force within society and especially to the institution of marriage.

The medicalization and social stigmatization was reinforced in media portrayal of the unmarried where negative representations served to warn women of the dangers of stepping outside the confines of marriage and motherhood. The messages communicated illustrate Peach's (1998) observations regarding the function of the stereotype as a means of social control. Without doubt, the combined weight of such social pressures led to a degree of desperation in the sphere of sexual relations, where pleasing a man was an all-important route to securing marriage in an era when competition to find a spouse was particularly fierce. Numbers of available men were decimated by wartime fatality, resulting in a situation described by Zeiger (2010, p. 130) who explains how an unfortunate "two to five million marriageable women in America [were] doomed to remain spinsters because of the male-female disproportion."

The anxieties around finding a partner were further magnified by women's changing status within the post-war workforce. Whereas in wartime, they were invited to take on paid work, replacing men who were away on active service, when the war ended, single women were forced to give up their jobs to returning servicemen. Those who continued to work were expected to take on more menial jobs for minimal pay, despite the fact that during wartime women in employment had gained a significant degree of financial and emotional independence. In Metzl's (2003, p. 247) words: "Often overwhelming social pressure sought to have women give up their jobs and return to their positions as happy, reproductive homemakers, in order to ensure jobs for the returning veterans." The positive gains women were experiencing could no longer be countenanced at the expense of the well-being of men, so they had no choice but to give up the freedoms and independence provided by regular employment.

While it was still commonly believed that looking after a family and running a home were the most suitable occupations for a woman, in the past, those who could afford to had been able to engage the services of a servant. However, the numbers entering domestic service were declining rapidly for as Palmer (2011, p. 2) writes: "World War II [was] the final moment when housewives in large numbers could hope to hire another woman to do part of the work designated as theirs." As a result, women in the 1950s were expected to do their own housework and to take pride in making the home clean and inviting for their husband and family. Furthermore, with the advent of cheaper electrical appliances it was difficult to justify paying for any help around the house and therefore women's domestic duties expanded, leading to endless days of childcare and cleaning. Housework may have been presented as an ideal occupation but the majority of women had been reluctant to give up paid employment and most preferred to work outside the home. This point is reinforced by Evans (1997, p. 247) who found that 80 per cent of women polled in a contemporary survey said they would prefer to return to their wartime jobs.

The beginnings of a backlash

The ascent of the nuclear idyll was short lived and by the early 1960s the first signs of a feminist backlash appeared. Between 1960 and 1961 *Redbook* magazine ran a series of articles on the subject of "Why young mothers feel trapped," a topic that quickly generated 24,000 responses from women desperate to express their dissatisfaction and isolation. The timing of the feature was significant for as Harvey (1993, p. 226) explains, 1960 was a 'demographic watershed':

> [This] was the year that the trend in early marriages began to reverse itself, and indeed the marriage rate itself began a thirty year decline. Although material changes in women's lives were still years away, the events of 1960 were harbingers of a revolution to come.

The *Redbook* article was followed by a more incendiary text in 1962 when Helen Gurley Brown's book *Sex and the Single Girl* was published. Her book not only gave women advice on how to become independent of men financially, it also discussed women experiencing sexual relationships before marriage and even *without* ever being married. Among other shocking topics, women were told where they might have to go find potential partners, how to look sexy, and how to enjoy a love affair—contentious subjects in an era when men were expected to make the key decisions regarding sexual matters and when marriage was considered the only morally and socially acceptable route for sexually active women.

In 1963, Betty Friedan's book *The Feminine Mystique* added fuel to the growing evidence of a feminist awakening. The book's opening lines identified a nameless problem which she claimed had "lay buried, unspoken, for many years in the minds of American women"; a problem likened to "a strange stirring, a sense of dissatisfaction," and "a yearning" (Friedan, 1963, p. 15). Distilling the results of a survey she had carried out on fellow students while at college, she explained how women who had given up their own education at the expense of their husbands' were left feeling bored and trapped by domesticity. Adding a further nail into the coffin of patriarchal theorizing, she also used her knowledge of psychology to critique Freud's work on the subconscious, in particular his view that women suffered from penis envy (Freud, 1933/1995, pp. 155–58).

Changing gender relations

Regardless of the negative public attitudes towards spinsters and the prevailing disapprobation surrounding sex outside marriage, gender relations were forced to change once the growing body of literature critiquing the constraints of contemporary femininity was accompanied by sweeping social reforms. These developments posed an even bigger threat to the status quo in terms of their effect on emancipating women. Safer birth control was approved by the US Federal Government in 1960, allowing married women to determine when or even whether they would have a family. Although the improved options were not yet available to single women, it did allow those who were married to make decisions about the timing and size of their families, a degree of agency they had lacked with the less reliable and more inaccessible contraception on offer prior to the 1960s. This emancipatory act was followed in 1961 by the Presidential Commission on the Status of Women, an initiative designed to research and report upon women's equality. The report findings criticized the inequalities faced by women in the United States; however, in Weigand's (2002, p. 157) view the fact that it went on to exalt their traditional role of homemakers as 'anti-communist' exposes the contradictory character of gender relations at this time. These underlying conflicts underpin the climate of gender relations in an era described by Marton (2001, p. 163) as "an edgy time of transition, change, and confusion." Moreover, as the decade progressed, the feminist call for equal pay, equal opportunities at work, and more egalitarian domestic relationships continued to disrupt the traditional dynamics of gender relations.

Conflicting media messages at the time highlight some of the irreconcilable issues as well as the difficulties women faced in moving forward towards greater equality. In particular, contemporary pop songs provide us with a window on the troubled terrain of gender relations and a society struggling to come to terms with female emancipation. On the one hand, lyrics and narratives appear to reinforce dependence upon men while simultaneously broadcasting a call for independence. For instance, in 1962 as female narrator of the popular song "Johnny Angel," Shelley Fabares wailed meekly that she would 'just' sit and wait when other men asked her on a date, adding that she would rather concentrate on her potential lover, Johnny Angel. The next year, Little Peggy March also chose passivity towards the male love object in the song "I Will Follow Him" (1963), proclaiming she would follow her male lover wherever he went, before proclaiming that he was her destiny.

By contrast Leslie Gore's 1964 hit single echoes Friedan's call to arms when she tells her man that it is not for him to decide what she can and cannot do. She reclaims the freedom to express herself and make her own decisions. The song reminds the audience that women no longer have to be controlled by men or spend their lives trying to please them. Just a year later the song "These Boots are Made for Walkin'" struck a chord with downtrodden American women, as Nancy Sinatra warns her cheating lover of the punishment he may soon receive— that her boots are going to walk all over him one day. Clearly, some women were struggling to make a break with tradition, to stand up for themselves, and to refuse to be dominated by men. These examples expose both the conflicts and the evolving character of gender relations as men and women tried to adjust to the fast pace of social reform.

On the highway to hedonism

References to the automobile in contemporary song also reveal a great deal about gender relations. It is not surprising since the car was central to many of the changes in American culture during the period in question: determining the nature of life in the suburbs and defining hierarchies of power and control. Evidence of the ascendance of car ownership is provided by Lewis and Goldstein (1983, p. 29) who note how, during the period between 1900 and 1980, the number of motor vehicle registrations in the United States soared from a modest 8,000 to 120 million. Owning a car was fundamental to the realization of the American dream, enabling men to travel to work and then back again to homes and families in suburbia. It also dominated the sphere of leisure where motor vehicles played a major role in the social lives of teenagers and young adults throughout the 1950s and 1960s (see Chapter 1 in this volume). At this juncture, the automobile became a potent symbol of freedom and modernity, introducing new ways of experiencing life and relationships. Although the fictional protagonists of Kerouac's legendary, freewheeling novel *On the Road* (1957/1991) make use of various alternative means of transport on their epic road trips, it is the car that captures most: the spirit and the dreams of an era uninhibited by fears of pollution and petrol shortages.

Cars were the transport of choice for a generation of young men who had access to either the family car or, in many cases, a vehicle of their own. As a result, they enjoyed levels of mobility and independence their parents and grandparents had never experienced. Contemporary styling ensured that cars reflected the forward-looking ideology of the era and for most men, the automobile symbolized success, freedom, and virility. In the culture of teenage courtship, cars provided the additional function of a private social space where, in relative seclusion, it was possible to conduct intimate relationships away from the watchful eyes of parents and others in authority. Its powerful hold on the national imagination ensured that cars featured significantly in popular culture: in films, advertisements, and popular music of the period, the vehicle's presence is indicative of its ubiquity and omnipresence in the collective consciousness.

If we examine lyrics of popular songs from the era, the car articulates a variety of messages about the dynamics of contemporary gender roles. The use of the car as a metaphorical device can be traced back to the 1930s and the work of bluesman Robert Johnson, whose gender-coded objectification of women surfaces in some decidedly misogynistic lyrics. In a study of the song "Terraplane Blues," Anne Lemon (1997) shows how the artist conflates his car with the female body, suggesting that a woman exists primarily, as a machine existing solely for the sexual gratification of a selfish male. We learn that the female protagonist of the song is not sexually responsive, comparing her to an engine whose batteries need to be charged. Johnson goes on to tell her how he plans to remedy the situation by fixing a loose connection so that her 'spark plug' will give him fire.

More recently, the artist Prince introduces the automobile as a feminine metaphor in the song "Little Red Corvette" (1983), where the line about his female lover, named after the car in question, being 'too fast', warns the female driver to stop playing fast and loose, and settle down. In fact, Prince relates the characteristics of the Corvette (fast, agile, dangerous) to the woman. In his song, he sees the car as being out of control, just as the woman, and it needs him to put things into order again. Examples like this illustrate the car's utility as a repository for unresolved thoughts and feelings regarding female sexuality, but it is in the work of vocal harmony group the Beach Boys that we find the motor vehicle's qualities explored most fully and, for this reason, their repertoire deserves closer investigation.

The Beach Boys: Sunshine, surf, and cars

The Beach Boys' fascination with the car can be attributed in part to their upbringing and proximity to the beach in the Hawthorne district of Southern California, an area where car racing was a popular leisure pursuit. During the 1960s, the group's eulogizing of car culture tapped into the collective conscious of young men who spent much of their free time in and around their vehicles. Many enjoyed the practice of 'hot rodding,' a way of customizing vehicles to make them run faster, and drag racing and parading were customary ways of showing off the results. One account describes a typical evening scene:

> After dark when all the stores closed and all the shoppers had gone home, the atmosphere for automotive carousing became electrified: Flashing lights, neon lights, blinking traffic signals, and glaring street lamps transformed the commercial corridor into a brightly lit automotive stage. (Witzel and Bash 1997, p. 44)

The preoccupation with car culture can be detected in many of the Beach Boys' songs, where popular vehicles of the day are lovingly referenced. From the nifty Deuce Coupe and the powerful 409, to the aerodynamically styled Thunderbird and Stingray, no technical detail was too small as the minutiae of individual car performance is painstakingly elaborated. In Schinder and Schwartz's words:

> To the generation that came of age in the first half of the 1960s, the Beach Boys will forever be identified with a bucolic vision of an innocuous, carefree, pre-Beatles America. The quintet's lengthy string of hits mythologized middle class teenage life and the mythical ideal of California, extolling the virtues of hot rods, surfing and youthful romance. (Schinder and Schwartz, 2008, p. 102)

When they are examined in more detail, however, the lyrics of many of these songs reveal something of the dynamics of power relations between the sexes, and themes of ownership and control are never far from the surface. The song "409," for example, refers to a new breed of cars with increased engine capacity designed to compete with heavier, more powerful domestic automobiles. With lyrics such as talking about how impossible she is to catch, and how she really 'shines' when taken to the track, it is the first in a series of car songs to introduce the use of the female metaphor. Assigning a female identity to the fast moving vehicle, the owner is clearly proud of its stylish appearance and capacity for speed. However, unlike the women of the early 1960s who were engaged in a determined battle for independence, the car is firmly under the control of its male owner.

A year later the group released *Little Deuce Coupe*, an album dedicated almost entirely to the joys of automobile culture. Within the recording themes of car ownership abound and while on the surface this may seem relatively innocuous, the possessive impulses reveal insights into contemporary gender dynamics. In "Our Car Club" the male narrator informs listeners how he and his friends intend to set up a boys car club, one that demonstrates 'class and style.' Innocuous enough, but the lines which follow reveal how they intend to get those cars. In this song, the use of the gender specific pronoun 'she' again confers femininity upon the vehicles, thereby casting the neutral object within an imagined binary of male ownership/female as object of possession.

In the song "Little Deuce Coupe," themes of ownership are further elaborated as the narrator boasts about 'her' expressing possession and using a diminutive. The male narrator continues, lovingly referencing the small car's automotive parts and technology. The gender-coding of the vehicle implies that while the car has the capacity for high speed (a quality which might enable it to go far), the male owner is still fully in control of the potentially wayward object. While the speed of the vehicle could be viewed as a metaphor for female freedom, the more intimate car interior takes on another set of characteristics that can be interpreted as the female body. In the song "Cherry Cherry Coupe" for instance, the narrator describes a quasi-sexual relationship he has with his vehicle, making sure to remind the audience that he is its owner. The car's interior is presented as inviting, alluding to the potential it is offering for a romantic encounter. Because the car is small and inviting, his thoughts dwell on the prospect of intimacy when moments of leisure are linked to pleasure and the potential for a sexual response from the vehicle in the repeated line about her getting 'sparks' when she begins to 'whine.' Another song, "Little Honda" contains encoded allusions to sexual relations as the narrator projects his fantasies onto a feminine-coded motorbike. The "Little Honda" is informed of the owner's plans for the day. What could be seen here is the male narrator's idea of making plans with a girlfriend, expressing traditional gender roles.

Having established the schedule, there are references to acceleration, which, in the context of the relationship formed with the motorbike, might be read as a metaphor for progressive levels of physical intimacy. In this light, the proposed trip comes with the expectation of some sort of release for the narrator as he assures the bike that it is alright to go accelerate further; faster is alright.

The examples mentioned thus far depict fast moving vehicles as instruments of pleasure, but the ever-present urge to control and take ownership of feminine-coded forms of transport takes on far more misogynistic connotations in "The Ballad of Old Betsy." Here, conflicted thoughts and feelings are projected onto a car which is now past its prime. In the disturbing tale we learn that 'Old Betsy' was once the narrator's attractive and youthful companion. The narrator confirms Betsy's fidelity. And yet, he goes on to question it, referring to previous encounters with car owners. The car owners can also be interpreted as previous partners. The fact that the car's innocence is compromised arouses the narrator's anxiety and he goes on to say that 'she' had her own 'favourites' before they met. A woman lacking in experience cannot make such comparisons, but her sexual experiences place her in a position to judge subsequent lovers. This leads to a sadistic turn in the lyrics when we learn that Betsy has been physically beaten. Meanwhile, the narrator sheds sentimental tears over the car's ageing form and beauty.

When girlfriends and women are referenced in a less oblique manner, they are still objectified and portrayed in terms of the language of car ownership. For instance in "Car Crazy Cutie" where the protagonist's girlfriend is admired not just for her looks but for her knowledge and dedication to the automobile: she knows about everything technical, 'man,' and has grease under her fingernails. The male narrator continues that it is difficult to decide whether he is more attached to his car than he is to the girlfriend, since the two are merged at some point with the 'car crazy cutie' providing the bridge between the car's identity and the women's identity. Either way, the narrator's main aim is to proclaim ownership and show off the object of his affection.

It is also interesting to note, by contrast, how women are described when they are in control of the car themselves, as is the case in the song "Fun, Fun, Fun," where a girl, having lied to her father and without his permission, has taken his car on what turns out to be a joyride. Here, the car becomes a metaphor for female emancipation. The female subject of the song is depicted as disliked by fellow women for her capability to drive at high speed, perhaps on the grounds that it is somehow 'unfeminine' to do so: the other girls cannot stand her since she drives like an 'ace.' In an era where the majority of women had to surrender their chance of freedom by sacrificing their jobs to men, this could be read as the general approbation expressed towards women who failed to conform. The song tells us that the men joined forces to compete with her (albeit unsuccessfully). Ultimately, however, the female driver must submit to the forces of patriarchy when her father, having found out about her lying, takes back the keys. At this point, the narrator assures her that although she can no longer drive independently, he has plans for her to join him on his rides. Hence, where the male is the primary figure of authority, the female driver's efforts to drive away at high speed might be read as an attempt to escape the predictable confines of femininity, and the father's reclaiming of the car key might be viewed as a way of reasserting masculine control. Furthermore, by exploiting the situation and establishing himself as back in the driving seat (and thus determining the character of any potential fun), the narrator colludes with her father to maintain patriarchal authority over the girl.

Objectification

The Beach Boys' objectification of women is not confined solely to songs about cars. Indeed, other material released by the group portrays women in a similar manner. In the song "California Girls," for example, American females are categorized according to their geographical location, with lyrics describing women from the respective regions almost entirely on the basis of their appearance and ability to satisfy male sexual urges. Where 'East Coast girls' are seen as trendy and the group love their dress sense, northern girls are praised for their kissing abilities and because they keep their boyfriends 'warm' at night. If we consider the persistence of this objectification from a feminist perspective, sexual connotations within the texts can be related to the requirements of patriarchy, where it is anticipated that men's sexual and emotional needs will be gratified first and foremost. The innocence of such fun-filled songs must be questioned for as Bartky (1990) points out, the practice of seeing someone as an object existing solely for the purpose of sexual gratification is a process where a person's individual needs are disregarded and their personal qualities and needs are minimalized or ignored. The media play a major role in circulating ideologies and informing preferred representations of femininity, many of which reduce women to the role of receptive and submissive sexual subordinates. While the Beach Boys are not alone in depicting women as objects, their work adds to the combined weight of demeaning and often sexist texts already in circulation. Nevertheless, the medium of popular music is particularly potent in providing rich and memorable representations, all the while acting as an emotional backdrop to social life. Presenting women as sexual playthings subliminally reinforces the assumption that, more than anything else, women are supposed to want and need men, and the primary female role is to please the men by fulfilling fantasies in their lives.

Freud on creativity and the subconscious

Clearly, when viewed as a means of expressing thoughts and feelings about women, the Beach Boys' collective outpourings show somewhat conflicted attitudes to the opposite sex. On the one hand, they demean women and deny their individuality and, on the other, they express a deep-rooted need for female company and support. Songs like "Help Me Rhonda" illustrate how, at the very least, another woman can assuage the pain of rejection when the male protagonist is cheated on by his fiancé. Fear of abandonment also dominates "God Only Knows" where in the event of a breakup, lead vocalist Carl Wilson laments that the world would mean nothing, thereby demonstrating the depth of his dependence on a woman. Women in the songs are objects of desire and a source of pleasure but this in itself creates tensions regarding security and issues of control. They may have minds of their own and fail to reciprocate male desire; they may even choose to leave a man or forsake one man for another.

From a psychoanalytic viewpoint the infiltration of the group's contradictory impulses is of interest and Freud's pioneering work on the subject of creativity has much to offer regarding insights into the way the mind processes conflicted feelings. Through his research, he came to the conclusion that unresolved desires were the primary impetus underpinning the creative process. In the essay "Creative Writers and Day-Dreaming" (Freud, 1908/2001), he suggests that daydreaming and fantasy are safety mechanisms for the subconscious and that these activities help to feed creativity. This view implies that well-balanced, fulfilled, and happy people may lack the driving force that moves others to produce art, for as Freud puts it, "happy people never make phantasies, only unsatisfied ones. Unsatisfied wishes are the driving power behind phantasies; every separate phantasy contains the fulfilment of a wish, and improves on unsatisfactory reality" (Freud, 1908/1968, pp. 34–43).

He goes on to argue that "unsatisfied wishes are the driving power behind fantasies; every separate fantasy contains the fulfillment of a wish, and improves an unsatisfactory reality" (Freud, 1908, in Arieti, 1976, p. 22). Like neurosis, which also arises from unfulfilled wishes and thwarted desire, the creative impulse necessarily draws on the sublimation of unfulfilled desires, very often of a sexual nature. In Freud's view, a preoccupation with matters sexual manifests itself in three distinctive and different outcomes: repression, compulsive defence mechanisms, or sublimation.

> [The] first is repression, which is quite energetic. The second outcome occurs when sexual investigation is not totally repressed but is coped with by thought processes or by compulsive defenses. In the third outcome, which is the "most rare and perfect type," sexual curiosity is sublimated into that inquisitive attitude which leads to creativity. (Freud, 1908 in Arieti, 1976, p. 22)

The exact nature of the source of musical inspiration is unclear, and as Sloboda (1985) points out, the secrets are yet to be unlocked as studies on the subject are currently limited. When questioned on the sources of his inspiration, the composer Beethoven allegedly said: "You ask me where I obtain my ideas [for a theme]. I cannot answer this with certainty: they come unbidden" (Kennedy, 1999, p. 157).

Transformation

According to Freudian theory, the subconscious mind bypasses the critical power of the superego by making use of what Freud calls 'transformations'—a means of processing information without the superego's usual censorship. Essentially, transformations are a mental toolkit that the subconscious mind can mobilize to obscure the content of uncensored information emerging from the deepest levels of the imagination. The transformations repackage these forbidden desires into more innocent and therefore more acceptable dream imagery. In this way, the id and the subconscious mind collude to resolve internal conflict by offering a sanitized version of an individual's primitive urges, ensuring that the unacceptable forces are thereby contained.

Freud suggested transformations could be divided into four distinct categories: symbols, representations, displacement, and condensation. Through the use of symbols problematic concepts can be converted into imagery, thereby turning unacceptable desires into something more palatable. As Freud believed that the majority of unconscious symbols are linked to sexual concerns, symbolic devices are able to act as a substitute for forbidden actions and unacceptable ideas. He uses examples such as sticks, tree-trunks, and swords and rockets which surface to symbolize the penis, whereas through transformation hollow objects like houses, boxes, and cupboards act as substitute for the female organs. The function of representations is broad enough to transform single thoughts into a range of more acceptable imagery. Through the process of displacement, an emotionally charged object can be replaced by a more acceptable substitute, which effectively hides the inadmissible archetype. By contrast, with condensation, different dream elements can work together linking ideas, words, sounds, images in ways that incorporate subconscious impulses. This allows groups to be formed out of disparate individuals on the basis of an element common to each of them. Hence, the Beach Boys' grouping of girls according to regional location in "California Girls" could be read as an attempt to transform the unresolved and conflicted desire to possess women into a more acceptable set of images.

The content of dreams was divided by Freud into two aspects: latent and manifest. Where the manifest content provides an acceptable version of what goes on in the dreamer's mind, the latent content offers insight into forbidden thoughts, desires, and motivations. Due to the censorious character of sexually motivated thoughts, information must be offered in a distorted or concealed fashion so that they can fulfil the dreamer's subconscious wishes, often at a fantasy level in dreams. Through the medium of songwriting, a similar resolution can be achieved when the artist projects deep-rooted desires upon a seemingly innocent text. For instance, an analysis of the lyrics of a singularly troubling song by the Beach Boys offers a potent source. In "Hey Little Tomboy," the narrator invites a young girl to sit on his knee so that he can offer her a word of advice. He explains to the 'tomboy,' who seems to be unaware of her feminine appearance, that she has come of age and must now turn her attentions away from sport to satisfying the sexual needs of men. Next he informs her of how he has been observing her and what she needs to learn in order to join other women in responding to the universality of male sexual desire. He suggests for her to wear clothes that show more flesh and is also prepared to teach her how to kiss, claiming that this is what women do everywhere.

The manifest message of the song connotes the timeless tradition where young people are given advice by their elders. However, the latent message can be deduced from the fact that the young girl must first submit to physical contact and to behave like a child rather than an equal. Although she is presented in the song as a child, presumably a symbolic device designed to assuage subconscious fears surrounding the dangerous character of adult femininity and sexuality, the man's intentions can be read as less than paternal. The desire to control and to manipulate the object of desire surfaces when the narrator informs his protégé of his intention to kiss her. Even then, regardless of how she may feel about these overtures, she is told how she ought to feel.

In conclusion, the Beach Boys were not alone in their objectification of women, and it is easy to find a conflicted message regarding gender relations in other artists' work from the period in question. What is striking about their music is the sharp contrast between the upbeat sound and carefree imagery of much of the group's repertoire and the troubled nature of the underlying message. As women struggled to gain greater independence through personal and collective political efforts, their endeavours were airbrushed from the lyrics and narratives. To all intents and purposes the women in the Beach Boys catalogue of songs during the mid-1960s are at odds with the prevailing mood of self-direction, liberation, and the desire for change expressed by women in so many quarters of society. The car at this juncture becomes emblematic of a battle between the sexes, symbolizing on the one hand a new-found freedom while simultaneously acting as a metaphor for containment and control.

3

Music is the vehicle: Queen's "Don't Stop Me Now," *Top Gear*, and the driving anthem

Roddy Hawkins

There is no immediate sense in which the Queen song "Don't Stop Me Now" is about cars, roads, or driving. And yet, in 2005 viewers of the popular British television programme *Top Gear* decreed that it was the "Best Driving Song Ever" (*Queen Win*, 2005). In fact, the same could be said for Toto's "Africa"—and, for that matter, "Bohemian Rhapsody"—and any number of canonical rock and pop songs that rotate and feature on drive-time radio, or in compilations or playlists of driving songs. To put it another way, what constitutes a driving song—and especially a driving *anthem*—has very little to do with the extent to which cars, roads, and driving are explicitly represented in song lyrics, though the two may coincide. Rather, a driving anthem is a song that music supervisors and record producers deem good to sing and to play—to perform—in the car: it is a song *for* driving, not *about* driving. But in a broader sense the driving anthem in *Top Gear* compilations is indeed *about* driving because the term 'anthem' is a marker of participation and imagined community.

What kind of driver and driving is imagined here? Given the impossibility of generalizing about what individuals may enjoy driving to, and how they drive, the musical criteria for a driving anthem ought to be impossibly broad. But British-produced lists of driving anthems are predictably narrow; indeed, they are very closely related to those lists that appear under the heading of rock anthems, indie-rock anthems, and other closely related titles. The driving anthem, then, is a product of the gendered, racial dynamics in popular culture that are partly constituted by representation itself—in this particular case, by the work of the cultural industries, rock aesthetics, and a regime of automobility specific to 'the open road' and manifest in the language of the epigraphical 'epic drive'.[1]

In order to probe the highly stylized and stereotyped 'soundtrack' to the 'epic drive' in more depth, I undertake a close reading of "Don't Stop Me Now" in the context of the position it occupies as a driving anthem within the *Top Gear* franchise. The first part of the essay provides some background to the production of *Top Gear* between 2003 and 2015, and considers the ways in which gender, speed, and sound are linked to the cultural politics and nationalism of early twenty-first-century Britain. Set against this account of "combustion masculinity" (Redshaw, 2008, p. 80) a second stage explores the musical detail of the remediated song text, focusing on speed and movement in particular. A third stage considers the history of the compilation album as a means for understanding the rise and resonance of the driving anthem prior to the online paradigm of algorithms and personalized playlists. The conclusion considers all this in terms of the tensions between the visibility of representation and the invisibility of everyday experience, especially as it relates to the performance of masculinity.

Underpinning my argument is the claim that the ordinariness of both compilation albums and driving can benefit from a mode of close listening, and of critique, that sits between two currently dominant approaches to music, sound, and their relationship to automobility. The first approach is shaped by a focus on the meanings and histories tied to car song texts: it ranges from the car as a site of female empowerment (Lezotte, 2013) to the road as a space for contested national narratives (Schiller, 2014) and is informed more generally by what Gordon Slethaug (2017) has called the 'semiotics of the road.' The second approach concerns the history and politics of sensory experience, where music or other cultural texts tend to serve an illustrative function in accounts attuned instead to the technological mediation of sound, mobility, and space beyond representation (see LaBelle, 2010; Bijsterveld, Cleophas, Krebs, and Mom, 2014). Situated between these two approaches, and untethered from the literal representation of cars and roads, I argue that the speed and movement of "Don't Stop Me Now" suggest how the automotive space beyond the text is, so to speak, also contained within it. In pursuing this synthesis of text and space my approach is similar to Justin Williams (2010a; 2014) in his studies of G-funk and automotive listening, though the emphasis here is on the packaging and consumption of automobility rather than its impact on music production. Beyond automobility, the argument follows Freya Jarman (2013) in her account of affective distribution in radio, compilations, and playlists. Viewed in this light, the ordinariness—and the normativity—of automobility provides the everyday space for the fantasy of the 'epic drive,' a space that is at least partially constituted by the politics—and texts—of representation.

Sounding out gender, speed, and banter in *Top Gear*

In March 2015, the news in Britain was awash with the story that Jeremy Clarkson, the lead presenter of the BBC prime time motoring show *Top Gear*, had been sacked for physically assaulting and verbally abusing one of the show's junior producers. The incident followed a decade of high-profile occasions where Clarkson appeared to provoke controversy and cause complaints with his offensive on-screen and off-screen remarks. In 2010 Frances Bonner, author of *Ordinary Television* (2003), attributed the "cheerful" reactionary politics of Clarkson-era *Top Gear* as the most plausible reason for its lack of scholarly attention. She warned that critical study of *Top Gear* ran the risk of falling foul of the disarming discourse that would mock those who took its socially conservative politics and brand of humour seriously (Bonner, 2010). *Top Gear* was "a potent mixture," Bonner concluded, "a slippery candidate for investigation" and part of a genre that she called "invisible television" (2010, p. 44).

With the benefit of a decade of hindsight, and following the rise of populist politics and the renewed confidence of authoritarian regimes across the world, Clarkson-era *Top Gear* seems both hopelessly out of date and a portent of the populism that has followed. But the show looks even older in its first, 1990s incarnation, prior to a relaunch in 2002 when the format of the programme changed to emphasize entertainment rather than information. The 2002 relaunch was hugely successful, with an alleged "one billion viewers across 117 different countries" choosing to watch across a range of formats and in a variety of ways (Bonner, 2010, p. 32). Based in an aircraft hangar, the studio, complete with live audience, formed the central location from which the revamped show was hosted. Importantly, the shift in format meant that from 2002 there were regular 'live' link segments between pre-recorded items filmed on-location; it was during link segments that the presenters (three middle-aged, 'Middle England' white men—Jeremy Clarkson, Richard Hammond, and James May) acted out their on-screen personas in the presence of the studio audience—a space where speed and power were discursively performed. Similar modes of discourse were performed during celebrity guest interviews and 'news' segments; elsewhere 'The Stig,' an anonymous male racing driver of suprahuman abilities, acted in a slightly different way, primarily as a blank canvas for some mildly ironic fantasy work—as encapsulated in the strapline "I am the Stig" which appeared on various items of *Top Gear* merchandise. In contrast, the older format had no studio, no audience, and little to no interaction between presenters; it tended instead towards factual reviews, industry news, more frequent analysis of 'everyday' cars and a now defunct section on used cars (Bonner, 2010). The shift might be encapsulated as a move from a magazine-style motoring programme based around consumer advice to a lifestyle, 'infotainment' programme. As Bonner (2010) has it, this change in format meant that although "information [was] secondary to entertainment . . . both [remained] predicated . . . on the centrality of cars to a life worth living" (p. 35), underpinned by, and manifest in, "a discourse of fantasy about cars and the pleasures of driving" (p. 7).

At the heart of this fantasy is speed. With Clarkson as the focal point, *Top Gear* asserted the importance of speed and power above all else, whether in self-mocking segments such as the "Star in a Reasonably Priced Car," frequent "Challenges" (in which the presenters competed against each other, typically in ridiculously inappropriate vehicles), or the more obvious testing of sports cars. Like an endangered species, the pleasure of driving was something which that trio of *Top Gear* presenters were concerned to protect, especially in the face of what some scholars of automobility, in more sober terms, describe as "a continuously increasing disciplining of drivers" (Böhm et al., 2006, p. 10). In April 2012, for example, Clarkson wrote about the need for speed in his monthly *Top Gear* magazine article. Clarkson opined that

> the green, the weak and the hopeless must accept the fact that the faster you go, the more you have to think and, thus, the safer you are. Speed focuses the mind. It cuts through the fog of drab everyday living and keeps us on our toes. Speed keeps us focused. Speed works. Speed saves lives. Speed is good. And we should have more of it, not less. The simple fact is this. We are told to concentrate more. But we can only do that if we are allowed to go considerably faster. (2012, para. 15)

We can take the style of the following excerpt as a mild version of what the British comedian Stewart Lee has described as Clarkson's "outrageous politically incorrect opinions which he has every week to a deadline in the *Sunday Times*" (Lee, 2012, p. 54). But whatever one thinks of Clarkson's use of humour, it operates as a result of his 'playing to type,' deriving its sense of mischief from a widely known public persona based around anti-establishment posturing.

In terms of how speed relates to gender in this discourse, it is typical of what Redshaw (2008) has called 'combustion masculinity': "where the aggressive and competitive demonstration and exercise of car handling skill is given prominence over caution" (p. 80). In the British context it is important to frame this 'combustion masculinity' against the emergence in Britain of 'lad culture' during the 1990s, where the British 'bloke'—a term whose adjective means "stereotypically male in behaviour and interests" (*Concise Oxford*, 2002)—becomes fused with the new, younger 'lad,' a fusion epitomized in the 1990s by the coexistence in Britain of men's lifestyle magazines such as *Loaded* and *FHM* and 'sitcom' television programmes such as *Men Behaving Badly*. Importantly, part of the success and, arguably, the power of the discourse and representations in publications such as *Loaded* (and programmes such as *Top Gear*) derive from a form of 'ironic' humour popularly described as 'banter,' a term which defines a playful, friendly exchange of teasing remarks that, while in no way confined to overt displays of masculinist representation, is nonetheless particularly associated with male social exchange and bonding rituals. In terms of a wider cultural context, where it is a popular idea, the deployment of banter helps to connect and reinforce assumed social bonds (and not simply those between men, as can be seen by the prevalence of informal modes of address and attempted banter in a wide variety of marketing materials and consumer packaging, from bottles of fruit juice to price-comparison websites). Lynne Segal (2009), for example, describes the discourse in men's magazines as a "sardonic, ironic, mild detachment from dominant ideals" of masculinity. This detachment, she writes, provides "inner self-confidence" even though it is precisely these same ideals that "are often most pronounced in boys and men most lacking in social power" (p. 142).

Within gender studies, this kind of 'banter' might be framed as a symptom of 'the crisis of masculinity.' As with Connell's conceptualization of 'hegemonic masculinity,' to which it relates, the notion that there is actually a crisis of masculinity is a controversial idea.[2] But at least in terms of the symptoms of discourse, crisis remains a useful category. For example, it is against the backdrop of the crisis debate that Carroll (2011) explores reactionary forms of white masculinity in the American post–9/11 context, utilizing an understanding of hegemony that captures its fluid form as well as its normative content. For Carroll, whiteness is an important factor that informs the liability underpinning the hegemony of masculinity in contemporary America: "whiteness," he writes, seeks "the validation for its own authority—which it believes it has lost" (p. 180). Reflecting on reactionary politics, Carroll is especially concerned to highlight how white masculinity adapts to and maintains hegemony in a geopolitical context where it is made all the more powerful by "appeals to injury, cries for recognition and critiques of power" (p. 180). A slightly different account of the relationship between crisis and masculinity has been undertaken by Eastman (2012a; 2012b). His work investigates the formation of 'hegemonic masculinity' by 'rebel men' in their participation and interaction with southern rock. He bases his analysis primarily on class antagonism to show how an implicitly white hegemonic masculinity is performed by artists and fans of southern rock but in a compensatory way, as it were, by emphasizing aspects of masculine behaviour which go against the perceived hegemony of a metropolitan, northern mainstream, precisely those who dominate the instruments of political, educational, and legal power in the United States.

As noted above, the presenters in Clarkson-era *Top Gear* were fond of acting out an 'underdog' subject-position, having frequently mocked the 'political correctness' of the metropolitan BBC. Viewed from this perspective, the banter in *Top Gear* provided audiences with what Bonner (2010) calls 'avenues for disavowal': specifically, banter serves as an alibi for "viewers wishing to defend their enjoyment of the show against charges of complicit misogyny" (p. 41)—to which we might add homophobia, racism, and xenophobia.[3] Positioned against appeals to injury or censorship, the 'epic drive' and the driving song in *Top Gear* are therefore bound up with the powerful rhetoric of individualism and patriotism—the 'everyman' political discourse so beloved of today's political class—that frequently and nostalgically yearns for the simplicity and values of the past, not to mention its music and highways. This configuration of identity politics cuts across music and sound prominently in an episode broadcast in 2013—which concludes with a parade of British automotive engineering prowess, past, and present, on the Royal Mall outside Buckingham Palace (Wilman, 2013). Prior to this spectacle, Clarkson undertakes a test drive of the Jaguar F-type sports car. In a highly positive review, which sees Clarkson drive around empty roads in the Scottish Highlands, the presenter extols the virtues of a car that harks back to the assumed authenticity of the 1960s, when the predecessor to the F-type, the iconic Jaguar E-type, was designed and first manufactured in Britain. According to Clarkson, the visual beauty of the car, its sounds, and its speed all reinforce one another, making it a "proper," powerful sports car. He states:

> It's got such a wide range of intoxicating noises [. . .]. When you change up [a gear], it snorts like a hippo; and then when you put your foot down it bellows; and

then when you take it off again . . . [the edited film cuts to the exhaust crackling as Clarkson changes down the gears, as if it were a part of his sentence] . . . . Honestly, have you ever heard a soundtrack like that? That is the sound of the sixties right there. (Wilman, 2013)

In the same sequence, Clarkson frames the power of the F-type by referring to it as a "X-rated, hard-core monster for the terminally unhinged"; it is almost banal to point out how the engine noises are likening to the explosion of rock music through misty-eyed references to the hedonism of the late 1960s (see Heining, 1998, for an early discussion of these links, and Lezotte, 2013, for an alternative account). Similarly, because this particular review falls at the beginning of an episode that concludes with a militaristic parade outside Buckingham Palace in an explicit demonstration of nationalistic pride—including the trio of presenters 'in formation' in new Jaguar F-types—it is suggestive of the wider cultural and political resonance of the sounds and 'intoxicating noises' highlighted in this example.

Music and banter combine beyond the broadcast episodes, too, as in the CD booklet that accompanies an earlier compilation album *Top Gear: The Ultimate Driving Experience* (2005a). By using musical stereotypes to reinforce the respective personas of the presenters, they inform readers that

we asked our presenters to pick a driving song favourite of their own. Unfortunately, James's suggestion involved a 16th century madrigal and Jeremy's was some terrible 27 minute prog rock workout so we threw them in the bin. Happily, Richard came up trumps with the excellent BodyRockers' "I Like The Way." (Various Artists, 2005a)

In terms of the emergence of the anthem compilations produced under the *Top Gear* branding, the positive framing of more 'recent' music against the 'uncool' tastes of older father figures is important in understanding the compilation process and the ways in which the then revamped *Top Gear* valued younger audiences. In particular, it is worth noting that commercially successful indie-rock bands, associated with (and in many cases descended from) the 1990s Britpop phenomenon with which Lad Culture shares its origins, account for much of the music to be found on *Top Gear* driving-song compilations.

However, when an audience poll took place during series six of *Top Gear* (broadcast during the spring and summer of 2005), none of the songs considered for the award of "best driving song ever" came from the 1990s. The poll consisted of five songs and acted as a precursor to the release in 2007 of the compilation album *Top Gear Anthems: The Greatest Ever Driving Songs*. Each week one of the five candidates was discussed by James May; audience voting, meanwhile, occurred throughout the series. During the final episode of the series, May revealed that Queen's "Don't Stop Me Now" (1978) had topped the poll and won the award. Golden Earring's "Radar Love" (1973) was in second place, followed by Meat Loaf's "Bat out of Hell" (1977), Steppenwolf's "Born to Be Wild" (1968), and Deep Purple's "Highway Star" (1972). While there is a slight stylistic difference between the piano-driven, vocal-led recordings of Queen and Meat Loaf and the 'classic rock' guitar sound of the other contenders, the *Top Gear* audience poll marks a clear example of a highly constructed and stereotypical conception of driving and its mediation through rock music. While all of the songs can be discussed in terms of speed, power, and masculinity, I wish only to outline those symbolic and sonic aspects of "Don't Stop Me Now" where speed can be heard.

Framing the fantasy: Speed and structure in "Don't Stop Me Now"

First released by Queen on their 1978 album *Jazz*, "Don't Stop Me Now" is a song whose title gets straight to the point. Framed by a dreamy opening sequence and a similarly dreamy comedown at the close, the intervening music suggests a drug-fuelled hedonistic experience where anything is possible. Lasting just over three minutes in its original recorded version, the song is structured as summarized in Figure 3.1 (see next page).

In terms of lyrical content, it is not hard to find references to speed. Each of the verses is based around a straightforward sexual metaphor. In the first verse, Mercury describes himself as being like a spectacular comet and a 'racing car'—which, he warns, cannot be stopped. In the second verse the cosmic references continue, this time with Mercury as a space ship on course for a forceful impact, plus, of course, a 'sex machine' primed and ready to detonate. These images are brought together in the service of speed in the most explicit fashion during the repeated pre-chorus sections, where Mercury frames the heat and intensity of his ecstatic experience by saying that he's travelling at supersonic speeds. Quite how this combination of references is interpreted in terms of sexuality is discussed below; for present purposes it is necessary to emphasize that the specific content of these references is less important than the simple observation that speed and a

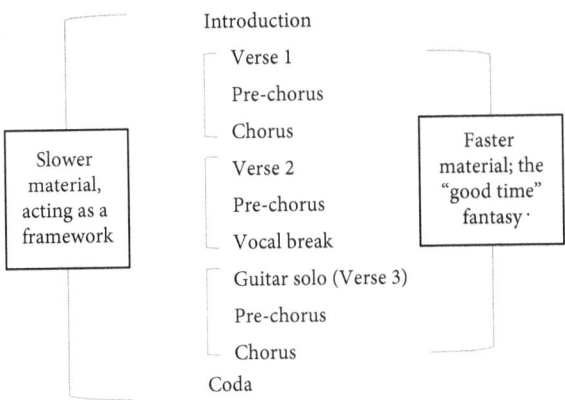

Figure 3.1 Overall song structure.

particular type of 'driving' or propulsion is hermeneutically audible in the lyrical content and its style of delivery.

Music on the recording reinforces lyrical expressions of speed in a number of ways. Throughout the song the vocal phrasing is structured around the symmetry of an arpeggiated rise and fall in pitch with a particular sense of acceleration. Indeed, the combination of a rise and fall in pitch could be applied to the musical structure more widely as a means of understanding the overall harmonic relationship between verse and pre-chorus. Specifically, the pre-chorus is characterized by the consistent appearance of the highest pitch in the vocal part (B flat), before leading back to the lowest (F) at the beginning of the chorus. This relation between verse and pre-chorus is in fact summarized within the fifteen-bar structure of the song's slow introduction where (with obvious adaptations) the first five bars are taken from (or recur in) the verse, the subsequent five in the pre-chorus, and the final five in the chorus. Harmonically, much of this material is organized in a way that pushes forward towards the next section, with the use of flattened seventh chords a particularly frequent means of either pushing the music into new frontiers, as it were, or sending it back from whence it came.

What, though, is really important in this effect is the rhythmic syncopation which provides the song's principal musical identity. It occurs at every level of the music, and can be heard most clearly as the main hook in the chorus, by extending syllables in the introduction, while in the coda it is heard as an echo throughout the vocal melody. What is important here is the way in which 'steep' pitch contours and rhythmic syncopation combine: in each case, steep, syncopated rises in the melody lead to a sustained note, whose process of arrival creates the effect of acceleration.[4] The effect of acceleration is important because 'combustion masculinity' suggests a mode of driving where acceleration and breaking are part of driving skill, in contrast to the monotony of motorway cruise control and sustained speed. After all, those alpine roads have frequent hairpin bends, which, as well as the absence of traffic, is part of their attraction.[5]

An analogous and more interesting example of this sonic effect occurs in the word repetition near the end of each verse. Each verse is constructed from two melodic phrases, identifiable lyrically by the onset of each new metaphor (the shooting star, racing car, etc.). At the end of each phrase, the verse ends with a simple cross-rhythm of three quavers against two, a figure which is both an extension of the syncopation already heard at the end of the first phrase in each verse and a link to the pre-chorus that follows. Unusually, the verse and pre-chorus are both organized in five-bar phrases of ten bars each, a grouping suggested by the harmonic structure underpinning the material; it is a structure which, by the use of a series of predominant chords, helps to propel the music forward and achieve a certain kind of fluency as a result of circularity. If this five-bar phrasing is somewhat unusual then it is not readily perceptible as such. For example, while the idea of a five-bar structure under each phrase suggests we hear a change of emphasis as the music arrives on the word 'me' over the chord of F major (bar 26; 0'51") our perceptions suggest something else. Upon listening to the song, an obvious structural shift is not what seems important: indeed it sounds as if the verse is continued, because the melodic phrase overlaps the harmonic transition, over-reaching it, as it were.

An alternative view might instead perceive this transition as a sudden increase and subsequent settling of momentum—and one achieved on the same stretch of road. In bar twenty-seven (0'52"), the flattened seventh is added to the previous chord of F major as we hear the first line of the melody to occur in the pre-chorus (when he 'burns' through the firmament). During this bar, the music appears to shift up a gear and increase in speed, signalled in part because the F major harmony is extended by the added seventh. But it is also manifest by the bass guitar's brief but forceful expedition into the higher register as the first line of the melody begins (up to the flattened seventh note, E flat) and its subsequent resolution (onto B flat, a vital pivot note towards the chord of G minor which, in turn, acts as the point of departure towards the chorus). With the B flat, the bass line settles back into its standard register (bar 28; 0'54") as the vocal melody arrives on one of its sustained notes, the cumulative effect of which is, to this listener at least, to make sonorous the image of having broken through the sound barrier: a sudden boost of speed and a brief feeling of weightlessness. With the bass and the melody as the points of focus in bars twenty-six to twenty-eight, one might yet deflect attention away from notions of structural change and instead towards continuity: more precisely, an acceleration (and a kind of perceptual suspension) prior to a return of equilibrium, with the chorus, less than ten bars later (and back in the home key) the immediate destination. What is important, then, is not the abstraction of song structure but listening 'with' the car (and those who sing in it).

In a similar way the framing of the song (by the slower introduction and coda) provides further instances of apparent acceleration and crossing of boundaries. At the beginning, the frame acts as a sort of 'starting grid,' as it were for what is to follow. Something is about to happen, but, crucially, the injection of movement has yet to occur: an intimate, pent-up Mercury sings of ecstasy, but we could also be waiting at a traffic light. As the music moves from this slower introduction to the first verse, the listener hears the song's first actual acceleration in the form of an accelerando. Actual or virtual sudden changes of speed also occur between sections in the transition to the guitar solo (2'13") and, most obviously of all, during the blissful transition into the post-coital coda (3'04"). To put it bluntly, it is not hard to hear this music in terms associated with 'combustion masculinity.'

Moving from sound to symbol, the framing device is doubly important because it enables—indeed, it enacts—a space for fantasy to operate, one which need not be *directly* related to the overt sexual and narcotic references of the lyrical content. For example, in his discussions of music, sport, and the spectacle of hypermasculinized rock anthems, McLeod (2006) observes how "homosexual anthems of liberation have [. . .] been successfully co-opted to serve traditional heterosexual masculine leisure" (p. 543); it is not a stretch to suppose something similar is at work here (nor in the infamous opening to the film *Wayne's World*). In a related way, it is important to remember that Queen were heavily invested in a male-centred discourse of authenticity specific to rock, in which the group's virtuosity and the spectacle of their live performances remain key (see Dickinson, 2001, p. 335). Certainly, this act of framing resonates with Bonner's observation that *Top Gear* is built upon "a discourse of fantasy about cars and the pleasures of driving" (2010, p. 7). That is to say that, beyond the very literal way in which fantasy is framed as such within the content of the song, the same structure also serves, metaphorically at least, to frame the wider conceptual tensions between representations and the reality of driving that this chapter seeks to complicate.

Taking for granted the obvious sing-along qualities behind Mercury's approach to melody, and not ignoring the infectious interaction of lead and backing vocals that precedes the guitar solo, these moments of acceleration, movement, and framing might help to explain how "Don't Stop Me Now" came to be voted the best ever driving song by *Top Gear* audiences. But what does it mean to frame this song (and others) as a driving *anthem*? In order to answer this question, the next section sketches out the development of what I call 'the normative anthem,' underpinned by a focus on the intersection of collective and individualistic forms of musicking (Small, 1998).

From the collective to the individual: Framing the driving anthem

In her doctoral study of the rock anthem, Dockwray (2005) draws on both textual analysis and listener surveys to identify participation as the main observable feature of rock anthems in a live context, examining how rock anthems are put together and the ways in which their lyrical and musical content helps achieve participation from audiences. She writes: "The key feature of rock anthems, which makes them different from other [rock] songs, occurs when every individual within a large group participates by adopting an identical (or similar) gestural or body movement in response to the music" (Dockwray, 2005, p. 57). However, participation would appear to be irrelevant when it comes to commercial, mass-produced compilation albums.

Dockwray's survey of listeners suggests that anthemic qualities coalesce around the ideas of songs as 'timeless classics'—in sonic terms, qualities identified as grandiose, uplifting, and imposing. Indeed, according to the *Oxford English Dictionary*, an anthem is "a rousing or uplifting song identified with a particular group or cause" (2002). The historical roots of the anthem derive from the sudden shift to a vernacular-based liturgy in sixteenth-century Reformation England, but it is only later, in the nineteenth century in particular, that the anthem became increasingly participatory, with a directness and relative simplicity in both sacred and secular contexts. This shift followed the twin developments of Wesley's church hymns and secular national anthems, the latter providing the clearest historical precedents for sung participation in the name of the modern nation; following its roots in religion, the anthem became "a secular, participatory song" (Dockwray, 2005, p. 19). There are, then, historical roots that link anthems with social, cultural, and political power. Over time musical anthems offered a space where, in today's academic discourse, collective identity work was undertaken. Whether written to celebrate God, monarchs, the nation-state, or its people, musical anthems are imbued with a history that asks large numbers of people to celebrate the collective, to delimit the power of the individual, and to do so with an increasing emphasis on participation in performance.

During the later 1980s and early 1990s, a new phase of musical anthems emerged when an expanding catalogue of compilation titles saw the following related trends take place: first, the anthem no longer related to national anthems or rock anthems in particular, but to a wider range of genres in general; and secondly, the term anthem came to stand in for, or appear alongside, heritage terminology designed to signal prestige and popularity, such as 'greatest hits,' 'best of,' 'best ever,' and 'classic,' a phenomenon that is logically (but not commercially) complicated by the combination of recent music and established 'classics.' While Dockwray (2005) asserts on the one hand that anthems lose their musical identity as they gain ubiquity across different genres and styles (p. 126), she insists that the net gain of this process has been the spread of the "anthem as a practice [of participation] to new constituencies through new styles" (p. 129). In any case, it is because of the mediation and proliferation of the term anthem, enabled by the recorded object and the enthusiasm of record companies to turn a quick profit, that the socio-musical features Dockwray identifies with the rock anthem become 'more ambiguous' (p. 174).

Nevertheless, within the sphere of representation specific to the promotion of rock anthems in 1990s Britain, normativity is predictably prevalent: while the anthem title appears alongside a range of music including independent and commercial dance labels (from Street Sounds to Ministry of Sound), it is, at least during the 1990s, the link between rock music and anthem releases which is of particular interest. One important example in this respect is the *Best Anthems* compilation series, produced by Virgin Records in the early 1990s (during the same period that saw the release of the first *Top Gear* compilation album and the first publication of the *Top Gear* magazine, both early moves in the development of the franchise by the BBC's commercial arm BBC Worldwide). The *Best Anthems* releases followed a sister-title called *The Best . . . Album in the World . . . Ever!* Both the *Best Anthems* and *Best Album* titles contained songs recently released by popular 'indie' and 'alternative' guitar bands from Blur to Skunk Anansie, alongside occasional 'classics' by bands such as the Smiths in earlier volumes and, importantly, recent tracks by electronic dance music groups such as Underworld, the Prodigy, and the Chemical Brothers. Furthermore, both titles were themselves part of Virgin's broader *Best Ever!* series which began in 1993 with *The Best Dance Album in the World... Ever!*, a collection of dance music based on commercial success in the main UK singles chart.

The *Best Ever!* formula allowed for many incarnations, including such titles as *Best Rock, Best Reggae, Best Punk, Best Rap, Best Irish, Best '80s,* and *Best Party.* But the *Best Anthems* and *Best Album* titles, set out below, differ in one important respect: they omit a specific genre (in these cases, 'indie') and insert an ellipsis in its place. The following list gives a sense of the evolution of titles from album to anthem, demonstrating a clear link between the words 'rock,' 'albums,' and 'anthems,' as well as the use of ellipses after the word 'best':

The Best Rock Album in the World... Ever! (1994)
The Best Rock Album in the World 2... Ever! (1995)
The Best... Album in the World... Ever! (1995)
The Best... Album in the World 2... Ever! (1996)
The Best... Album in the World 3... Ever! (1996)
The Best... Album in the World 4... Ever! (1996)
The Best Rock Anthems in the World... Ever! (1996)
The Best... Album in the World 5... Ever! (1997)
The Best... Album in the World 6... Ever! (1997)
The Best... Anthems... Ever! (1997)
The Best... Anthems 2... Ever (1997)
The Best Rock Anthems... Ever! (1998)
The Best... Album in the World 7... Ever! (1998)
The Best... Anthems 3... Ever! (1998)
The Best... Anthems 4... Ever! (1999)

Many of the artists whose careers are documented in *Best Album* releases continue to feature on the *Best Anthems* releases, suggesting that this mode of presentation serves in part as a means to refresh the 'albums' formula. For present purposes what remains significant is that both titles refuse to specify genre. I understand this trend in compilations to result in 'normative anthems.'

In retrospect, the list also shows how the earlier 'rock album' and 'rock anthems' titles act as symbolic precursors to a new generation of 'bands,' 'albums,' and 'anthems'; we might consider such a process as canonization, which is to imply that anthems and albums become normalized as a result of these discursive practices. In this light, albums and anthems become, at least in marketing terms, genres in and of themselves: with the mere use of an ellipsis they stand in for 'greatest rock and indie hits.' Without wishing to simplistically 'gender' all forms of canonization as masculinist, it is interesting to begin by noting the ways in which, according to Leonard (2007/2016), heterosexual masculinity is inscribed in the rock canon by specific aspects of industry practice; in terms of representation, for example, this means the use of heteronormative discourse in the packaging and presentation of *Greatest Hits* and *Classic Albums* (pp. 26–31). Indeed, this point is especially important when one considers the extent to which the term 'anthem' has come to stand in for, or appear alongside, the same heritage terminology identified by Leonard and, elsewhere, by Bennett (2009). Thus a type of canon of popular music is manifest at the same time that the roots of rock culture themselves become historicized amidst a gendered discourse of prestige and value which includes the liberal use of the term 'anthem.'

Similar anthem compilations released after the millennium reveal genre relationships that support this terminology and provide further context for approaching *Top Gear Anthems: Greatest Ever Driving Songs* (2007a) in terms of normativity. For example, three further series by Virgin Records demonstrate the ways in which the above formula is rebranded: both *The Album* (2001a; 2001b; 2002a; 2002b; 2005a; 2005b) and *The Anthems* (2006; 2007b; 2009) are two related titles each with multiple volumes while *The Best Bands Ever* (2002c; 2004) is interesting for the way in which the redundant exclamation mark follows the discarded '*in the World*' in a trend of shorter and bolder titles. Beyond compilations released by Virgin, more recent examples of mainstream indie-rock compilations have continued to capitalize on these naming trends, influenced by the post-millennial boom of music festivals; this has led to such 'anthem' titles as the wonderfully concise *Epic* (2010; 2011; 2012). Such practices have only continued and proliferated as online playlists have emerged as the new means by which playlisting companies, record labels, and streaming services promote music.

Even this most simplistic of comparisons highlights the culturally specific context in which masculinity, neoliberalism, rock music, and driving are represented. In particular, whether it is 'the world' or the epic, the titles that frame anthem compilations privilege 'bigness' in a way that resonates both with the historical roots of the anthem and with global consumer culture and its army of representations. Furthermore, when framed as an object, the compilation album poses additional questions for the status of participation as the defining feature of anthems at the end of the twentieth century and, therefore, the question of individualism. With reference to the role performed by vocal harmonies, Dockwray incorporates the recording into her argument by explaining:

> The recorded version of the song indicates that there is to be vocal participation, particularly in the chorus through its use of multi vocals and vocal choruses [as is the case in "Don't Stop Me Now"]. The listener is made aware of the vocal participation and is able to participate while in a concert setting or indeed any performance of the song before a crowd. (2005, p. 67)

We might also add that listeners are able to 'participate' where there isn't a crowd, too, such as a car or truck. To say that participation remains central to anthems in the era of compilations requires a serious consideration of the ontological complexities posed by the recording as a material object (in the case of rock music see, for example, Moore, 2001/2016; Gracyk, 1996; and Auslander, 2008). That is, to ignore the variety of spaces in which compilations are actually experienced is to ignore elements of listening practice that may undercut—or at the very least complicate—those notions of participation derived from consideration of the rock anthem in a live context. And since the recording enables new contexts in which participation becomes more diffuse, it is therefore important to conceptualize how participation might yet remain important in the often private, idealized listening spaces enabled by recordings; it is important, that is, to imagine the ways in which driving while listening provides a literal and metaphorical space where fantasies are enacted, even when the traffic doesn't move.

Bennett (2012) explores a similar tension when he engages with the participatory nature of large rock concerts and the complications posed by recordings (and specifically the 'live recording'). Emphasizing the interdependence of, on the one hand, ownership and individuality (recordings) and, on the other, community and participation (live performance), Bennett problematizes this opposition to show that ownership or possession is not yoked to the material, recorded object. Conversely, "Audience participation in the live rock performance can be aligned with the symbolic appropriation and cultural 'ownership' of rock texts as an aspect of [the] late modern lifestyle project" (2012, p. 294), part of the rise of the so-called 'experience economy.' In this context it is worth bearing in mind the words of Born (2009) when she writes that the recording acts as a second primary object in the case of popular music, such that we can talk of a "double ontology" that does not privilege live performance over the recording or vice versa (p. 294). Participation, then, can be conceived as an aspect of both the live and the recorded experience, but if conceptualized as part of the latter its mediation should be understood in its own terms and not against norms based on live performance. In this context, it is important to underscore how the recorded object shifts the emphasis from collective to individual listening practices, just as the individual as such is increasingly courted by the discourse of contemporary consumer culture.

Of course, whatever they are, the unimaginable myriad of sounds and fantasies that occur within automobiles today makes a mockery of attempts to represent them. Nevertheless, with both its symbolic and material aspects taken together, the driving-anthem compilation album occupies a space where, in neoliberal Britain, the collective is imagined to the extent that it valorizes the individual, while the emphasis on participation is confined to a privatized listening space. As Bennett (2012) suggests, following countless others, today it is the late modern lifestyle project which is the object of worship. Of course, the move towards individualized bigness is visible in the design of cars, too, most especially the SUVs already alluded to above. In the context of driving anthems, then, it is no surprise that the 'epic drive' and speed are seen to coexist so naturally with music that is similarly assumed to be powerful and individualistic.

Conclusion: Music is the (invisible) vehicle

Against such dominant tropes as that of the American frontier, and set alongside a history of blues and rock music since the 1950s, where roads, journeys, and isolation feature prominently—not to mention the examples that link together women and cars as objects of desire—the web of relationships between representations of driving, masculinity, and music offer much potential for cultural critique. Importantly, a history of technological developments in the mediation of recorded and broadcast sound underpins the way rock music and driving have come to be imagined together; these range from the development of in-car entertainment systems to the network of local FM 'classic rock' radio stations that, in the United States at least, broadcast a significant share of 1970s British rock, a sound that, according to Cross (2004), was written for the American rather than British landscape (p. 253). Building on this theme, Cross also describes the way in which the car windscreen frames and mediates the view (and, one might add, the sound) of a landscape made famous on cinema and television screens. Recalling a geological formation of unusual hills reminiscent of a scene from an old Western, Cross advises us not to 'leave the car.' Instead, he writes:

> Keep the buttes framed within the windscreen. To leave the car is to remove the frame, the animation of movement and the significance given it by Hollywood. In fact, it is on the screen that the buttes are best seen. Viewed for real in the open air, these otherwise highly aesthetically and culturally charged rocks lose any dimension, like discarded props. (p. 256)

The overall implication is an important one: mediation takes ontological primacy, which means that representations are not simply distortions of everyday experience.

In terms of a critical engagement with the representation of the 'epic drive,' what is significant about driving anthems is not, as *Top Gear* would have had us believe, the immediacy of their experience within the automobile, but, instead, precisely their mediation outside it: on television, film and, in this case, compilation albums based around the 'normative anthem.' It is through such sites of mediation that the image gains its discursive resonance; after all, it is not as if many people possess the means necessary to experience something like this ideal of driving. Sargeant (2002) encapsulates this problem nicely when he writes:

> Cars remain the ultimate realization of individual affirmation. [...] Cars are the great enablers of freedom; to drive is to engage in the promise of the open road. Except that such visions are not—and never have been—true [...]: people always get in the way. (p. 312)

In the absence of open roads, the most suitable listening environment for the driving anthem may not be the car, even as it remains the ideal one.

In the transition from sensation and everyday experience to ideological critique, it is perhaps predictable that the scholarly gaze should seek out the apparently rich configuration here between music and cars, and between listening, automobility, and masculinity. In this latter respect the underlying idea has been invisibility: the invisibility of hegemonic masculinity; the invisibility of consumption and listening practices and of everyday automobile experience; and the invisibility of compilation albums and 'ordinary television' as objects of academic study. I have sought to highlight some conceptual points of similarity which may be useful in approaching, first, the re-packaging of a rock song as an 'anthemic' driving song, and, secondly, what this tells us about the ideological values invested in expressions of power, freedom, and escape in contemporary Britain—values by no means confined to the white, heterosexual, middle-aged men embodied by the presenters of *Top* Gear, even though it is they who most overtly perform them. Furthermore, by conceptualizing driving, listening, and anthems in relation to the materiality of their mediated experience (in cars and recordings, for example), I have attempted to lay the groundwork for further study of both driving songs and 'normative-anthem' compilation albums.

The claim I make here is that automobility and music offer a compelling double act, as it were a configuration with which to think about the materiality of mediation. Metaphorically at least, the materiality of *Top Gear Anthems* (2007a) suggests ways in which participation can be understood in a double way: simultaneously, the image of the collective and the reality of the personal. If, as Cross (2004) has it, the windscreen provides the automobile with a fusion of representation and perception, made in Hollywood, then it should be borne in mind that this ontological formulation also affects how the soundtrack is heard (and, therefore, how movement is perceived): in this sense, the structural organization of Queen's "Don't Stop Me Now" can be read as providing a sonic windscreen for the *Top Gear* 'discourse of fantasy,' suggesting, in its structural organization and movement, how this mediated fantasy might be integrated into the perception of everyday life.

4

The passenger? Gender, cars, mobility, and dance music

Katie Milestone

How do gender, cars, mobility, and music culture fit together? While the issue of masculinity, music, and cars has been explored in academic literature (see Heining, 1998, and Nayak, 2003) there is very little existing work that considers the relationships between women, popular music, and cars. A notable exception is Best's (2006) work on girls in car-based youth subcultures in California and Lumsden's 2010 piece on 'girl racers.' However, in both of these studies music is not a primary focus of interest. In this chapter, I begin with an overview of the key work that combines gender, cars, and music before moving on to a discussion specifically about women that introduces the theoretical terrain to date.

To start with, in the broadest sense, cars and pop music share many commonalities. They are both 'modern' inventions and play a central role in everyday life. As Edensor (2004, p. 102) notes, automobility is a realm that includes "humans, machines, roads and other spaces, representations, regulatory institutions and a host of related businesses and infrastructural features." This analysis highlights the far-reaching complexity of car culture. Likewise, popular music is a sphere that includes a comparably multifaceted circuit of production and consumption, involving a range of technology and an intricate industry structure encompassing songwriters, musicians, performers, producers, artist and repertoire personnel, audiences, fans, groupies, concert goers, disc jockeys, record collectors, music journalists, and so on.

Significantly for the discussion in this chapter, both music and cars are entities that have great symbolic value in modern culture and society (albeit in very different ways). Urry (2004, p. 26) highlights that automobility is a powerful symbol of 'the good life' in consumer society and a central focus of citizenship, mobility, and a potent inspiration for art and popular culture. Urry acknowledges that the car and all it represents is laden with meaning, value, and symbolism. A dominant feature of twentieth- and twenty-first-century life, the car is an evergreen and recurring focus of attention in films, pop music, television, art, and literature.

Popular music, notably from post Second World War and beyond, is a similarly centrally prominent feature of everyday life. The sound track of our lives is provided to us via music, accessed through our smart phones, our domestic music transmission technologies, music radio, music television, film, advertising, and so on. Both the car (see Dant and Martin, 2001) and popular music are ubiquitous elements of modern life. Most people encounter both on a daily basis. Popular music and cars are important in terms of representing or signifying a sense of identity. Cars are highly visible status symbols, carriers of meaning, and 'positional goods'. Music taste, just as with car preference, says something about who we are and how others judge us. Access to both entities is not universal but contingent on financial resources and other forms of capital. Frith (2004, p. 38) acknowledges that music is profoundly important in forming taste cultures, building social alliances, and is a medium that produces intense emotion.

While acknowledging that cars and popular music are very different types of cultural products, their centrality in culture, their role in signifying identity *distinctions*, and the passionate reactions they both invoke also reveal their similarities. Crucially, music and cars are frequently consumed in conjunction with one another, as Bull (2004) has emphasized. It is the aim of this chapter to explore the relationships between cars and music from a perspective that prioritizes gender.

Gender is not something that we are, but something that we do. As both Erving Goffman (1959) and Judith Butler (1990) elucidated, gender is socially constructed and performed. Gender is not a static, 'natural' identity but is instead the end result of a range of activities and traits that, over time, have become attributed to masculinity or femininity. These qualities are emulated and then eventually solidify into behaviours defined as gendered. Finding its origins in feminist thought, gender studies explores the gender inequalities of patriarchal society. It increasingly focuses on examining both masculinity and femininity. Popular music lyrics, music video, cinematic representations, magazines, and other media forms play a central role in creating and maintaining ideas about gender roles.

Musicologist Susan McClary (2002) skilfully maps the terrain of key issues in terms of gender and music. To summarize, McClary identifies five key areas of concern in terms of music and gender: musical constructions of gender and sexuality, gendered aspects of traditional music theory, gender and sexuality in the music narrative, music as a gendered discourse, and discursive strategies of women musicians (in terms of negotiating the barriers they face within the music industry). Within the confines of this chapter, it is only possible to briefly touch on some of the important areas she has laid out.

On scratching the surface of both automobile culture and popular music culture, the persistent gendered hierarchies (where women are the less equal party) are loud and clear. Car culture is perhaps even more overtly masculinized than popular music culture. The gendering of car culture is deep rooted and long-standing. As Lumsden (2010) argues, "Just as the history of the car is gendered, so too are accounts of participation in various forms of car culture which emphasize its relationship with men and masculinity" (p. 2). Both cars and popular music are established as entities connected more with men than with women. It goes without saying that women make and listen to music and drive and are involved in the production of cars. However, both car and popular music culture are largely controlled by men and are culturally ascribed as masculine realms. The automotive industry is male dominated in terms of the design, production, and buying and selling of cars. At the level of consumption, there are stark contrasts in the discourses about how men and women interact with cars. Racing drivers are usually male, and media products about cars, such as the long-running British television show *Top Gear*, are predominantly aimed at male audiences. Unlike the male experience, women's relationships to cars are not normally represented as being about speed, sex, and the car as a status symbol. Instead, women are typically linked to types of cars described as 'run arounds' that are functional, practical, and frequently connected with domestic labour (such as going to the supermarket or taking children to school). Cars marketed to women tend to be small, economical, and 'feminized,' such as the Fiat 500 and BMW Mini. Myths about women and their lack of knowledge about the technology of the automobile and their allegedly substandard driving skills continue to circulate in media and popular culture. Women are frequently positioned as being inferior drivers to their male counterparts in spite of the fact that figures consistently highlight that they are safer drivers than men (see Al-Balbissi, 2003). Even the speed at which it is considered culturally appropriate to drive at is gendered. In some countries women have, until very recently, not been allowed to drive (see Jarbou, 2018, for a discussion).

The car often symbolizes something different for men and women: freedom, escape, and status for men compared with service, care, and chores for women. As Lezotte (2013) points out:

> The woman's car—a household appliance that often took the form of a nine-passenger station wagon—not only aided the suburban housewife in performance of daily tasks, but also defined her cultural role. Rather than grant her mobility, it effectively condemned the suburban housewife to a life of domesticity and serving others. (p. 170)

Not all female driving is connected with the drudgery of errands and care work; the pleasurable 'just for fun' element of driving is, however, less accessible to women. The cliché of the car figuring as a phallic symbol for men contrasts greatly with the car as symbolic of the womb for women because the car operates as a space of nurturing and support. Within this space, that for women frequently remains intrinsically connected with the domestic sphere, listening to the radio or car stereo is a key experience, as Bull's (2004) work has shown. Although women are the dominant audience for radio, the majority of prime time DJs are male (though this is gradually changing). During peak times, such as breakfast slots and 'drive hours,' only one in eight voices on the radio is a female one (O'Carroll, 2013). If women's voices are heard at all, they are much more likely to be reading the traffic news or the weather report than introducing and discussing music. These are just a few examples of the patriarchal modus operandi of car culture.

The way in which popular music is gendered has remarkable similarities to that of car culture. Music production, band management, A & R, music journalism, and DJ culture have all developed as predominantly masculine spheres. Of course, women have taken on all of the roles cited here, but the balance is tipped powerfully in the direction of male domination in all sub-sectors of the music industry. When the focus on automobiles and music is combined, this gendered dichotomy between masculine and feminine involvement remains powerfully distinct.

Men, music, and motor cars

Within rock and pop music, culture songs about cars, motorbikes, scooters, driving, and escape predominantly emanate from male songwriters and male voices. Women tend to feature in these representations in terms of minor and passive roles such as passengers, muses, or groupies. Both well-known pop songs about cars and cinematic portrayals have reinforced ideas about male mobility.

In hard rock and some pop music, cars have been associated with a sense of male autonomy and freedom. In his recent book on 'road music,' for example, writer John Scanlan (2015) examines the importance of cars, travel, and the road for pop musicians such as the Doors, Led Zeppelin, and the Rolling Stones. The milieu that Scanlan describes is one centred on men, masculinity, escape, and freedom. Powerful social constructions of gender norms expressed in hit songs have helped solidify gendered cultural constructs in the popular imagination. In Prince's 1982 song "Little Red Corvette," the car is portrayed as a wild, lusty woman who needs to be tamed and to 'settle down.' Another strategy occurs in Bruce Springsteen's 1984 track "Pink Cadillac," a song that simultaneously feminizes the car, via colour and 'crushed velvet' seats, while also making it function as a metaphor for the female body. Bette Midler recorded a version of Springsteen's song but was allegedly barred from releasing it as the song was deemed by Springsteen as unsuitable for a woman performer (Ken, 2018). Springsteen later relaxed this opinion and the song became a global hit for Natalie Cole in 1987.

Although rock and heavy metal are arguably the most extreme and intense examples of genres connected both with automotivity and masculinity, other genres appear not to be dissimilar—notably hip-hop and rap music. These are the genres that have been explored in detail in terms of the linkages between music, cars, and masculinity (see Forman, 2001; Adams and Fuller, 2006). This is not the music of "the privileged White male" (Laderman, 1996, p. 43), but more typically of the oppressed, underprivileged African American male. The automobile is an important component of hip-hop culture and numerous music videos, song titles, and lyrics make frequent reference to the car. A content analysis of rap lyrics revealed that Mercedes-Benz was the car brand most frequently cited, closely followed by Cadillac and Chevrolet (MC Big Data, 2015). Hip-hop has also been an important soundtrack for mobile youth in the urban environment.

A recurring representation of hip-hop culture in cinema and music video is that of young males cruising around the streets with the windows wound down, pulsating music being transmitted, and sometimes the car having been 'pimped' to judder in time to the beat. In this case, the car becomes part of the music and an extension of the body at the same time. As Murray Forman observes, the car alters both the landscape and soundscape of the city:

> The transformation of the urban soundscape since the early 1980s has been partially accomplished via the rolling bass beats of hip hop music booming from convertibles, Jeeps, customized low riders and tall SUVs, luxury cars and sedate family sedans. The fetishization of bass and volume in tandem affect the sonic character of the city. (2001, p. xvii)

For Paul Gilroy (2002) the centrality of the car within hip-hop culture is a tragic symbol of the depoliticized and disenfranchised nature of black America. Adrienne Brown's (2012, p. 267) discussion of Gilroy's work notes that the car functions, for Gilroy, as "a consolation prize for certain black subjects barred from other avenues of citizenship." However, Brown takes a more positive and optimistic view to that of Gilroy and argues that "the hip hop car often remains rooted in the social, deriving its value from the commons of creativity" (2012, p. 272).

Cinema provides a key source in further establishing the connections between music, cars, and the masculine realm. Wolff (1995) highlights that there has been a persistent gendering of narratives of travel. A narrative of male mobility persists within masculine rock music culture on film.

The 1969 film *Easy Rider* (Hopper) is arguably one of the most iconic films in terms of culturally establishing the freedom of the road (albeit on motorbikes rather than four wheels) via rock music as a masculine space. The film's director and leading co-star, Denis Hopper, began his career in the picture that linked cars and youth culture, *Rebel without a Cause* (Ray, 1955). The Steppenwolf track "Born to Be Wild" that features in the film is one of the quintessential songs of the counterculture, and the sound track of the entire film is revered and memorable. This film represents an important cultural moment in solidifying 'natural' connections between men, music, and the open road. Laderman (1996, p. 41) argues that the automobile emerged concurrently in society with the growth of new youth cultures and films aimed at the youth market and thus a symbiotic relationship emerged. Referring to iconic youth cultural films such as *Rebel without a Cause* through to cinema of the late 1960s American counterculture, he points out that "young people weaned on the automobile seemed to appropriate it from its drab nine-to-five or weekend leisure routine and transform it in to a literal vehicle for their restlessness and rebellion" (p. 41). Groups of male friends are offered mobility, escape, and adventure via cars and motorbikes. The features that Laderman (1996) uses in his discussion of road movies, including *Easy Rider* (Hopper, 1969), in turn draw on motifs and themes raised in a wide range of literature, including Jack Kerouac's influential male road trip novel *On the Road* (1957). In this novel, Laderman (1996) argues, "Sal and Dean use women to satisfy the sexual drives they sublimate through driving; conversely, the female characters ultimately become distractions from their freedom on the road" (p. 43). This sentiment is one that has resurfaced in road movies time and time again. A range of youth cultural films focus on male buddies on a tour or pilgrimage. Esperanza Miyake's recent publication *The Gendered Motorcycle* (2018) provides a detailed and important analysis of masculinization of vehicles across a range of forms of popular culture.

Established myths and constructions about hegemonic masculinity in terms of car and music culture remain powerful. For example, a recent North American advertisement for Mercedes-Benz cars (Coen brothers, 2017) blatantly references *Easy Rider*. The advert shows Peter Fonda (one of the stars of the 1967 film) in a Mercedes car (rather than a Harley Davidson motorbike) on Route 66. It cuts to Fonda entering a saloon bar filled with Hells Angels, and Steppenwolf's "Born to Be Wild" blasting out of the jukebox. The only female to feature in this advert is placed there in a sexual context (although Fonda/the car are also represented as objects of desire). In these discussions, Hirschman's (2003) work on the semiotics of rugged individualism is useful to draw upon to examine the hegemonic masculinity of the rock music and automobile paradigm. The rugged (male) individual is the dominant 'ideal type' within rock music culture. The music of *Easy Rider* is principally that of early heavy metal which has long been established as a masculine realm (see Walser, 1993). At the level of music consumption, too, the connections between pop music and the car are dominated by images of men. Car scenes in notable music films such as *Northern Soul* (Constantine, 2014) and *The Blues Brothers* (Landis, 1980) feature males as both drivers and individuals in charge of the car radio or cassette deck. The combination of cars and pop music are symbols of mobility, hedonism and escape, and are overwhelmingly discussed and represented in terms of male culture.

In popular culture designed for men, women are portrayed in certain ways. The objectification of women in hip-hop videos has been widely discussed. Equally, if they feature at all in cinematic representations of road culture, they are not usually shown in a positive light. In the spoof rockumentary *This is Spinal Tap* (Reiner, 1984), which focuses on the band on tour, the female character is portrayed as both a threat who is going to 'break up the band' echoing the narratives that haunted Yoko Ono, and as being naïve and ignorant about the technical aspects of music. The success of this film and its 'authenticity' is the extent to which it draws on (and parodies) 'real' narratives and discourses about rock bands on tour. The only high-profile road movie that focuses on women is the film *Thelma & Louise* (Scott, 1991). Unlike the iconic soundtrack that accompanies *Easy Rider*, the sound track of this film is far more understated and not foregrounded.

Do less overtly masculine musical realms, such as mod culture, suggest a different picture? From the early 1950s onwards cars, motorbikes, and scooters became an important feature of youth culture and many subcultures, as highlighted in some of the work of the Birmingham Centre for Contemporary Cultural Studies (CCCS). Given that popular music is central within 'ordinary' youth culture and in youth subcultures alike, the connection of motor vehicles to subcultures also links them to popular music. Paul Willis (1978) wrote about the motorbike boys, Dick Hebdige (1974) about the mods and their scooters. As McRobbie and Garber (1991) argued of subcultures in the 1950s to the late 1970s, girls were largely invisible in the CCCS work, and if present were physically and metaphorically 'riding pillion'. Films such as *Quadrophenia* (Roddam, 1979)—which is based on The Who's 1973 rock opera—repeated the narrative that men were the drivers of scooters and women always the passengers (see Singleton, 2018, for a detailed analysis of women's subordination in mod culture and the film *Quadrophenia*). This masculinization of the scooter within mod culture is curious given the 'feminine' qualities that have been attached to the scooter and the fact that Piaggio marketed Vespa scooters to young people in general and women in particular. Arvidsson's (2001) work on the scooter in Italian society notes:

> For women, it seemed, the scooter had mainly a psychological value. More than any other pragmatic concern, mobility meant autonomy, visibility and self-affirmation. To be able to drive around freely meant to be able to control one's life, if only on a symbolic level. The result was a campaign that stressed that the scooter's mobility enabled a new, more autonomous and emancipated kind of femininity. (p. 64)

This was not an ethos, however, that translated into representations of scooter use in the UK. Cinematic representations of mods in films such as *Up the Junction* (Collinson, 1968) and iconic photographs of scooter runs show scootering as a male activity in the UK context. In other words, both research by female academics and analysis of relevant films suggests that women's connection to vehicles has been located as passive and secondary: passengers, as opposed to drivers.

Women at the wheel?

Having explored the intensely strong relationships between men, motors, and music, we will now examine some key examples and debates in relation to women, music, and cars. It seems that because motor vehicles mean something profoundly different to each gender, women rarely sing about them. In "Leader of the Pack" (1964) by female group the Shangri-Las, for instance, the (deceased) subject of the song is a male motorbike rider. The female figure evoked in this song watches passively and adoringly from the sidelines while her risk-taking, motorbike-riding lover meets his fate on the open road. It is almost impossible to imagine the lyrics of another example of popular music describing a scenario where the gender roles are reversed, since the normative ideologies surrounding masculine mobility and feminine passivity within popular culture are so powerful. Arguably the most famous song written by a woman about a car is Janis Joplin's (1969) song, "Mercedes Benz." This song is not about the car at all. In this song, the car functions as one of a range of examples that represent shallow status symbols from a materialist culture.

A key point to highlight is that both car culture and popular music culture are technologized aspects of social life. The technological aspects of car culture—from building cars, repairing and maintaining them through to driving them—are spheres from which women are largely excluded or deemed to be lacking in aptitude. Likewise with popular music culture there are a plethora of examples where women are excluded or absent from roles and practices within the music industry and club culture. Stereotypes about women's lack of aptitude in the use of technology have been well documented (see Wajcman, 1991); because of the key role of technology within pop music, they have also served to exclude female participation. In ways echoing the discourse of car culture, certain instruments and performance style have become masculinized, as authors such as Simon Frith and Angela McRobbie (1978) and Mavis Bayton (1997) have suggested. Mayhew (2004) argues that, although the recording process has been important in popular music since the 1940s, women have on the whole been able to access this space only as singers or to a lesser extent as instrumentalists. At the start of the 1950s and the dawn of rock 'n' roll culture, women were not major players in the emerging music industry. From the outset, they were all but absent from most aspects of the landscape. Those who assumed the position of pop singer were often devalued through a construction of femininity as an unskilled, and/or a "natural" musical position (p. 150). There was no female equivalent to a performer such as Elvis or a music producer such as Phil Spector, for example. Rebelliousness and overt sexiness were at odds with the categories defining the femininity of the time, which were connected with domesticity and demureness. In 1978, Frith and McRobbie (1978) wrote about the 'cock rock' attitudes of rock culture. Many other musicologists have noted how these gender strategies continue to imbue the popular music world (see Bayton, 1997; Cohen, 1997; Leonard, 2007/2016; Richards and Milestone, 2000). Girls' and women's relationship to rock 'n' roll was frequently limited to the fan or groupie. This was exploited by the music industry, which saw the economic benefits of the gendered fan/consumer relationship. Popular music lyrics were, more often than not, focused on heterosexual sexual courtship; male pop stars were produced to be idolized by their adoring female fans. This pattern echoes the separation of women from technology that can be seen in numerous areas of popular-cultural production, such as DJing and computer gaming.

Second-wave feminism has had a significant influence here and led to some transformations in most sectors of the labour market. Slowly and over time, increasing numbers of women have made inroads as musicians and behind the scene roles. In the mid-1970s, the arrival of punk saw the emergence of new female musicians such as Patti Smith and Poly Styrene, who did not conform to traditional notions of what female performers should look and sound like. Kearney (2006) claims that during the late 1970s there were significant transformations in terms of gender and power in music production. This was made possible by the invention of accessible and low cost music production technologies which allowed for a step change in terms of female interactions with popular music culture. She states that "the broad diffusion of inexpensive media technologies and entrepreneurial youth cultures during this period allowed more girls to gain access to the tools and infrastructures of cultural production than ever before" (p. 48). Kearney goes on to argue that punk and subsequently hip-hop were notable as music genres where girls were able to carve out creative roles. However, in spite of some progress, there are large enclaves of the music industry where women remain woefully on the margins. Within dance music culture, for example, we have to ask ourselves where the female 'superstar DJs' and music producers are represented. As British female DJ Lisa Lashes commented in a press interview in 2014:

> A lot of my female friends who were DJs have now given up and been forced to get a different job. It wasn't until I was asked to give a speech at a music conference that I started looking into it properly. Of all the major music events

like Creamfields and Global Gathering, female performers represent under 1% of the line-up. Why should it be that way when we are almost 50/50 in this world?

These findings from British electronic dance music culture are mirrored in North America. Rebekah Farrugia's (2012) research about women and electronic dance music traces a long heritage of the gendering of music and music technology. She cites research about how women were being driven out of radio industry in the 1930s and the 1960s, which saw the arrival of hi-fidelity as technology aimed squarely at men. Farrugia's (2013) experience of discovering electronic dance music in Detroit in the 1990s—especially as the music went more mainstream—was one which saw her encounter the distinct gender boundaries:

> Men would often dominate the area in front of where the DJs performed. . . . Women were often distanced—physically, and at times even aurally—from the music and the technology so central to dance music and culture. For the most part they were relegated to the sidelines, encouraged to participate primarily as patrons on the dance floor. (p. 4)

The location of women in symbolic spaces of club culture tells us a lot about the gendered hierarchies that remain within electronic dance music. While many social revolutions have emerged from club culture, persistent under-representation of women in the production side is reprehensible.

It appears that women's relationship to music culture often mirrors the way that women encounter automobile culture. They rode on the back of the motorbike or sat in the passenger seat, but they were rarely represented as being in control as the driver of the car or bike. Women are passengers, consumers, fans, audiences, muses, groupies, but all too infrequently are they the DJ, the rock star, or the celebrated producer. Girls and women with passion and talent are being shut out of the possibility of being solo performers or in bands, even at high school age, and there is clear evidence that the education system itself reproduces and enforces the idea that music, notably popular music, is 'for the boys.' Armstrong's (2011) work, which explored the gendered inequalities of music education in schools, found clear evidence of the 'hidden curriculum' which actively distanced girls from music making. What is highly problematic is that since the arrival of the computer and its role in music composition in the classroom, girls have been increasingly pushed out. This is emphasized by Born and Devine (2016), whose research revealed that 90 per cent of students on undergraduate music technology degrees were male. Neoliberal voices claim that when it comes to 'talent' and creativity, the 'market will decide.' The market does not truly decide, because the majority of female musicians do not make it in the market, the festival line-up, or get the prized recording contract in the first place. Analyses from 2017 of a range of music industry reports by the *Guardian* newspaper highlights that women are faced with barriers and are significantly underrepresented in all areas of the music industry (Larsson, 2017). Just as men control the steering wheels of the car or motorbike, so, too, do they control of the 'wheels of steel' in the DJ booth.

This chapter has considered well-known fictional cinematic examples that combine a focus on cars and music and highlighted music genres where the car is an important and much fetishized object of desire. I have touched upon a range of examples of the relationships between music and automobiles with gender as a key focus. It is clear that the fields of both music and cars are culturally ascribed as masculine. This is the case in terms of both fictional representations and 'real life' examples drawn from the popular music industry. With a few notable exceptions, such as *The Girl on a Motorcycle* (Cardiff, 1968), a significant majority of films about cars and other vehicles represent drivers as men. There are many parallels, in terms of gender relationships, between car culture and popular music culture. In both realms, women are on the periphery and this, of course, has an impact on women's status and power (or lack of it). What is patently clear is that, given the intense ways in which both car culture and popular music culture have been inscribed and represented as masculine domains, women's access to these spheres has been rendered patchy and sporadic. For men, cars operate as an outward facing public symbol; music is played loudly and ostentatiously. For women, social norms encourage cars to be encountered more typically as a private, intimate space. Given the centrality of automobiles and music to everyday life, the designation of these entities as male preserves must be challenged. The irony, in terms of the labour market, is that challenges to gender inequality in the UK began in the car production at the Ford plant in Dagenham in 1968, when working-class women took industrial action for equal pay. Half a century later, gendered inequalities in the labour market (and pay) remain stubbornly persistent. Women's struggles in the music industry are problematic in ways that are arguably more significant than the fact that car production remains a male-dominated sector of the labour market. Working on a car production line is not most people's definition of a dream job; 'making it' in the music industry is, however, a highly desired and much sought-after prize. Endlessly repeated messages, that women are somehow lacking the genius of the male creative, or are inferior drivers, continue to reverberate.

5

Rave journeys: Intimacy, liminality, and the changing notion of home

Beate Peter

Historically, raves in Britain were understood to be outdoor, electronic dance music gatherings which took place in particular geographical spaces. Their sites were often located just outside of cities, and it was not uncommon for raves to happen in locations accessible only to those who drove or knew someone with access to a motor vehicle. Despite the crucial role that cars, vans, and buses played for visitors to be able to participate, the importance of ravers' journeys has been largely ignored by music historians. This chapter presents the results of interviews with people who used to go to raves by motor transport. Between December 2017 and January 2018, semi-structured interviews were conducted with eight such participants. All self-identified as having been to raves in Greater Manchester, and beyond, between 1985 and 1995. The respondents were a self-selected sample of committed contributors to the Lapsed Clubber project who had all been involved in research for this project for a couple of years.[1] None of them owned a car during their rave-going days, so they all depended on others' willingness to offer lifts. Interview questions were designed in order to ascertain their motivations for rave journeys, discover the conditions under which people travelled, and understand the social significance of the car as an immediate means of transport. George McKay has claimed:

> One central way in which cultures of resistance define themselves against the culture of the majority is through the construction of their own zones, their own spaces. These can be distinguished in part through the subcultural elements of music, style or favoured drugs (if any—there usually are), but space itself is vital. (1996, p. 7)

For rave, this space was the English countryside (see, for example, Hill, 2002; John, 2015). Transport in the form of cars or vans was vital to get to key places in the countryside, and the crucial role that automobile journeys played—namely, to provide a safe space for people to develop a notion of home and belonging—was dismissed once raves were criminalized. Drawing on my interviews, this chapter discusses the significance of the car journey in the wider context of the rave experience.

It is important at this point to distinguish between early rave culture and club culture as it is understood today. Steve Redhead (1993, p. 4) defines early rave culture as being both a youth culture and a 'deviant' activity. At the same time, however, he acknowledges rave culture's embrace of materialistic values and commercial practices. Some scholars argue that this embrace was the result of Thatcherism (Hill, 2002; John, 2015; McKay, 1996). However, the "double relationship between the subculture and Thatcherism ... reaches beyond simple opposition" (Hill, 2002, p. 91) and allowed a youth culture to develop alternative practices while fully engaging in entrepreneurial activities and commercializing a subculture. "Rave culture's ability to alternately contest and mimic Thatcherite ideology" (John, 2015, p. 162) might be the reason why George McKay (1996) struggles to see rave culture as a counterculture in a historical sense. And yet, McKay presents rave culture as part of a tradition of free festivals in Britain. In doing so, he provides a narrative of countercultural values that did not appear out of nowhere. Instead, he argues that the cultures of resistance (which include rave) partly "constitute a politics of the disenfranchised, wherein the youth and marginal left out of Thatcher's revolution find their voices and use them to express their resentment and opposition" (p. 1). McKay traces the values informing those voices back to the 1960s, thus allowing us to read rave culture as part of a legacy that is represented by rave's PLUR (Peace, Love, Unity, Respect) ethos: "Castlemorton was literally a displaced hippy event" (1996, p. 120).

Not all members of 1980s to 1990s youth culture internalized or celebrated the PLUR ethos, either across the whole demographic or for the initial period that rave existed. Redhead characterizes rave events as having been "notorious for mixing all kinds of styles on the same dance floor and attracting a range of previously opposed subcultures from football hooligans to New Age hippies" (pp. 3–4). Members of previously different subcultures harboured diverse values. McKay also hints at the fact that even within the traveller scene, motivations and values were shifting at the time, and that moving goalposts allow for the amalgamation of different youth cultures (p. 71). He states that "the pinnacle of the festival/rave crossover to date was undoubtedly reached at Castlemorton Common in Hereford and Worcester in May 1992" (1996, p. 120). McKay argues that the 1994 Criminal Justice and Public Order Act—commonly referred to as the Rave Bill—presented a most oppressive piece of legislation that criminalized rather than challenged certain lifestyles associated with raves, but not limited to ravers. The affected groups shared certain lifestyle aspects, including the free use of open land and the playing of music at these sites. With the prohibition of such practices, rave culture's transformation into a fully commercial mainstream culture seemed logical. Brian Ott and Bill Herman (2003) argued that the changing rave sensibility from a countercultural resistance towards its commodification resulted in a loss of "transgressive potential" (p. 249). I argue that this 'potential' was partly formed during rave journeys.

Like McKay, Jaimangal-Jones, Pritchard and Morgan (2010) note that space plays a crucial role in the construction of dance music culture. They argue that event spaces (festivals) are "places which, whilst on one level . . . are operational entities, can also be interpreted as liminal thresholds of transition and transgression" (p. 253). Jaimangal-Jones et al. place particular importance on the role of the journey to create a specific space in which a culture can flourish. They state that "travel to dance events is socially constructed by their participants both as a rite of passage and as a pilgrimage or source of spiritual fulfilment" (p. 254). Ott and Herman (2003) similarly assert that "the secrecy surrounding the location of underground raves also served to heighten a sense of community by uniting ravers in specialized knowledge and transforming the quest for the location into a ritualistic pilgrimage" (p. 24).

Findings from the interviews established that car journeys functioned as community-building processes upon which a positive rave experience could be based. Generally, all passengers, including the driver, would participate in the rave. The journey itself became understood as starting when the driver picked up fellow passengers and spent time at their flats or houses. Individual processes linked to each part of the picking up led to the establishment of strong bonds between the passengers. This impacted on their sense of physical and mental well-being, and helped to create a safe space inside the car, once all passengers were collected. Themes that emerged from the interviews highlighted how important each journey was for the overall rave experience, not only as a means of getting to and from the rave itself but also as a base *during* the rave. Each vehicle was a chill-out room, a drug den, and a meeting point, all in one. This space became crucial for the rave itself, as people would feel listened to, looked after, and cared for—and all of this before the dance spectacle had even started. In this chapter, I therefore argue that ravers developed an idea of home and belonging that was not built on geography but instead based on social bonding during a car journey. It was this idea of an emotional and spiritual home of bonding with fellow ravers that shaped early rave culture, both within and in relation to wider society. The chapter therefore seeks to explain the importance of rave journeys, particularly the ways that they physically and mentally facilitated intimacy and helped to develop a sense of community prior to the participants arriving at the rave.

Getting ready, or fine-tuning, for the journey

During the interviews it became clear that getting ready, in the context of a rave, could refer to three distinct types of activity. These not only helped people focus their minds on the forthcoming rave, but also helped them to adjust to one another.

First, ravers would get specially dressed for the event. However, in the context of raves that could mean something completely different to what might be inferred. Respondent 6 commented on his ritual of dressing up as 'dressing down.' Dressing down, for this raver, was meant to distinguish himself from the 'Balearic heads,' a group of other dancers that would exhibit not only other clothing accessories but also a different behaviour. Here, reference was being made to style (sub)cultures and their desire to distinguish themselves from perhaps more prominent cultures. This discussion, in Britain, is mainly informed by the work of scholars belonging to the Centre for Contemporary Cultural Studies (CCCS) in Birmingham in the 1960s and 1970s, who focused mainly on class belonging, but also on style, as an expression of opposition and resistance. Respondent 6, however, a male respondent, referred to dressing down as a new-found freedom.

Previous dance experiences in the city not related to house music required men to wear shirts, ties, and shoes rather than trainers. A lack of dress code at raves was experienced as both personal and physical freedom: personal in that a choice was given as to what one can wear, physical because the clothing would facilitate dancing. Baggy trousers and lose-fitting t-shirts became associated with rave culture for quite some time. And yet, tight-fitting clothes also featured on the rave scene. The first respondent referred to a ritual of dressing up in such clothes and characterized the rave experience as beginning with the choosing of clothes. One could argue that the anticipation would start to build when people began to dress up. The level of anticipation would increase over the course of an evening, as arriving at the site of the rave was hours away.

Secondly, getting ready could also mean that the driver would pick up their fellow passengers or pieces of music equipment (something mentioned by half of the respondents). That ritual would often involve a stopover. In this context, the journey would involve not only driving from one place to another but also socializing with potential fellow passengers before setting off for the actual rave. This social aspect of the pickup allowed passengers to co-create a positive, trusting atmosphere that set the tone for the journey. Because of the preliminary interactions, any inhibitions that might prevent people from creating and enjoying an intimate atmosphere in the car could be overcome, in other words, meeting up with fellow passengers before being squeezed into a car allowed everybody to bond. At the same time, it increased the level of anticipation, especially when rituals associated with the rave space were practised. These rituals, according to respondents 4, 5, and 6, included taking drugs as well as dancing in somebody's private space. Occasionally, it would mean, according to respondent 4, that they "would have taken all the drugs before setting off and peak somewhere in the middle of nowhere, stuck in the car." This experience had to be facilitated, and the mutual support that people gave each other, before as well as during the drive, would enhance the process of forming a strong bond with fellow passengers.

Thirdly, getting ready could also be understood as a way of building critical mass, often achieved by meeting other ravers (and their cars) at service stations. All respondents commented on the effect that meeting fellow cars on the journey had on their mood and levels of anticipation. Four and five commented on their feelings of exhilaration when spotting other 'rave cars' at service stations. Recognizing that others were part of a group that was about to engage in illegal practices generated a strong bond between people that might never have met before. Knowing about other people's intentions was crucial for the sense that they were going on an adventure together. It began to generate a shared perception that there was a critical mass of rave goers.

The interviews revealed that each rave journey encompassed more than an actual drive from a geographic origin to destination. Rituals preceding the drive were important for the people who became fellow passengers, as they allowed them to establish a strong bond, and to be on the same wavelength before entering the confinements of a car. Those preconditions had to be met in order for a joint drive to become a transformative experience.

The drive

All of the people who were interviewed about their journeys confirmed that they would never share a journey with people they did not know. Other participants had to be friends, or friends of good friends, in order for everybody to be willing to share the car. All but one respondent referred to the close-knit Manchester rave community where everybody would know everybody else, and it would be the same set of people who would travel to raves outside of the city. As respondent 2 confirmed: "You would see the same faces in Manchester, Leeds, Sheffield, Liverpool and North Wales. It was almost like a tribe moving to different locations in search of the ultimate rave experience." The respondents explained the importance of mutual acquaintanceship with the practices that passengers engaged with during the journey, and the threshold level of trust that was needed in order to enjoy those experiences. Contrary to popular assumptions, building trust included not just practices related to drug taking but also sharing conversation topics, listening to music together, or lying to the police when stopped on the way to a rave.

Most of the respondents referred to the vehicle as an intimate space. Respondent 1 referred to it as a "mini living room" because "you would talk, come down together, be silent together, listen to music together and take drugs together." The level of intimacy experienced inside the car was sometimes described as making you feel safe and protected, similar to a 'cocoon.' The fact that the 'mini living room' was not stationary, but mobile, meant that a protective environment created by both the car and its people transported the passengers 'safely' to the site of the rave.

In their study, Jaimangal-Jones et al. (p. 257) found that "a journey can heighten the enjoyment of a dance event as it increases the build-up and excitement; indeed, often the greater the commitment and effort required reaching an event, the more it was anticipated and enjoyed." The first five respondents in this study confirm this point. They provided examples of trips to the countryside in North Wales, which verified that the level of excitement would increase the longer the journey took. The duration of the journey was not necessarily linked to geographic distance, respondent 1 explained. Journeys could be prolonged because of the exact destination of a rave being unknown. Also, being stopped by the police in remote places and lying about the destination of the car journey, according to the first two respondents, had a positive impact on the level of excitement. Moves to define the rave journey as both starting with rituals of getting ready and involving the drive itself can be seen as a tool to build up positive emotions. However, they can also be understood as facilitating or being part of, an act of transition.

Although music and drugs might already have featured in people's houses before driving to the rave, being together in a car meant that each transgressive journey could include the change from the city to the countryside. Respondents repeatedly pointed out the fact that in the 1980s and 1990s, people did not have mobile phones nor were they able to use satellite navigation systems in their cars. Leaving the city with signposts aplenty and attempting to find a secret location in the countryside was almost a journey by instinct. Anecdotes from respondents 1, 2, and 4 included hours of searching for the right location, often attempting to follow the music. In a sense, this experience could be described as 'homing': people returning, almost by instinct, to *their* territory. It is what McKay (1996, p. 7) describes as the construction of zones for cultures to engage with their specific practices. Additionally, raver territoriality effectively involved arriving at a site of rupture from everyday life. Jaimangal-Jones et al. (2010, p. 257) compare the change of an "individual's self-consciousness and conformity to social roles" in such zones with the behaviour of tourists in unfamiliar surroundings, only that the ravers developed a sense of arriving 'home' when reaching the site of a rave.

The notion of home

At the time for all of the respondents, the notion of home was strongly linked to a community of like-minded ravers rather than to a particular geography or family. One of the reasons why this community felt so tight-knit was, perhaps, the understanding of its members that their experiences were not ordinary. By leaving the city behind and producing meaning in the countryside, ravers became resistant bodies, refusing the division of life into opposites: day and night, work and leisure, us and them, or buying and selling. Respondent 4 remarked on how the lack of buildings that are frequented by office workers or shops with specific opening and closing times also added to a feeling of suspense and "the capitalist world was left behind." The nurturing of a specific positive atmosphere, the building up of excitement, and high levels of anticipation—all of them experienced in the car—meant that people were ready to embrace the rave once they had arrived. For all but one respondent, that process of embrace included interaction with other ravers at the site. In fact, according to respondents 1,

4, and 5, fellow passengers would rarely stay together at the rave but instead meet and engage with other people. Again, respondent 5 commented on how they would always end up talking to strangers, often for hours on end. Some of those people they would never see again. Others would become friends for life. Respondent 3 associated the making of memories with the making of friends. That would not just include the people who they had shared a journey with but also new people that they would meet at the site of the rave. It suggests that a certain attitude existed among the ravers, and it included openness towards strangers, trusting them to be part of a community that jointly created the rave.

Practising the community ethos, all respondents reported that the cost for the journey would always be split, and respondent 1 noted that typically they would be inclined to "pay over the odds" because you would want a lift next time. Payment was not always in the form of money, but could also be in the form of drinks or drugs (respondent 4). Also, all passengers on a journey were aware they were engaging in risky behaviour. The risk of being stopped by the police while trying to find a rave was permanent and made them come closer to one another (respondent 4). The secrecy of, and communication about, locations had a similar impact on the bonding as a community. The notion of being part of a culture that is different to the model of youth, that is advocated through the media and enforced through policies, acted as another bonding agent. Although respondents 4 and 5 stated that being part of rave culture was related to getting to know new music and to being able to dance, the sound systems at raves were often bad. This is partly linked to the DIY ethos that existed at the time and the fact that sound equipment had to be taken to remote places in the same way as ravers travelled to such sites. As many raves were based on donations, professional equipment would not be rented, but borrowed instead. Half the respondents explained how the sound systems that they helped transport would be collected from various houses that were visited before people set off to leave the city. Sound systems and collectives were each known for their particular music style, but people did not— respondents 4, 5, and 6 noted—seem to be too selective over the kind of music that would be played at a rave. In this regard, the idea of home was also linked to a particular attitude towards capitalist commerce. All respondents except for 3 and 7 commented on the role of new music as constituting resistance. The period in question preceded internet radio, file sharing, and digital music production, so going to events was often the only opportunity to actually consume new music. Meeting to hear new music was perceived as a form of activism, and the unknown—in this case music—was not feared but embraced.

The celebration of the community spirit stood in direct opposition—according to respondents 4, 5, and 6—to the values that ravers perceived to be promoted by a Thatcherite government: individualism, private entrepreneurship, and an assumption that all people are driven by the desire to climb the social ladder. Such resistance to conformity did not exclude entrepreneurial activities. Motivation for such activities lay in the desire to create a community in spirit, one that could "have the potential to change the world" according to respondent 4; they referred to a sense of unity and belonging and their belief that the rave community would be able to change society: "We felt that something bigger was about to happen." The respondents did not, however, perceive rave culture's exploration of its commercial potential as exclusively negative, as bigger raves were seen as opportunities to experience more new music on the one hand, and gathering momentum on the other.

All respondents confirmed that their reason to drive to a rave was to dance. Through dance, ravers defined their (counter)cultural spaces and their relationship with fellow ravers. It was through dance that new music was experienced on a physical level. According to McNeill (1995), dancing together for a prolonged period of time is a form of muscular bonding that shifts the focus away from the individual towards the community. He argues that, similar to marching, dancing together in sync allows people to experience "muscular manifestations of group solidarity" (p. 10). McNeill goes on to suggest:

> An important feature of emotional bonding through rhythmic muscular movement is that it affects those who take part in it more or less independently of how they may have been connected (or divided) by prior experience. Hence dance could and did become a way in which all sorts of new groups could define themselves, both by differentiation from within existing communities and by allowing marginalized persons or complete outsiders to coalesce into new, more or less coherent groups. (p. 52)

Over half the respondents referred to a spiritual home that was created by being part of the rave community, and, from this safe space, long-lasting friendships were built. Those friendships transcended into everyday life and blurred the lines between countercultural spaces and civic life. All respondents described the period between 1985 and 1995 as a time in which they experienced significant sociocultural changes. For some, those changes were experienced as rupture and, at the same time, as an opportunity to experiment with new forms of community.

Liminality

The feeling of being totally free at a rave was described by all respondents in one way or another. In a field, according to respondent 4, ravers were not confronted with the visual cues of civic life and the unspoken requirement to engage with it. Respondents referred to the absence of (rush hour) traffic, office workers, and public buildings; Goethe's words seem quite fitting here when he says "music is liquid architecture; architecture is frozen music" (reproduced in Sussman and Hollander, 2015, p. 129). It appears that the kind of music that was played at raves not only created a countercultural spiritual space but also created associations with the actual landscape and architecture in which raves would take place. The suspense of time was clearly felt, at least for respondents 4 and 5, because rural areas did not provide the typical time markers that people would experience in the city—for example, opening and closing times of shops, peak travelling times, or even public clocks. Another aspect that promoted the shared sense of being in a liminal space was the idea that nobody knew when the rave would end. An absence of schedules and timings allowed people to fully immerse themselves in the moment without thinking ahead in time and thinking of possible (negative) consequences. Apart from witnessing day and night in the open, ravers would be unable to fit their experience into the everyday framework of a working day or even a 'normal' weekend; this impossibility of mapping the experience against ordinary life was embraced.

In addition, the lack of physical boundaries such as walls, buildings, or roads added to the experience, for respondent 5, of being removed from the everyday. The same applies to the notion of being somewhere far away from civilization, as the absence, according to respondents 4 and 5, of 'normal people' such as shop owners, ordinary dwellers, or inhabitants was strongly felt. Being 'alone together' was described by respondent 5 as "being away from people who do not belong but being together with people who do belong." I argue that 'the rave car journey' also fits this description, and by 'the rave car journey' I also mean the return trip.

The journey back

Until now, journeys in relation to raves or big EDM gatherings have been discussed only with regard to getting to these places. However, the journey *to* a rave is fundamentally different to a journey *leaving* the rave, not least because, as over half the respondents said, the destination of your return journey was not always your physical home or the place you started your journey. Respondents 4 and 5 described the return journey as being of the same liminal quality as the rave itself. They both agreed that it was unknown when the rave would end. This meant that passengers did not quite know when to congregate in order to drive back. Uncertainty about the agreed departure time was embraced rather than dreaded, as it allowed ravers to enjoy the moment without having to plan ahead or even position the rave experience within a wider context of everyday life. And yet, all respondents agreed that it was the driver who would decide when to leave the rave. The role of the driver is of importance in this context and needs to be discussed further.

Considering that all respondents said that they would know the driver, and not enter the car if this person was not known among friends, three respondents noted that they also needed absolute faith in the driver and trusted that they would always get home. The first two respondents explained their attitude towards the driver needing to "stay straight" with previous traumatic experiences. Other respondents blindly trusted the driver's ability to be in command of the car, regardless of their level of intoxication. Respondent 6 said that "back in the days everybody thought that you could drive on pills." They go on to explain that there was this myth that mixing alcohol and MDMA was not good, so people chose MDMA over alcohol, and assumed that MDMA or other drugs did not have as profound an impact on the driver's ability as alcohol. Respondents 4, 5, and 6 agreed that there would be ways in which the driver's decision to leave a rave could be influenced; providing drugs for the driver was one of them.

Occasionally, a driver would be rented together with a minibus, so that all passengers could fully engage in the event. On those occasions, according to the first two respondents, the driver would wait in the car or minibus and a time would be arranged to start the return journey. That was not necessarily the case when the driver was from within the rave community. The car constituted a meeting point during the rave, and people would treat it as an intimate space, to which they could retreat. Ravers would regularly move, according to respondents 4 and 5, between the overall dance space and the car to catch up with the driver. It provided an antidote to what was happening at the rave: the rave knew no physical boundaries, but the car was small and intimate; raving meant active participation for hours or days on end, whereas retreating to the car provided an opportunity to rest. For respondents 4, 5, and 6 it constituted an alternative venue, in which the suspense of time was felt even more than at the rave.

The way that ravers described their transitioning between the intimate space of the car and the wider rave space suggested that there was a need for people to retreat temporarily in order to immerse themselves in the bigger event for a prolonged period of time. The atmosphere created in the car, even before driving to the rave, constituted a crucial element for passengers who dispersed once they arrived, but were then able to return to intimacy inside the car when they left the rave together.

Each return journey was fundamentally different to the journey at the beginning of the night. Often, people would not listen to music but talk or, in fact, be silent together. Regardless of the mood in the car, all respondents confirmed that you would look out for one another during the journey. Arranging breaks, supplying water, resting, turning down the music, or engaging another person in a conversation were all reactions to a fellow passenger in need. The idea that people would look out for one another increased the level of intimacy and added to the notion of not only being in when respondent 1 called a 'mini living room' but also being with one's family, according to respondent 4, with regard to care, respect, and empathy.

Not knowing where you were going was not just something experienced during the drive to the rave but also extended to the return journey. Respondents commented on the desire to extend the rave at other locations, but with the level of intimacy that was felt in the car. Ravers would sometimes drive to other remote places in the countryside or to somebody's house. Half the ravers mentioned that the desire to stay together as a group was felt very strongly and would only be overridden by the need to go to work or similar such commitments.

Later, things changed. Respondents 4, 5, and 6 struggled to establish a causal relationship between the change in music ("it became," as one noted, "cynical and dark"), the changing effects of ecstasy pills ("they became trippier," said respondent 6), and the change in the character of events (most respondents said when "alcohol appeared and people became more aggressive"), but they all agreed that the general atmosphere in the rave community transformed. The rise of the superstar DJ was commented on, as well as the establishment of super clubs; both of those were identified as being part of a changed rave culture.

Conclusion

Journeys by means of cars or vans form an important part of early rave culture, not least because the events themselves took place outside the city, and it was impossible to reach many locations by public transport. The car, then, can be seen as an enabler for participation in raves. Each vehicle, however, was not just a means of transport but also a safe space in which an intimate relationship with fellow passengers was formed or maintained. Several factors contributed to the car being understood as a safe space: its size, joint listening to music, the knowledge of engaging in illicit practices, and a joint sense of adventure as the rave *had to be found*.

This chapter has shown how the perceived protection that the car provided on the journey was also the result of a build-up of mutual trust and a form of fine-tuning of moods hours before the drive. Because of this, the car journey has to be understood as an experience that starts much earlier than the actual drive. First, the rave experience started for many with the ritual of getting dressed. The practice was presented here as an act of freedom (of choice) that was in stark contrast to the dress codes required by nightclubs in the late 1970s and early 1980s. The absence of a formal dress code for raves was a sign of individuality and freedom of expression; something that rave culture embraced through its inclusive approach. Secondly, picking up fellow passengers was another crucial element to the rave journey, as the time spent in other ravers' houses prior to departure allowed people to adjust and adapt their moods and create the intimate atmosphere that would be intensified when people entered the confinements of the car. Finally, meeting up with cars full of other ravers at service stations was important because participants felt the build-up of critical mass and momentum, which, in turn, impacted on their sense of belonging to a specific counterculture. That feeling of belonging to a strong, close-knit community of like-minded people did not end at the rave. In a similar way to the outward journey, the intimacy of the car facilitated communication and further bonding. A form of decompression was possible when fellow passengers decided to spend more time together by driving to other locations.

Taken those aspects together, the rave journey itself has to be recognized as a liminal experience, both physically and mentally. Leaving the familiar landscape of the city, home town, or village to drive to a remote field, ravers would experience geographical detachment. Entering an unlicensed, unregulated space facilitated a liminal experience. This was further helped by the absence of physical boundaries at the rave and an undefined dance floor. In addition, raves did not operate within time limits; curfews were not enforced. Consequently, the whole rave journey was celebrated by its participants as an experience suspended beyond time and space.

When basic conditions were met, ravers could redefine their idea of a home both geographically and mentally. Forming bonds with like-minded people that were perceived to be stronger than blood relations is one such result. Long-lasting friendships transcended the boundaries of rave culture and helped to incorporate rave values, as expressed through the PLUR ethos, into everyday life. This understanding of rave culture provides an alternative reading to the common assumption of rave culture having been an apolitical, purely hedonistic culture that had no significant impact on people's lives.

What does this mean for analysing current club culture? The sonic landscape of electronic dance music has changed so much that it has become almost impossible to compare it with early rave culture. And yet, there are developments in which one might be able to find traces of early rave culture. The festival market, for example, has changed considerably over the past few years. According to UK Music, the number of people who attended live music events rose by 12 per cent between 2015 and 2016. That equates to almost 4 million people attending festivals in the UK (2017, p. 6).

It is worth mentioning that 67 per cent of festival goers still travel by car according to the UK Festival Awards' *Market Report 2017* (p. 5). Contemporary car journeys can last for hours and, like rave journeys, they take passengers to a site of suspense both in terms of time and space. Music is stated to be the most important reason for attending a festival (64 per cent), followed by a concern to hang out with friends (19 per cent). There seems to be a clear desire to connect with other people and to spend prolonged periods of time together. Interestingly, the second most prominent age group after twenty- to twenty-five-(18 per cent)-year olds were forty- to fifty-year olds (18 per cent)—people who enjoyed their teenage years during the second summer of love in 1989, and the explosion of acid house in the UK. So, one could wonder whether old ravers are discovering festivals, rather than nightclubs, as sites to continue or repeat their rave experiences.

To finish, I will outline some directions for future research based on the findings presented in this chapter. Such research could explore the similarities and differences between early rave culture and contemporary festivals in more detail. Can festival sites be seen as similar sites of liminality? What role does the journey play? Is there a shared ethos that is common to all festival goers? Do experiences at festivals have a similar impact on people's everyday lives to the impact rave culture had? Finally, how are these experiences contextualized by their participants?

6

Driving on the A470: Cars and roads in Welsh-language popular music

Craig Owen Jones

In his final published work before his death, *The Psychology of Distance* (2003), the academic and Welsh assembly politician Phil Williams related an anecdote the contours of which will be familiar to most Welsh people. As a student, Williams hitchhiked from the town of Aberdaron in North Wales, and accepted a lift from a local farmer. They fell into conversation, and when Williams revealed that he was from South Wales, the farmer responded in all sincerity that he had visited Dolgellau once—the joke, of course, being that the prominent market town lies on a line of latitude no more than ten miles south of Aberdaron. As Williams noted, "The psychology of distance has never been based on cartography" (2003, p. 4).

This anecdote is emblematic of the perverse attitude towards geography that, it seems, is inherent in the Welsh psyche. It may be that such attitudes are common to all peoples living in a distinct and compact area, a natural corollary to the 'small town' mentality. It is axiomatic of Welsh-speaking society that, on meeting a stranger, one typically asks where they come from. And, typically, if the answer contains a town or village known to the interlocutor, the following question will ask after any possible mutual acquaintances, which, at least as often as not, proves a productive line of questioning; one of the most common Welsh proverbs is *byd bach* ('small world'). Another equally emblematic characteristic of the Welsh mind, if less well-known outside Wales, is *hiraeth*, a word that has no direct translation in English, which can be thought of as conveying feelings of sadness and nostalgia due to the absence of a place, usually one's home town or neighbourhood. A concept invoked with cloying frequency and regularity by Welsh expatriates, it was Peter Finch who pointed out the ridiculousness of the Welsh obsession with home and *hiraeth* in his poem "A Welsh Wordscape," which, in his customary sparing language, defines the concept as encompassing "the incredible agony/of an exile/ that can be at most/a day's travel away."[1] Even when Finch wrote the poem in the 1970s, a time when Wales' road network was less developed than today, this was doubtless true: there is no village or hamlet anywhere in the country that is more than four hours' drive from the English border.

Welsh landscape and automobile culture

From the streets of Dylan Thomas's Llareggyb to the musings of John Evans's drug-addled protagonists, there is a fascination with the Welsh landscape that borders on the obsessive in art and literature, and it is within this framework that I wish to situate the present discussion of automobile culture. As will be demonstrated, both cars and roads contribute to the narrative of landscape in Wales in surprising ways, helping to answer the question of how the space between places both within Wales and beyond its borders is traversed. So, too, with popular music: it was singer-songwriter Heather Jones who combined the imagery of *hiraeth* with the landscape of the South Wales valleys in her 1978 track "Cwm Hiraeth" (Hiraeth Valley), while the Carmarthen rock band Galwad Y Mynydd (Call of the Mountain), with their 1972 song "Niwl Y Môr" (Sea Mist), elevated an afternoon on the shores of Cardigan Bay to the level of spectacle worthy of a painting by Kyffin Williams, Richard Wilson, or Sidney Curnow Vosper. Against this background, roads and cars are frequently treated in idiosyncratic fashion: not necessarily as adorning the landscape, or allowing movement from one part of it to another, but rather as forming part of it. Notions of mobility that loom large in the cultural narratives of other nations when invoking 'the open road' are less apparent in Wales's case—a result of the nation's peculiar geography, one that encourages travel links that run from west to east rather than from north to south. Invocations of, say, cars, roads, and motorbikes therefore have fundamentally different connotations to those found in, for example, the songs of Steppenwolf or the cover artwork of records by ZZ Top— the roads form an integral part of the landscape, but are frequently stripped of the connotations of movement they hold elsewhere. More surprisingly, vehicles depicted also become part of the landscape, either literally or figuratively in the case of abandoned wrecks. What follows will seek to explore these tendencies in greater detail, concentrating for the most part on the utilization of these symbols by rock musicians.

'Come for a spin in the charabanc': Rejecting the car as the 'great liberator'

The advent of Welsh-language popular music can be dated to the early 1940s, but what became known as the '*byd pop Cymraeg*'—the 'Welsh pop world,' which has produced artists such as Mike Stevens, Gorky's Zygotic Mynci, and Catatonia— began life as a musical movement rooted in protest (see Hill, 2007). The gradual realization of the imperilled status of the Welsh language, which had been losing speakers at an increasing rate since the end of the First World War, came to a head in 1962, with the radio broadcast of essayist Saunders Lewis's "Tynged Yr Iaith" ("The Fate of the Language"), which drew attention to the language's plight and the lack of civil rights for speakers, and the subsequent formation of the pressure group Cymdeithas yr Iaith, the Welsh Language Society, in South Wales later in the year. Early campaigns included the occupying of post offices and public thoroughfares in order to demand greater engagement with the Welsh language from local authorities, public bodies, and other organizations prominent in Welsh life.[2] Concomitant with this was a renewed appreciation of aspects of Welsh culture associated with the language, such as the centuries-old tradition of the *eisteddfod* art and music festivals,[3] indigenous forms of literature and poetry such as *cerdd dant*, and others. A great deal of emphasis was placed on revitalizing the language in Anglicized areas of Wales, and on maintaining the language in speech communities, where it was still spoken by a majority of the population, and resistance to avowedly Anglo-American styles of popular music in general, and rock music in particular, was therefore widespread among older social commentators who feared the debasing influences on usage of the Welsh language of a youth culture in which English slang was prevalent. While it would be going too far to say that this factor was alone responsible for the somewhat belated appearance of Welsh-language rock bands in numbers—other factors were in evidence, not the least of which was the substantial financial investment required to found such a band at a time when electric instruments and amplifiers were prohibitively expensive for most amateur musicians—there can be little doubt that it was influential. A further obstacle to acceptance was the violence commonly associated with rock music in the early 1960s. Welsh-speaking Wales was not impervious to these problems. On Anglesey, Benllech Beat Club in particular gained a notorious reputation in the mid-1960s for the rowdy behaviour of the mods and rockers who attended it; while in Barry, in May 1964, a riot involving mod and rocker gangs attracted much negative press coverage. Acoustic styles of popular music were, however, integrated into Welsh-speaking society with far more ease and enduring success; singer-songwriters such as Dafydd Iwan and Meic Stevens, taking their cues from Pete Seeger and Bob Dylan, wrote songs addressing the independence issue and the language struggle, and celebrating Welsh culture in general, even if both dallied with rock music from time to time in the 1970s as the genre began to gain acceptance.[4]

During this period, uses of automobile imagery were, then, defined in the first instance according to their relation to or evocation of the Anglo-American youth culture, as can be seen in the cover to Edward H. Dafis's second album, *Ffordd Newydd Eingl-Americanaidd Grêt O Fyw* (*A New Great Anglo-American Way of Life*), released by Sain in 1975 (see Figure 6.1).

The palm trees and the American car model are all suggestive of a more exotic location than rural Wales; indeed, for the initiated the title acquires added meaning in light of the band's first album, *Hen Ffordd Gymreig O Fyw* (*An Old Welsh Way of Life*), released the previous year (see Figure 6.2).

These titles underscored the tumultuous process of stylistic change Welsh-language pop was going through at the time. What was being referred to as the triumph of 'dance bands,' or the 'electrification' of Welsh-language music—the

Figure 6.1 Edward H. Dafis, *Ffordd Newydd Eingl-Americanaidd Grêt O Fyw* (*A New Great Anglo-American Way of Life*) (Sain, 1975). By permission of Recordiau Sain.

Figure 6.2 Edward H. Dafis, *Hen Ffordd Gymreig O Fyw* (*An Old Welsh Way of Life*) (Sain, 1974). By permission of Recordiau Sain.

avoidance of the word 'rock' is significant, placating, as it did, older generations averse to the appearance of Welsh-language rock bands (see below)—was changing the nature of both the record industry and the live scene in Wales. The former had entered a rut by the early 1970s, with falling sales reflected in the stagnant pop chart published every week in the Welsh-language newspaper *Y Cymro*. At the same time, the declining popularity of the '*noson lawen*' or 'merry evening'—the live event of choice for acoustic artists and close harmony groups in the 1960s, aimed at a wide demographic including children, teenagers, and adults of all ages—coincided with the rise of the rock disco and the rock gig. By 1975, these older, more conservative infrastructural elements had been in place for the best part of twenty years and had become an accepted part of Welsh-speaking culture. Their relegation to a peripheral position within that culture due to the rise in popularity of discos and rock bands is, in its way, the subtext of these two albums: the juxtaposition of the intimate photograph of the band's five members with the anonymized, brash landscape of the later album underscores the transition that the band's own brand of R&B–based rock represents, even as their ironic employment of the anthropomorphic car, the palm trees, and the outlandish 'neon' writing casts doubt on the influence it exerts on the culture in which it resides. Though the proclivities of Fleet Street journalists led, in the 1990s, to a tentative identification of a 'Cool Cymru' sound exemplified by groups such as the Super Furry Animals and Gorky's Zygotic Mynci, predicated on an exoticism rooted in use of a Celtic language mixed with the visual and aural trappings of psychedelic rock, it is plain that neither the so-called Cool Cymru bands nor their 1960s and 1970s predecessors viewed themselves as exotic. *Ffordd Newydd Eingl-Americanaidd Grêt O Fyw*'s cover gives the impression of exoticism, though its audience knows better.

The car and significance

What, though, is the wider significance of the car? It is perhaps the most exotic element present; it is clearly an American model and is in no way designed to evoke vehicles seen on the streets of Cardiff or Caernarfon. We may conceive of it as a representation of the car as a 'great liberator,' in which terms Sean O'Connell described it in his analysis of the car in early twentieth-century British society. For O'Connell, "Car ownership had an emblematic status from its inception" (1998, p. 94); it denoted, in Britain as in the stylized America represented on Edward H. Dafis's album cover, prosperity but also defined the ways in which people conceived of their own aspirations. For Edward H. Dafis, however, it is present only as a palimpsest. The album cover of *Hen Ffordd Gymreig O Fyw* allowed for the construction of the band's role as interpreters of a shared heritage, even if only by inviting the audience to be complicit in a fictive past evoked by the soft-bordered, sepia-toned image of the band. This was doubtless deliberate and motivated by considerations of audience. By the early 1970s, Welsh-language rock bands were increasing in number, but acceptance of them—and more specifically, their music—by opinion-formers in the Welsh press and society in general was halting and qualified. There are indications that alleviating the perceptual difficulties encountered by older audiences due to the rise of rock music in Welsh-speaking Wales lies behind the design of *Hen Ffordd Gymreig O Fyw*. Far from presenting, say, an image representative of a 'high-technology group' "a literal signifier of the psychedelic effect [the band] hoped to achieve," as Sheila Whiteley (1992, p. 105) characterizes the prism that graces the front cover of Pink Floyd's *Dark Side Of The Moon* (1973), in *Hen Ffordd Gymreig O Fyw*'s case the record buyer is required to acquiesce to the harkening-back to earlier times that the image connotes and anticipates a listening experience that, though grounded in the rock genre, contains abundant points of contact with earlier musical styles and cultural reference points (as indeed the album does).

Conversely, by situating its imagery in a suburban American locale, the album's successor distances the audience from the sentiment expressed in its title. The 'great new' way of life—signified by 'Anglo-American' culture, the English language, and the car, is a chimera; the incongruity of social liberation is reinscribed upon the car that supposedly brings it. Where appearances of cars on record artwork have often been seen as representing a band or artist's flaunting of an (achieved) lifestyle, the logical culmination of 'rags to riches' aspiration so lavishly indulged by Elvis Presley through his automobile-buying habits (as Patrick Field has noted), the amateur nature of the Welsh-language pop world combined with the relatively small audience for Welsh-language records restricted the amount of money musicians could expect to make from their releases, effectively preventing any such largesse.[5]

A similar though more complicated relationship with the car can be seen in "Siarabang," a song by Llanrwst group Y Mellt. Originally formed as an English-language band the Lightning Rwsters around 1966, the band soon changed their name to Y Mellt and began playing gigs in 1967. After splitting in 1970 following an injury to one of the band members, the group reformed the following year as a three-piece and released two EPs on the Sain label before splitting up for the second and final time in late 1974.

The second of those EPs, "Mari, Mari" (1974), is notable in the context of the present discussion for its inclusion of the song "Siarabang" ("Charabanc"), one of the earliest Welsh-language rock songs to feature the car as its subject. The singer describes his car in effusive terms, detailing not only the pride he takes in its appearance, but explaining exactly why it looks as it does.

When the singer extols the virtues of his car, it is both as a piece of cherished property and a badge of his identity. Painted in red, white, and green—the colours of the Welsh flag, and also of Urdd Gobaith Cymru (The Welsh League of Youth), the nationwide Welsh-language youth activities organization—the car bears the dragon's tongue: obviously a reference to the Welsh national symbol, but which would also have been readily understood by listeners as the logo of Tafod, the Welsh Language Society's youth wing. The car's journey and that of the narrator are conflated—the destination cannot be reached on any metaled road, but is, rather, salvation through espousal of Welsh patriotism as expressed through the Welsh language.

This, it can be seen, is a long way from the accepted role of the car in rock music as an uncomplicated indicator of masculinity. It is self-evident that Y Mellt's "Siarabang" does not stand for the financially affluent, sexually confident, rock 'n' roll–obsessed teenagers of the 1950s and 1960s, whose way of life found such regular and emphatic expression, for example, in the early works of Chuck Berry. Indeed, this is obvious from the cover, which shows the band posing on the bodywork of a vintage car of the prewar years—hardly the vehicle of choice for young men of the 1970s—and also the deployment of the anachronistic term 'siarabang', long abandoned by all but the oldest generation of Welsh speakers in favour of 'modur', or even more simply, 'car' by the early 1970s.

In all seriousness, such imagery would be completely incongruous in a Wales of whose teenage men such as R. S. Thomas once wrote that a twenty year-old Welshman had two options—either to act like a fifty-year-old or to turn into an Englishman. Other objections include the incongruity of the connotations of car as sexual symbol. Writing in 1980, Paul J. Karlstrom wrote of American society that

> for much of the present generation, the relationship with the automobile has been and continues to be an extremely intimate one . . . the experience gained behind the wheel or in the back seat as an adolescent has a lasting effect. In many communities, cars provide freedom beyond simple mobility and escape from parental restrictions. Social development and sexual experimentation routinely take place at drive-in theatres, on country roads, or at scenic spots overlooking the lights of the city. (1980, p. 18)

In Welsh-speaking Wales, such ideas were faintly ridiculous; after all, in the 1970s, cities and drive-in theatres were noticeable by their relative absence. Similarly, the idea of car as status symbol in "Siarabang" lacks validity: although the singer values it for what it represents—that is, his steadfast adherence to the patriotic cultural revival convulsing Welsh-speaking society in the 1960s and 1970s—and the listener by implication acknowledges this, the status his stance confers is not transferable, and certainly not universal, achieving currency only within a select group of similarly interested members of Welsh society. Indeed, compared with other early rock songs about cars, the song is noteworthy for what it does *not* contain; there is no 'baby beside me at the wheel,' no notion of a (physical) destination in sight, and no reference to speed or the car's performance. Rather, what "Siarabang" reflects is one of the more important strands of usage of the symbolism of the car by Welsh-speaking popular musicians of the period: a conceptualization of the car as an instrument with which to advance the language struggle, rather than an indicator of social milieu (or, conversely, an actuator of social mobility).

Examining the context of the song's release is also instructive in this connection. One of the other tracks on the "Mari, Mari" EP was specially recorded to commemorate the opening of the preeminent music and arts festival in Wales, the National Eisteddfod in Rhuthun—a sure sign of the band's willingness to conform to wider social norms; indeed, production of "Siarabang" seems intended to engender the goodwill of older Welsh-speaking record buyers unfamiliar with (and, in many cases, hostile to) rock music, with its bizarre mixing-back of the drums and guitar, and prominent placing of lead vocals and harmonies.[6]

"Siarabang," then, demonstrates the extent of the disinterest of Y Mellt towards the usual symbols of automobile culture, a disinterest that we may take as being emblematic of Welsh-language rock music for much of the rest of the 1970s. It is perhaps also for the same reason that the 'biker' song, exemplified by the Shangri-La's "Leader of the Pack" (1964) or Steppenwolf's "Born to Be Wild" (1968), is almost completely absent from the canon of Welsh-language popular music; the only notable exception of the 1960s and 1970s was "Olwen Dwy Olwyn" ("Olwen Two Wheels") from 1978 by mid-Wales blues-rock band Seindorf.

Later generations of Welsh-speaking musicians, however, shortly began exploring the image of the automobile and the road as it appeared in the Welsh landscape—either anecdotally or in actuality as an abandoned wreck. The sort of photographs employed, for example, on MC Saizmundo's records in the 2000s (see Figure 6.3) bear considerable resemblance to the works of photorealist artist

Figure 6.3 Photograph used on CD booklet artwork of MC Saizmundo's *Malwod a Morgrug: Dan Warchae* (Snails and Ants: Under Siege) (Slacyr, 2005). By permission of Deian ap Rhisiart.

John Salt, whose series of paintings of wrecked American cars bore a broadly similar rhetorical force: a reminder of rural poverty, of disenfranchisement, and a lack of upward mobility.

Yet where Salt's work is frequently devoid of conscious narrative, so many of these images bespeak decay: the transformation of the object itself but also the society it signifies. Such ideas are also of relevance in considering the manner in which the symbolism of the road is deployed in Welsh-language popular music.

Cemeteries and 'L' plates: The Welsh road

It is ironic that such a small country as Wales should have such poor transport links. There are only two motorways, the M4 and the M48, both of which service the industrial south; the M56 motorway that services towns and communities in Cheshire and the Manchester area adjoining North Wales terminates a mere mile and a half from the Welsh border. Until recently, those wishing to travel from the north's largest town, Wrexham, to Cardiff found themselves in the curious position of having to go down English 'A' roads to do it; the next best Welsh road that accomplished the task added an hour to the journey. Since the 1970s, the road network has undergone steady improvement, but in the opinion of Phil Williams, the money spent on constructing and improving east-west road links such as the M4 and North Wales's arterial road, the A55, should be complemented by similar expenditure in improving north-south road links, "a small price for consolidating national unity" (Williams, 2003, p. 59).

It is, then, no surprise that the Welsh road has seldom been celebrated in art and literature. Artists, with the notable exception of Stuart Burne's award-winning 2006 photographic study of the A55, have largely ignored the creative possibilities of the road. In cinema, too, less than half a dozen Welsh-language movies eulogizing travel are in existence, of which only *Gadael Lenin* (Emlyn, 1994) and the road trip movie *Patagonia* (Evans, 2010) deserve notice.

In some ways, this is surprising, as the campaigns for bilingual road signs, driving licences, and learner's plates—displaying a 'D' for *dysgwr* rather than an 'L' for learner—formed important battlegrounds in the 1960s and 1970s for Welsh Language Society activists. Many members of the society were given hefty fines as result of their participation in campaigns of civil disobedience that included the painting out (or wholesale removal) of monolingual English road signs, and some were imprisoned, including several members of Welsh-language rock bands. Indeed, Eurig Wyn, a guitarist who formed one of the earliest rock bands, Y Tarddiad (The Origin), was the individual responsible for bringing the learner plates issue to prominence when he was stopped by a police car in 1967 for driving with a 'D' plate rather than an 'L' plate, in contravention of the law as it stood at the time (see Stephens, 2004). Protest songs were written on some of these issues, most notably "Rhaid Yw Eu Tynnu I Lawr" (They Must be Pulled Down, 1971) by Y Chwyldro (The Revolution), but as a rule, the road did not prove a fertile subject for songwriters of the period.

Nevertheless, by the 1980s more rock bands were in existence, and the increasing success with which language campaigners raised the status of Welsh began to subtly alter the extent to which groups felt the need to explicitly address the language struggle in their songs. For groups such as Datblygu (Develop), such approaches were dispensed with in favour of a broader social commentary. Formed in 1982, the trio—sometimes referred to in the press as 'the Welsh Fall'—were a favourite of John Peel and recorded several sessions for the *John Peel Show*. Examples from their output demonstrating the self-reflexivity that had, by the 1980s, been developed by them and so many of their contemporaries are legion. Of particular interest is how the band appropriated the symbols of the earlier generation of language campaigners, as, for example, "Dafydd Iwan Yn Y Glaw" ("Dafydd Iwan in the Rain," 1990) demonstrates. Indeed, in the light of Y Mellt's evocation of the Tafod tongue logo noted above, it is provocative to consider Datblygu's reference to exactly the same logo twenty years later, in "Cân i Gymry" ("Song for the Welsh," 1993). The logo—a stylized 'T' twisted into the shape of a dragon's tongue—which formerly connoted the non-violent protests of the Welsh Language Society for more rights for Welsh speakers to use the language in everyday life in the 1960s, 1970s, and 1980s, suddenly bears a new and pointed reinscription. The language campaigners of yesteryear, having benefited from the increased legislation in favour of the use of Welsh, and the investment in Welsh-language radio and television caused by the advent of Radio Cymru (1979) and S4C (1982), now find themselves in positions of affluence and power. The radicalism they espoused for the sake of the language struggle, like that of the singer of "Siarabang," finds expression in "Cân i Gymry" through the bestowing of the Tafod logo on their car, but the car itself—a well-heeled family saloon—denotes an altogether different social standing.

The settled, cozy life of the Welsh-speaking middle class is here both pilloried and unfavourably compared with the activism of youth; with wealth has come a certain malaise, and the maintenance of Welsh and the perks that go with it—such as visits to Breton-speaking parts of Brittany (not France) mentioned later in the song—is no longer the grave and urgent matter it once was, but has become a lifestyle choice.

This tone is typical of Datblygu's works, and so it is all of a piece to find the band offering a new conceptualization of the road, even if it is one that is not particularly closer to anticipated notions of mobility. The act of driving appears in their 1988 track "Mynwent" (Cemetery) in the context not of conveying one from one place to another, but as a funeral procession. The road of which lead singer David R. Edwards speaks, wending its way up through the heart of Wales from south to north, can only be the A470, Wales' main arterial route, and one which was eulogized in a rather more conventional fashion by Fflur Dafydd on her 2009 concept album *Byd Bach* (*Small World*). However, the road itself creates the landscape it passes through; assuming the proportions of a nationwide allegory, Wales becomes a cemetery. Rural flight, either due to a lack of job opportunities or spiralling house prices caused by lifestyle tourism—the notorious *tŷ haf* (holiday home)—is the subject of countless songs in the Welsh-language canon, including MC Saizmundo's "Pentre Marw" ("Dead Village," 2005), and new wave band Ail Symudiad's "Twristiaid Yn Y Dre" ("Tourists in the Town," 1981); yet it is only on "Mynwent" that it is not the Welsh language or Welsh culture subsumed in these concepts that is made mortal, but the landscape itself, encapsulated in the road that links north and south, and the flagging communities that line it.

To paraphrase Karlstrom, this is the physiognomy of the Welsh roadside (1980, p. 22): a bleak, depressing environment in which whole communities seem to cease to exist. These are, indeed, the 'dead villages' of which MC Saizmundo would later rap—the 'grey houses' are without lights because they are only inhabited during the holiday season. The language deployed is so flat—there is a single adjective in the Welsh original—that we may even permit ourselves to think of the landscape of Wales described here as liminal: life begins again, in the most attenuated form, only when the journey concludes, and even then in a Caernarfon glossed as joyless.

However, in the end the abiding message of "Mynwent" may be that the road itself is just as legitimate a place as the two destinations it links, for in the most direct sense, it is where the things it describes occur. John Frow (1991), in an essay on tourism and semiotics, establishes that the 'formal essence' of a thing in a previous text (in his example, a tree described in a poem), once known to the traveller, dictates how it will be perceived from that point of comprehension onwards:

"all later seeing is governed by the possibility of conformity to this pattern . . . the authority of a poetic tradition that constantly refashions the essence of the tree, its normative beauty . . . constrains the visitor to a recognition of essence" (p. 124).

Edwards's journey through Wales is a procession in more ways than one. The 'places that aren't on the map' evoke the brutal geography of what the poet Harri Webb once famously described as 'the green desert': the unpopulated midland districts of Wales, in which valleys such as the *Clywedog* and the *Tryweryn* were drowned, and hundreds of Welsh-speaking people uprooted, during the twentieth century in order to make way for reservoirs, the latter painfully and pointedly eulogized by Huw Jones's single "Dŵr" ("Water," 1969). If we invoke, as Frow does, the conceptualization of the 'tourist gaze,' the notion that "things are read as signs of themselves" (p. 125), and accept the concomitant point that the process of gazing changes that which is gazed at, we may arrive at a firmer understanding of meaning of "Mynwent." All that is seen in the song is seen from the road; without the experience of the journey, it would be impossible to apply Edwards's observations to the landscape.

Conclusion

It is not at all clear how the conceptualizations of the car and the road outlined above will fare in Welsh music. It may be that we are witnessing the passing of these types of signification in Welsh-language popular music, as they become so prevalent that they come to be representative of a particular, but strangely unspoken and uncelebrated, mode of emoting—what Jameson (1992/2007) referred to as the "quasi-material 'feeling tone'" (p. 17) which occupies a transient position within any given narrative. For many of the artists discussed above, the key note of their discourse is decay—decay of a language, of a way of life. Welsh artist Iwan Bala's (1999) concept of 'custodial aesthetics' may well be of relevance in this regard, centring around the notion of the '*cof cenedl*,' the 'memory of the people,' which he sees as intrinsic to Welsh identity, and as informing the artistic endeavour; Welsh artists create so as to preserve the understanding of what it means to be Welsh. The regular recurrence of certain topics in pop songs—the post-war drowning of Welsh valleys, sporting defeats and victories, and the sacrifices of medieval Welsh princes and language campaigners alike, the whole communicated from the perspective of a chronicler, or even a participant—would seem to lend Bala's notion credence: Huw Jones, MC Saizmundo, and their contemporaries have remembered (and continue to do so) that we should not forget. The danger with such an approach, however, is in the fossilization of those memories; they become so familiar that they no longer effectively convey the cultural information they once did. Writing in 2002, Patrick Field, in his analysis of automobile and road culture symbolism in early rock 'n' roll songs, made reference to "the aching, impossible desire for unlimited mobility and party-without-end that dominated the popular culture of the twentieth century" (p. 64). For Field, this desire was impossible to satiate because the very means realized to enable it—the invention of the automobile—removed the very factor that actuated its own pursuit:

> The power to go anywhere we choose deprives us of motivation. Dominance of the natural world forces us to redefine our existence without our former adversary, raw nature . . . . The automobile's promise to take people from one place to another, leaving them, their origin and destination, and a route between unaffected by the trip while entertaining them with the thrill of operating a powerful machine and affirming their power and status, is equally unsustainable. Cars may be useful for moving people and goods from place to place; they may be enjoyable cult objects for play, display or tests of skill and nerve. Continuing with attempts to fuse these practical and aesthetic functions will only destroy the possibility that either can be satisfactorily attained. (2002, p. 64)

The above may yet stand as an epitaph for the appearance of cars and automobile culture in Welsh-language popular music. If the imagery of the car and the road may be approaching this point, today's artists would do well to revisit the imperatives that caused their forebears to dwell on them in the first place.

7

"*Ich will Spaß, ich geb Gas*": German pop between fun and subversion

Barbara Hornberger

It is said that Germans have a particularly intimate bond to their cars; they associate cars with both their motorways and their freedom. Thus, one might assume that there have been quite a few German pop songs where cars play an important part. Strangely, that is not the case. I remember exactly three rather popular ones: the song "Autobahn" by the internationally renowned electro band Kraftwerk from 1973, the Schlager[1] "Im Wagen vor mir" from 1977, and Markus's Neue Deutsche Welle (NDW) song "Ich will Spaß"[2] from 1982.

"Autobahn" is recognized as a minimalist masterpiece of electro-pop that fostered a style in its own right. "Im Wagen vor mir" remained on the German charts for thirty-three weeks. It is played at certain parties in Berlin due to the 'cult' character it has achieved these days, which is also reflected in the number of cover and spoof versions. The third song, "Ich will Spaß," was a number 1 hit in the charts for twenty-four weeks. It marks the full commercialization of the NDW, a genre finally allowed German musicians to sing in German. Because of its commercial success, the majority of critics and academics usually dismiss it for lack of critical thought. This chapter will focus on exactly that song and argue that by using the strategy of 'tactical affirmation,' it is, indeed, subversive.

NDW translates literally as New German Wave.[3] Assuming that it is an equivalent for the Anglo-American post-punk new wave would only be partially correct. Like new wave, NDW emerged from punk. However, in the context of West Germany (FRG), its development was something quite different. For West German youth, punk was initially—like rock 'n' roll and beat music—merely another imported genre that could be listened to and copied. The novelty of NDW, in contrast, lay in the development of one's own culture through embracing an import: German pop and NDW bands used the raw energy and DIY ideology of punk in their own way. Punk's demand that people immediately express their own real world experience led to a preference for writing in German. Karl Heinz Schott, a German underground punk musician, explained in 1978 that he could not sing "I'm cruising down the highway," when in fact he was driving down the Rothenbaumchaussee. Hence, he would try to find adequate forms of expression in music and lyrics (as cited in Hilsberg, 1978, p. 23).

In addition to German lyrics, which are certainly the most prominent symptom and feature of this cultural transfer, there was also a differentiation and extension of musical, textual, and performative modes. This, eventually, was fully embraced by NDW, especially at its later stages. The style broadened the raw sound of punk through synthesizers and sequencers, through the application of classical instruments and through elements of other styles such as funk and reggae. The use of German lyrics—instead of the usual English—was, especially at the beginning, verified by and related to the claim to portray reality. In punk music, lyrics should be simple and direct: an immediate, undiluted expression of one's living conditions, and one's attitude towards those conditions. Such living conditions were experienced as dissatisfying, alienating, and alienated. At the time, many young people felt estranged, unable to see prospects or a future for themselves. 'No fun' and 'no future' were the corresponding slogans. The themes in punk and early NDW songs were not utopian world designs, visions, or fantasy worlds. Also, they rarely touched on aspects of love or grief. The songs were rather concerned with finding a new, unadorned, personal access to, and grasp of, the present. At this point, NDW saw itself—and was understood—as a kind of pop avant-garde.

While the German press initially approached first punk and then NDW with varying degrees of benevolence, NDW itself changed and became even more experimental, generating extreme variations. On the one hand, Einstürzende Neubauten worked with avant-garde machine sounds, while on the other a series of bands developed a great zest for playfulness, the bizarre, and the comical. According to the scene and critics who championed it, however, the latter development was where the calamity could come from: where trivialization and commercialization were lurking, where the mainstream 'threatened' to encroach. Markus and his song "Ich will Spaß" originated precisely from that place.

At first glance seemingly daft, Markus's song attracted a great deal of criticism. Some said it satisfied a dead-on desire for kitsch (Döpfner and Garms, 1984, p. 32), others diagnosed an inexorable loss of standards (Longerich, 1989, p. 193) or a trivialization of underground music towards harmless dance delight (Kemper, 1999, p. 188). Indeed, critics stated that the song was nothing but a well-constructed product geared towards commerce, which drew on clichés in an arbitrary and senseless way, yet still managed to cleverly hit the nerve of its time (Döpfner and Garms, 1984, p. 60). According to Giessen (1992), "Ich will Spaß," accomplished an extreme form of depoliticization. Both calculus and success account for a need of clumsy, simple "fun" that dreads to think of or refer to any kind of problem: "acceleration" is only fun, as long as the police do not see it, and thus the consequences—traffic hazards, increased pollution of environment—are not even mentioned (p. 267).

The song was, therefore, supposedly superficial, conservative, stupid, and even dangerous, at least in the eyes of journalists and academics.

The song "Ich will Spaß"

Initially, the lyrics of "Ich will Spaß" describe an occupation of public space full of relish with and through the car. 'I want fun' here means the same as 'I want to drive,' and to have fun, in this context, means driving fast. Although this appears to be the essential message of the song, it is somewhat ironic. The astronomical petrol price of DM 3.10 mentioned in the lyrics excessively exaggerated prices after the oil crises of the 1970s. In reality, the average petrol price in 1982 was DM 1.36. Furthermore, the song deals with a notion of megalomania. The line "Germany, tonight I'll make you mine" can be understood in a sexual as well as a militant way, something that can be interpreted as a self-aware, ironic form of arrogance. So, it is no wonder that the petrol station attendant referred to in the lyrics is happy to see his best customer!

The music is a rocky version of Schlager, arranged for a rhythm machine, a sequencer (replacing the e-bass), drums, and guitar. It is a simple verse-chorus-verse composition in four-four-time with the conventional chords C major, F major, and G major7—tonic, subdominant, and dominant—and additional A minor in the bridge after the second chorus. The beat is a straight eight-part rhythm, and there are no traces of soul or blues in the harmonic or melodic structure, nor are there any in the singing. The most striking feature of the song is its continuous synthesizer pattern in the verses, and a sing-along melody, which guarantees the catchy tune.

From this first and rather superficial overview, "Ich will Spaß" may appear as a calculated retort song: a daft, childish, and unprofessional song with a hedonistic message. However, upon close inspection, both the text and its performance emerge as an accurately staged fall back on German pop culture and youth culture traditions. By portraying the occupation of public space through and with the car as an experience of pleasure, "Ich will Spaß" corresponds to the palpable historical prototype of 'motorcycle gangs': the 'young and wild,' 'rebel without a cause' culture of the 1950s, initiated and represented by Marlon Brando and James Dean (see final chapter, this volume). In Germany, such attitudes were revived in the 1980s in the form of *Halbstarke*.[4] To examine the link, it is necessary not only to analyse the song's lyrics and music but also to pay particular attention to its performance.

Between the 1950s and 1980s

Both the song and performance worked in close relation to a widespread revival of the 1950s in the early 1980s.[5] This is visible on the cover of the record: aspects from the 1950s are combined with those from the 1980s. The quiff, a cigarette, a leather jacket, and tie are as much part of the *Halbstarken* as are defiant, rebellious facial expressions. Similarly, the script is a typographical pointer. Still, the white leather tie, the cigarette lit with a plastic lighter (instead of a Zippo), and Markus's half-finger gloves are clearly indicative signs of 1980s fashion. This line of investigation is further supported by Markus's repeated performances of the song in fairly similar ways, frequently seen on German television during the time. The best known and most famous perhaps was shown at the weekly German Schlager chart show *ZDF-Hitparade*, a well-established and very popular show during the 1970s and 1980s on German television.[6] Here, similar to the record cover, the singer and band wore outfits that corresponded to the fashion of the 1980s. Yet, these are combined with obvious nostalgic elements (see Hyvernat, 2014). The men were in white shirts and—particularly striking— dark blue Bermudas with white belts. Markus himself, in addition, wore a dark blue jacket, the keyboard player a small, short tie—typical both for the 1950s and 1980s—and the drummer wore knee socks. These, together with their white calves and bawdy, ankle-high boots presented attire that resembled sailor suits, and a dress sense from the period up to about the 1960s, where boys were seen as children until they were confirmed by the church at the age of fourteen. Until then, they were wearing shorts. The female keyboard player also added to the nostalgic effect: a skirt, fitted at the waist, and a frilly white blouse, citing a version of Dior's 'new look' in a somewhat petit bourgeois manner. Her white socks in half-shoes—not dissimilar to 1950s trainers—combined with pig-tails gave her a naïve, childlike look.

1950s style and the motif of rebellion

The most significant and perhaps interesting reference to the 1950s in terms of *Halbstarke* culture is the motif of rebellion: 'loitering' teenagers appear as a threat to the public order. 'Conquest' of public places and the street comes to the fore as an expression of juvenile delinquency and emerges as a rebellious act. Indeed, this act showed a gap in the amalgamating society of reconstruction. Some young people refused both subsumption and the pressure to follow work ethics or contribute to productivity. Hence, they became a provocation for the 'society of reconstruction' of the Federal Republic of Germany (FRG).

With the occupation of public places they were able to rebel in a threefold manner. First, their occupation of the street was an actual acquisition of public space. In the post-war era, tiny flats offered little space and even less privacy for youths who were used to roaming around the ruins of bombed-out cities unsupervised. Spatial freedom was exchanged for confinement within the nuclear family. Instead of unregulated play, parental supervision began to prevail. The *Halbstarke* occupancy of public space emerged as a compensation for such restrictions. Secondly, being on the streets means visibly and demonstratively eluding parental control and societal regulations. The provocative loitering of the *Halbstarken* demonstrated their desire for freedom and breaking out of a society that was committed in its entirety to reconstruction and rehabilitation. It was a rebellion against the newly established authorities, which were met with scepticism particularly by the male *Halbstarken*. Finally, in the 1950s access to mobility was a status symbol. Car ownership and the level of motorization made the economic success of the new society apparent. Even though *Halbstarke* seized this development with their use and display of mopeds, they did not, however, relate it to an attitude of economic success through hard work, respectability and adulthood, but rather promoted hedonism and adolescent mindlessness. Through the occupation of the street, and mopeds, young people assumed a status and a place that was commonly owned by their bosses and parents, by adult authorities.[7]

The historical context of the song

A key aim of the 1980 Kohl government was precisely to revive the 1950s idea of work ethics to support a new society of reconstruction. In his government declaration from 1982 Kohl bridged, in an explicit manner, the economic miracle of the Adenauer era with the current times: what worked in 1949 under strain and with emotional wounds and material burdens should be possible and necessary in 1982 as well. The Kohl administration demanded a Renaissance of the notion of work ethics and an alliance with—as in following of—the reconstruction efforts and achievements of the 1950s. In this context, the rediscovery of the 1950s, in terms of aesthetics, was a particularly appropriate occurrence. Wolfgang Kraushaar noted how a series of seemingly antiquated values were reactivated: the nuclear family, the Christian sense of values. Yet, only images of the 1950s were prominent; a resurgence of the same or similar family situations and socialization aspects did not take place. He was convinced that the function of the revival of the '50s at the beginning of the '80s was one of mere relief or discharge. One simply needed an optimistic incentive or push, a release from all these scenes of crisis and self-problematization (Wagner, 1999, pp. 140–41).

At this point, the question remains whether Markus, with his references of the 1950s, acted affirmatively or provocatively in regard to Kohl's restorative stance. Here it is essential to, first, note that both the motif of mobility, as well as the *Halbstarken* rebellion, found their revival and appropriate—as in contemporary—translation in the song "Ich will Spaß." The racy ascending of the Italian sports car obeyed solely the principle of fun. In Markus's interpretation, automobility was not the business of grown-up citizens, something deployed to reach one's goal, to navigate through space or to display success. It was simply fun: driving as an end in itself, and the street as a playground. The song's reference to both the Opel[8] as proper car of the petit bourgeois and the '*Ente*' (Citroen 2CV)[9] as a declared hippy vehicle evoked two concepts of the enemy already cultivated by punk: petit bourgeois and old hippy. The song, therefore, built a bridge between the past youth culture of the *Halbstarken* and current punk culture. Resistance against the wider societal notion of work ethics, a postulation of a strategy of public presence, and a tendency towards aggressiveness without political ideology were common to both.

Markus evoked speed by stating that his Maserati makes 210 kilometres per hour, being aware of navigating in a regulated space, but one in which the police failed to register his speeding. The song was an ironic culmination of the West

German slogan "Freie Fahrt für freie Bürger" ("Free driving for free citizens"): a phrase that was circulated in the 1970s by car associations and industry alike, as they connected the (democratic) right to freedom and citizenship with the individual right to motorized speed. In the song, the civic call for freedom became a kind of offensive unreasonableness: don't want to save, don't want to be reasonable, only premium petrol will do, I'll have fun (Klopprogge, 1982).

Tactical affirmation

"Ich will Spaß" was denied any kind of ironic stance by its critics: to assume a subtle irony in this song was seen as mere over-intellectualization (Döpfner and Garms, 1984, p. 60). Still, self-irony is evident.[10] Taking about the petrol station attendant as a good friend because he spends so much money on petrol is recognizing flawed relationship. The same applies to thoughts that are spent on how expensive the petrol is, and that it will work out, somehow.

In addition, the performance itself amplifies this notion of self-irony. The band looks like an aged kindergarten group. This impression is further strengthened by the somewhat bouncy dance style, the slight squeaky, seemingly breaking voice with which Markus sings and the replacement of the drum kit by two big, colourful rubber balls. Fun is promoted here, yet simultaneously its demand is, to an extent, exaggeratedly integrated into a children's birthday party scenario. Critics' nagging missed this point. Nothing needed to be discovered or unmasked as clumsy and hedonistic by them. The performance itself already exhibited all the song's demands as childish, hyped-up fantasies. Ferocious waving of little German flags when Markus wants Germany to 'feel him' transforms a potentially aggressive scene of threat into a childish fantasy of almightiness. Similarly, outwitting the police did not appear framed as a traffic offence, but rather a comedy version of 'cops and robbers.' Both in content and form the song therefore articulated a radical claim with regards to fun, and, thereby, provoked a criticism that saw "Ich will Spaß" as a representation of a reckless, selfish, environment-destroying, hedonistic attitude. Critics, however, ignored the song's contextual correlation. They did not grasp the specific cultural context (Hügel, 2007, p. 17) in which the song developed its effectiveness and its popularity. Instead, they obeyed a logic that defined the economic binary between mainstream and independent music as an aesthetic-ethical one.

Indeed, "Ich will Spaß" began a break from both the content and aesthetics of the hegemonic culture, and the strategies of rebellion conducted and circulated by the preceding generation—including its gestures of enlightenment and its related belief in an ability to change the world for the better. In this context, the song thus managed to alienate almost everybody who ethically formed the FRG of that time. The culture of debate of 1968 and the corresponding political concepts and ideologies had nothing in common with the reality of young people's lives in 1977 and were, therefore, rejected. Similarly, the ecological and peace movements emerging alongside punk, that were still drafting utopias, exercising gestures of fraternization and preaching commitment, were despised as heirs of the 1968 generation. Subcultures after punk abandoned, to a large extent, declarations of protest, constructive social criticism, and progressive utopias. Protest did not need to be verified and reasoned for; an opponent did not need to be named anymore. Belief in the ability to reform the system from within through rational reasoning and constructive collaboration appeared absurd to the fans of punk and NDW. Consequently, NDW developed a strategy that was unheard of and unknown to pop culture: tactical affirmation. This strategy of subversion functioned in a way that was no longer openly oppositional, but rather did the job through hidden operations: an infiltration strategy that unmasked through irony (see Hornberger, 2017).

NDW positioned itself not in opposition, but rather crosswise to society by utilizing deception and confusion instead of protest. Essentially, this worked as provocation: many did not comprehend the tactical affirmation as an ironic strategy of (re)presentation, but rather perceived it as an ideology of compliance and belittlement. My analysis, however, shows that Markus's "Ich will Spaß" was a Punch and Judy show that only *seemed* affirmative. In an exemplary manner it portrayed the entire recklessness of the German 'car madness,' only to surrender it immediately to mockery and ridicule. In addition, it maintained a claim for fun, which situated NDW as culture for young people in contrast to the preceding hippie culture, as well as the logic of achievement postulated by (conservative) adults. The song remained a playful, anarchic, irrational resistance to reason, sustainability, work ethics, and adulthood. With the aid of tactical affirmation it disassociated itself from the strategies of subversion that were valid *until then* and, thereby—aesthetically and in terms of its historical mindset—indicated and even anticipated the epochal changes that marked the 1980s era.

8

Las chivas: Fiesta in motion

Santiago Niño Morales

An accelerated process of urbanization in Colombia has led to drastic changes in the meanings of traditional cultural practices and symbols. Once a prominent feature of the countryside, *las chivas* are old wooden buses. In modern times they have not disappeared, but have instead been incorporated into the cultural dynamics of cities. Refurbished with sound and lighting equipment, *las chivas* are now referred to as a form of 'nightclub in motion.' Their automotive mobility and status as spaces in transit make a certain kind of dance party possible. *Las chivas* bring diverse cross-sections of society together to drink, dance, and enjoy music. People from various class backgrounds rent them out in groups to experience a party that moves through different areas of the city. Most of the urban inhabitants of Colombia have rural origins; *Las chivas* communicate the heritage of many. Their repurposing demonstrates the urbanizing population's changed relationship to the countryside. In this context, cultural meanings of *las chivas* express one of the many forms of transition between urban and rural cultures.

Las chivas

Las chivas is the name of a popular means of transport that circulates in various geographic regions of Colombia. Each is based on a chassis, upon which local craftsmen build wooden bodywork. With such adaptation, this type of bus has travelled the rural geography of the country for more than ninety years. However, rapid urbanization means that, unlike other cultural expressions, *las chivas* have been reused in urban areas, not as a means of utility, but signifying something opposite: automobiles adapted as vehicles for fun and entertainment (see Figure 8.1).

Figure 8.1 1952 Ford Mercury *chiva* in the Flowers Festival. Medellín, 2015. Photograph: Juan Mario Rubiano Durán.

Music is an important factor when explaining the transformation of meaning of the 'bus.' In fact, musical sounds occupy a central place, in modes of everyday life both associated with the buses as rural means of transportation and—through *las chivas*—also with the city.

The mobility of music promoted by *las chivas* was originally a fundamental way of creating dynamic social interactions and related musical practices in rural areas. Because *las chivas* now pass through both rural and urban environments, they embody the transformation of rural music that is taking place. Changes in the meaning and value of this particular mode of transport indicate that *las chivas* function as a cultural object that expresses the transformation experienced by Colombian society.

Brief historical background

At the beginning of the twentieth century, the first large road vehicles arrived in Colombia, mainly in the form of chassis from the United States. Owners took chassis mass produced by Ford, Chevrolet, Dodge, and GMC (but also International and Fargo) and began to adapt them—either as trucks or buses—depending on their needs. They commissioned local furniture workshops to build the required bodywork from wood. In Medellín, the engineer and mechanic Luciano Restrepo kept records showing that he and his carpenter

Robert Tisnés built the first recorded wood bodywork on a Ford chassis in 1908. Other workshops were active in Barranquilla and Bogotá.

Wood bodywork formed a basic structure which was covered in canvas with inlets on each side. The canvas was subsequently replaced by a solid roof that allowed people, animals, and goods to be transported. Some vehicles had ladders added at the rear of the bodywork; those are also known today as 'ladder busses.' Widespread use of particular types of wood—including teak, carob, and sapan—offered a certain robustness, ease of maintenance, and economy; a solution that continued, with few variations, to characterize this type of transport. Similar designs were replicated across Latin America—specifically in Ecuador and Panama. Buses had special importance in Colombia, however, mainly due to the extraordinarily difficult terrain. Because of the comparatively slow development of the railroads, for most of the twentieth century, many people used them as their sole means of motorized transport.

Evidence of cultural syncretism in *las chivas*

As the result of their production through local practices of woodcarving and popular art (see Figure 8.2), the bodywork of *las chivas* has become an object that mediates the functional and symbolic, a key space which expresses a blending of cultural practices from different regions. In their role as rural transport, *las chivas* initially announced their proximity to country towns with a bell. Later, the buses were equipped with powerful horns placed on the roof of the cab. Decoration took place gradually over time. Its style was not

Figure 8.2 *Chivas* painter decorating a wooden bodywork. Popayán, 2015. Photograph: Juan Mario Rubiano Durán.

the same throughout the country. Today, profuse decorations derived from indigenous, Afro-Colombian, and Spanish traditions are visible. *Las chivas* decorations from the Caribbean region, for example, are characterized by solid backgrounds and primary colours.

In combination with geometric figures, musical notes, representations of music (see Figure 8.3), and dance, ensembles are often used as visual motifs. In the northwest region of Colombia, background art often consists of a delicate filigree of abstract motifs, most likely of indigenous origin, which generally accompany Catholic religious images (see Figure 8.4) or landscapes.

Figure 8.3 At the foreground, a 1952 Chevrolet 3100 Caribbean *chiva*. At the background, *chiva* with decorative motifs of musical instruments. Santa Marta, 2015. Photograph: Juan Mario Rubianurán.

Figure 8.4 Musical angel motif in a 1964 Ford-350 Antioquia's *chiva* (Northwest Andean region). Medellín, 2015. Photograph: Juan Mario Rubiano Durán.

Las chivas also include other elements of decoration, such as painted glass, decals, and chrome finishes. Vehicles from the Andean region tend to be decorated in pastel shades, and feature beads—usually made from primary colours.

The impact of population dynamics in culture: An ethnography of *las chivas*

Colombia has experienced rapid growth in its urban population in the last sixty years. According to a 2010 report by the United Nation Population Fund (UNFPA) and National Statistics Department (DANE), the country went from being a predominantly rural state to an urban one during that time. Now almost three quarters of the national population is concentrated in cities.

Population movements have had significant and measurable effects on both rural and urban cultures. In the cities, rural migrant communities have manifested their experience of change by drawing on local traditions to meet their new challenges. Fresh subject materials and experiential themes have been introduced to both urban music and arts, aiding this reconstruction of a rural identity.

As part of the complex process of response, *las chivas* have changed in both use and significance and found a role as uniquely 'rural-urban' spaces. In that way they have come to embody the powerful sociocultural transformation of Colombia by allowing rural migrants to preserve their local identities through remarkable new practices of re-signification (see, for example, Figure 8.5). The

Figure 8.5 'Thanks to the Lord. The Friend That Never Fails' is the slogan of a Dodge-600 Cauca's *chiva* (Southwest Andean region). Popayán, 2015. Photograph: Juan Mario Rubiano Durán.

music played in *las chivas* exemplifies this important relationship between economic shifts and the urban signification of rural culture.

There have been three key historic moments associated with the transformation of the *las chivas* music. From around 1910 to 1940, music associated with *las chivas* was rural, rooted in a local, agrarian way of life. Urbanization, industrialization, and economic changes have transformed the old buses in many ways, partly because of the power of broadcast radio (Toynbee, 2000). When this music was played on the radio and on phonogram between 1940 and 1960, it became part of urban entertainment. After 1980, such music was further incorporated into the service sector economy. Such changes depend, however, on a precedent set by traditional relationships between movement, music, and context.

Exchange and coordination of cultural meanings form crucial elements in both the affirmation of identity (Macdonald et al., 2002) and social communication (Cross, 2006). In order to foster such elements, *las chivas* continue to function as a facilitative space specifically for musical experience. Music is particularly important because the transit between rural and urban cultures is implicit in the experience of physical mobility associated with musical performance. The experience of travel is embedded in playing, listening, and dancing—all syncretic practices that have, in themselves, smoothly integrated elements from both rural and urban cultures. Although a transformation in the structural conditions of the Colombian economy explains major changes in the music of *las chivas*, the role that the music itself plays as a facilitator of social interaction has not altered significantly over time. Popular music has allowed transit between rural and urban culture. As a symbolic mode of communication, *las chivas* therefore provide, in a proactive way, both the means to decode different cultures and strategies for participation (Tagg, 1987).

Popular music, transit, and movement: Some results

In the nineteenth century, popular musicians from different regions made the long journey from the countryside to towns and cities on foot, often tens of miles, playing their instruments while they marched. One reason for their long walks, many of which took hours, was that they often met other musicians on

Figure 8.6 The chivas still have a crucial role in cultural and economic relationships among Cauca's communities. Dodge-600 chiva for goods and passenger transportation. Popayán, 2015. Photograph: Juan Mario Rubiano Durán.

the road and formed small bands. The process strengthened links between the communal identities of places they had come from and the cultural and musical practices that they pursued. Such links are not just historic throwbacks; they continue today.

Particularly in the southern regions of Cauca, Colombian musicians can be seen playing flutes and drums along the roads. *Las chivas* are nearly always present as a key feature in this ongoing social interaction (see Figure 8.6).

The first moment: Movement and popular music

The sight and sound of musical groups walking along country roads to celebrate local festivities was often a highlight of events in rural areas. However, it was not the only occasion musicians would play. A meeting of people from each village to celebrate Sunday Mass was, and is still, a pretext for the gathering of Colombian musicians (Bermúdez, 1994). Impromptu ensembles also met repeatedly on Saturday and Sunday in different municipalities to perform their music in bars and cantinas.

At the beginning of the twentieth century, a spread of *las chivas* allowed musicians from different regions of the country to avoid long marches on foot. When this new mode of transport appeared, they played music for the celebration of each feast or Sunday Mass on the busses, something that established strong cultural links between transportation and festive musical performance. Diverse ensembles of musicians from different regions of the country were transported. Many retained and exhibited the music cultures from which they came. In the Caribbean region of Colombia, papayeras bands and vallenato ensembles were dominant (see Figure 8.7), while in the western Andean region, plucked-string ensembles were more usual.

In the Pacific region, small groups of flute players and drummers were most common. All instruments in these ensembles could be transported. Some were sufficiently portable to be played during the trip.

In general, these musical assembles sat above the ceiling on top of the bus, or inside, on the last bench. That is still a popular tradition across the country, with the last bench of buses called the 'the musician's bench.' Transportation of people between the rural villages and their involvement in festivals has established a deeper relationship between musicians and displaced celebrants. *Las chivas* continue to increase a capacity for mobility that is already characteristic of popular music from the regions (Connell and Gibson, 2001). They are a predominant element in rural musical practice,

Figure 8.7 Long-play cover of an album by La Chiva de Palo, 1970s papayera band. Codiscos.

one that also has the potential to connect people both socially and culturally across different regions.

The second moment: The appearance of the radio

Multiple musical traditions from within the country and across Latin America have diversified and come into contact, not only with the performance of music within the vehicles but also through the installation of radios in *las chivas*. Since the 1950s, *las chivas* have had radios that operated continuously during their daily trips; mostly playing local stations which transmitted music associated with regions (see Figure 8.8). They often consist of a schedule featuring the more dominant Colombian and Caribbean music traditions, which include vallenato, bullerengues, porros, and other genres. These were produced mainly in Cuba, Mexico, the Dominican Republic, and the United States. Examples include sones, boleros, corridos, rancheras, méringues, and salsa.

Radio contributed significantly to the commercialization of music (Wade, 2002). *Las chivas* were and are a privileged place for music listening of radio broadcasts. The mobility afforded by *las chivas* may have resulted in the displacement of the musicians of the regions, but, combined with the influence of the radio, transformed the tastes and musical experiences of the listeners.

Figure 8.8 A radio receiver in an Antioquia's *chiva*. Medellín, 2015. Photograph: Juan Mario Rubiano Durán.

According to Bermúdez (2006), two of the most significant genres of popular music in Colombia today are parranda and despecho. These arose in the decades between 1950 and 1970 in the city of Medellín and its surrounding area. The dynamism of the city, which became the epicentre of the nascent recording industry and radio broadcasting, not only reached urban populations but also the rural areas. A related outcome has been the popularization of music genres like *guasca, carrilera, despecho*, and *parranda campesina*. Produced for a national and even international market, they have been locally modified and become part of *las chivas*.

The third moment: *Chivas* urbanization

The presence of *las chivas* in the cities was initially marginal. In the 1970s, however, they became a familiar sight in different cities. *Las chivas* were and are still related to specific functions, all of which transport goods and people to and from rural areas—for instance servicing market places, transport terminals, and storage facilities with raw materials. For the first generations of migrants, a specific sense of the bus as a working vehicle remained throughout the 1970s and 1980s. The size and intensity of rural migration to cities created a cultural effect, particularly in urban transport, by incorporating a number of practices and expressions from rural contexts into the urban bus system. Not only was this because many drivers came from the countryside; it was also an aspect of rural and urban cultural hybridization. The informality of passenger transport in the Colombian cities is still evident, in everyday events on the city buses. Due to rural tradition, in Colombian cities, music is a persistent part of urban transport. In a practice remnant of musicians in rural areas, players frequently appear on board and do a few numbers in exchange for money. They play their instruments and sing while the city bus travels along its route (see Figure 8.9).

Due to the diversity of musical practices that the city promotes, the range of the music heard on the city bus is very broad. Musicians of the Colombian eastern plains, bolero trios, rappers, vallenato ensembles, pop or rock singers, and more, share space with storytellers, performance poets, clowns, and vendors of all sorts of objects.

Like their country counterparts, city buses have also adopted lush ornate decorations that include religious images, coloured lights activated by the brake, embroidered blinds, small models of classic sports cars, photographic portraits

Figure 8.9 Musicians in urban bus. Bogotá, 2017. Photograph: Juan Mario Rubiano Durán.

of the same bus, baby shoes, and all sorts of stickers. These objects are used to decorate the interior of the buses, especially the driver's cabin. Similarly, the radio is used on city buses as a means of musical entertainment for permanent use on all routes, a practice inherited from *las chivas* from the 1950s.

These practices are a manifestation of ways of doing things that prevail in rural areas—practices which in themselves are partially promoted by the weak enforcement of traffic rules.

The persistence of *las chivas* in the cities is also due to each owners' constant care of their vehicle and their use of it for a multitude of tasks. Instead of replacing the buses with new models, in the city, *las chivas* serve as vehicles for transportation of household or commercial goods, and for transport of most of the general population (see Figure 8.10).

Moreover, for their owners, the vehicle represents some important values that go beyond practical considerations: decorum, dignity at work, traditional identity, memory, and cultural resistance.

The prevalence of *las chivas*: 'El hechizo'

Las chivas owners do not care about the concept of conservation or originality. They have no wish to preserve a 'classic.' For each of them, the important thing is that their *la chiva* continues in its role as a working vehicle, contributing to their community and financially supporting their family. Unlike in many other cultural contexts, where newer cars are more valuable, many of the buses are decades old

Figure 8.10 Everyday *chivas*' work: Cauca's *chiva*, a Dodge-600. Popayán, 2015. Photograph: Juan Mario Rubiano Durán.

and *chivas* owners are proud to keep them active. Phrases like '*Orgullo del 57*' ('Pride 57'), '*Calidad del 62*' (Quality 62) or '*Viejito pero cumplidor*' ('Old Man but Compliant'), often painted in highly visible locations, such as the windshield or hood, are intended to be read as expressions of pride. Tags and artwork identify the owners and their communities while also advertising the continuing availability of the vehicle.

Las chivas are kept in operation by the ingenuity of local mechanics and technicians called '*el hechizo*' ('the spell'). Faced with the impossibility of acquiring spare parts (as they were discontinued many decades ago), *hechizo* have turned to creative solutions, using all available resources. *El hechizo* often adapt parts from other cars and trucks in their efforts to solve the *chivas*' technical problems. They have been known to restore, rebuild, or replace old parts, often turning to various ingenious methods or constantly applying 'palliative' solutions to keep the bus running for a few weeks, only for it to be repaired time and again. Despite the advanced age of the vehicles, *el hechizo* therefore enable *las chivas* to be maintained at low costs.

Urban party: The new cultural place of *las chivas*

Technically, many *chivas* are obsolete, but decades of communal musical and social practice mean that the buses now embody culturally valued traditions.

Because so many owners have preserved them against a prevailing logic of replacement, they have come to symbolize a certain relation to identity and stand for an attitude that advocates finding creative solutions to technical problems.

Given their close relationship with various festivities and music, as well as their extraordinary ability to capture attention, since the 1990s local companies have used *las chivas* as a means of advertising and promotion. These companies adopt them as a means to promote products and services, particularly those related to traditional customs and national identity.

In addition to providing advertising space, some *chivas* have taken on another role. In cities, they are often used to stage parties and act as venues for late night clubbing—something that gives them relevance even to younger generations. This new role has emerged as a natural outcome of existing cultural practices that play on the tradition of rural music already associated with the buses. Rooted in rural culture and itinerant music, *las chivas* have maintained associations with their origins even while they are used in new ways (see, for example, Figure 8.11).

Now, *las chivas* of the cities are involved in the entertainment business, and are often called '*chivas rumberas*'. The new role has meant that some buses have undergone adaptations. These have included the creation of a wider space for musicians by removing benches and putting them along the sides of the vehicle, or making use of folding benches to create a dance floor. Some '*chivas rumberas*' have adopted sound systems which allow recorded music to be used inside. In

Figure 8.11 Tourist guide in a Caribbean *chiva*. Santa Marta, 2015. Photograph: Juan Mario Rubiano Durán.

this way, the buses can carry musical ensembles—mainly papayera bands and vallenato ensembles—or use a lighting and amplification system, and act as mobile discotheques.

A moving party

Las chivas have become a place to party and dance. Nevertheless, they remain a flexible, mobile, and changing location. Their increased capacity to change and meeting different needs does not mean older functions have been left behind, far from it. *Las chivas* are still seen as an essential part of more traditional festivals and celebrations in the cities. In Bogotá, the journey can take several hours as partygoers are transported from area to area. Some even go to nearby municipalities such as Chía, in the northeast, and La Calera, to the east of the city.

Dancing in *las chivas* is a challenge for passengers, especially when alcohol is consumed. Their experience involves an unusual kind of body movement that aims to take into account the motion of the bus. Music invites nearly all passengers to dance during the journey. In this way, *la chivas* both engender movement from the dancers (people dance while the bus is in motion) and represent a continuous manifestation of movement through the city (see Figure 8.12). During the night, celebrants periodically descend from the vehicle to dance at different venues. These places offer various kinds of dance music. Celebrants need to adapt their dancing skills in order to be active at the different places of the city—clubs, discotheques, bars, and the street.

Figure 8.12 Dancing in the *chiva*. Santa Marta, 2015. Photograph: Juan Mario Rubiano Durán.

Indeed, links with the music are not fixed (Cross, 2006). Movement is instead emphasized, in this case, by placing cultural significance on music and dance—something that might explain the importance that celebrants and musicians attach to participating in such activities. Along with the demands of the tourism industry, each new generation of urban youth requires buses to adapt in new ways. Owners have responded by incorporating exotic designs and offering an alternative to nightclub-based party culture, alongside the provision of a utility service to vast rural areas of the country.

In sum, the *chivas* are embodiments and communicators of both the historical and contemporary cultural landscape. They remain active, continually updating their meanings and expressing various forms of identity, all of which are rooted in rural cultures. The key message they express is one of adaptation and transition from rural to urban culture in Colombia. *Las chivas* have, therefore, created a place for social interaction, establishing and maintaining cultural ties by expressing a dense set of associated meanings, especially meanings related to music and dance.

Motivations for decoration and music

Although, as this chapter has described, *las chivas* are unique in many ways, use of art and music in relation to utilitarian public transport vehicles is an international phenomenon. Why is it that we find it in so many developing countries? A facile answer to the question might be that the vehicles need to be painted for their preservation against the elements (see Figure 8.13), so why not spend a little more money (when one has it) and make them look attractive?

Decoration, however, usually means more than just painting. It includes music. Even 'just painting' can be expensive. Not only is there the cost of the original installation; the art must also be refreshed regularly to counter the effects of climate and highway conditions. Additionally, beyond using the radio, any music supplied has to be updated to conform to current tastes and trends.

In the absence of a straightforward functional explanation, motivations for vehicle decoration remain an enduring puzzle. Interviews with the owners and/or drivers who commission and pay for the artists who execute their creations fail to elicit explicit reasons for it. Vehicle owners usually describe their motivation as a case of copying someone else; any deeper explanation of the motivation for decoration in any particular environment is necessarily speculative.

Figure 8.13 A *chiva* mechanic refurbishes the bodywork paint. Popayán, 2015. Photograph: Juan Mario Rubiano Durán.

In spite of the uncertainty—or perhaps because of it—commentators offer no reasons for vehicle decoration (see, for example, Harris 1988; Giucci 2012). One can, in any case, break any possible motivations down into roughly two categories: externally driven (motivated by public demand) or internally driven (motivated by the owner and/or driver). Regarding externally driven motivations, the most obvious—and perhaps also the least likely—is economic, meaning to attract customers away from other vehicles or other forms of transportation. This assumes that art and music effectively signal the quality of less tangible attributes of the services offered: reliability, safety, security, comfort, entertainment, clientele, and so on. It also works if the customers believe that the art and music signal something about them as people, such as their wealth, status, personality, or taste. Both assumptions presume that customers have a choice of which vehicle or form of transportation to use. Less obvious—but probably more likely—is a rather amorphous collection of reasons that might fall under the label of 'traditional identity'. Here, in short, the visual and auditory decoration of a vehicle identifies it as belonging to a particular route, to a particular neighbourhood or village, or to a particular culture.

Identification with a particular route borders on the economic, that is, passengers know which vehicle to take in order to get to where they want to go. Connecting with a particular culture might be another way of saying 'tradition', that is, a vehicle is decorated in a certain way because that is how vehicles have 'always' appeared and how the public expects them to appear. This does, however, beg certain questions about the origin and the perpetuation of such tradition.

One internally driven motivation for vehicle decoration is religious: the decoration may be a way to protect the driver—and the passengers and/or cargo—from the threats inherent in road travel (recall, for instance, Figure 8.5). Of course this might also be considered externally driven; that is, it is the passengers that demand the protection that the driver provides. Another internally driven motivation is psychological: for the driver and/or owner to make a personal statement. Many scholars have asserted that in countries at the stage of development during which decorated vehicles are likely to be found, drivers play a distinctive role within society and behave (or aspire to behave, or are thought to behave) in certain ways. They display a form of power or independence that others do not have.

The notion of the 'driver' is a familiar stereotype, perhaps not without foundation; something for each driver to live up to. Decoration arguably therefore signals the driver's individualism or machismo (see Figure 8.14). This idea presumes that each driver has some control over the decoration and that owners consider drivers' desires. If a small-scale owner rather than their driver determines the decoration, the message might presumably be somewhat different. Since the owner is likely to have been a driver, or still be a driver, or has a close relationship with the driver, however, the possibility of significant difference is not especially great.

While pieces such as this one analysing *las chivas* show there has been considerable research on specific types of decorated vehicles in single

Figure 8.14 The uses of music and bodywork decoration imply a considerable effort on behalf of owners and drivers. Photograph: Juan Mario Rubiano Durán.

countries, there are abundant opportunities for future scholarship regarding vehicle decoration and the associated relationships between automobiles and musical practice. The general phenomenon has been—and continues to be—so widespread that it may offer an important means of satisfying deeper social and psychological needs. *La chivas* are therefore an example of a particular object that has found a place in narratives of city life. The associated music presents a form of the cultural heritage for local communities that George Yúdice (2003) refers to as a 'cultural resource': provision of significant elements of culture to meet the socioeconomic needs of populations, offering them a strategy that allows them to participate in the logic of development without abandoning the determinants of their cultural identity.

9

Listening to music in cars while black: Popular music, automobility, and the murder of Jordan Davis

Amanda Nell Edgar

On November 23, 2012, four teenagers pulled into a gas station in Jacksonville, Florida, to buy some gum and a pack of cigarettes. Only three would live to see the next day. The fourth, seventeen-year-old Jordan Davis, was gunned down while the car's hip-hop soundtrack played in the background. The trial's collective testimonies reveal that Davis and his friends were listening to music in his friends' SUV while they waited for the driver to return from making the purchase. Michael Dunn pulled in next to the vehicle and asked the teenagers to turn their music down. Though the teenagers initially complied with Dunn's request, a verbal disagreement ensued, and Dunn responded by drawing his gun, firing ten shots into the vehicle. Davis was hit in the legs, liver, lungs, and aorta; he did not survive the shooting. Dunn claimed the shooting was in self-defence, arguing that he felt threatened by the teenagers, but in 2014, a jury rejected this argument. They convicted Dunn of first-degree murder and several counts of attempted murder and sentenced to life without parole (Ohlheiser, 2014). Many news outlets (for example, see Reed, 2014; Scherer, 2016) referred to the shooting as 'the "loud music" murder,' naming the music as sufficient provocation for Dunn to justify taking Davis's life.

Davis's murder highlights and complicates the disproportionate dangers African Americans, and particularly black male teenagers, face on the open road. The term 'driving while black' has been used to reflect a national conversation about the disproportionate likelihood for black US Americans to be pulled over by police as compared with their white peers; African Americans are also more likely to be shot and killed by police during the interaction (Sides, 2018; Gabriel, Sagara, and, Grochowski Jones, 2014). This case, however, offers an unusual perspective on such discourses. The four teenagers in the vehicle were young black men, but Davis was not driving, and his white middle-aged aggressor, though armed, was not a police officer. This, then, was not a typical example of 'driving while black,' but rather it demonstrated that anti-black violence can even be provoked simply by listening to music in a car while black. Considered in conversation with 'driving while black' narratives, the murder of Jordan Davis presents evidence that suggests it is not simply the act of driving or of listening to music, but the act of African Americans taking up public space that has historically been met by white vigilantes with deadly violence. The 'loud music' murder of Jordan Davis demonstrates that many white US Americans assert the right to dominate public spaces, particularly when presented with black assertions of rights to exist in such spaces.

In this chapter, I argue that the intersection of automobiles and popular music should be understood as deeply entrenched in US America's history of white supremacist violence. Specifically, the discourses surrounding black teenager Jordan Davis's murder at the hands of white vigilante Michael Dunn demonstrates harmful everyday white American logics that position the 'open road' as white public space. Within this space, hip-hop music is audible only through a lens of criminality and positioned as oppositional to black middle-class respectability. Together, these three socio-spatial logics, of the white open road, the 'thug' space of rap, and the 'polite society' of a gun-saturated culture, work to frame the contemporary musical space of the automobile as violent and unfriendly to black travellers, thereby connecting contemporary US American culture with the supposedly vestigial violence of Jim Crow. As a result, I argue that within US American history the technologies of cars and music cannot be understood as separate from racist logics of white supremacy.

Contemporary white attempts to limit and control black bodies in US culture reveal the enduring reverberations of a system of oppression that has shaped the nation since the chattel slavery era. Following the emancipation of the enslaved, Jim Crow laws and practices levied formal and informal codes that segregated US Americans according to race and sanctioned anti-black violence and discrimination against African Americans accused of disobeying them. Under this system, black US Americans were disallowed from sharing space with white people in places ranging from schools to public transit to restaurants and restrooms and beyond. In other words, Jim Crow laws responded to the emancipation of the enslaved by formally excluding new black citizens from the right to enjoy public spaces. As Alderman and Inwood (2014) write, Jim Crow was "inherently socio-spatial" (p. 69), in that it formalized the previous practices of racial discrimination in public spaces and, in future developments like the US highway system, shaped the rights and responsibilities articulated for newly developed public utilities (Seiler, 2006). In essence, Jim Crow defined space as white. In doing so, it sanctioned violence against any black US American who asserted their right to public space, either actively or through simply 'existing while black.'

Limitations on black mobility and the 'republic of drivers'

The mass availability of automobiles beginning in the 1920s, followed by the development of the US Interstate Highway system in the mid-twentieth century, meant that full citizenship in US America was increasingly defined by the ability to move through space as an independent agent. From at least 1940, ability and access to driving were integral to accepted notions of US American citizenship (Blanke, 2007). For many, particularly white US American citizens, the highway represented a modern articulation of democratization through technological accessibility, since, as Klinger (1997) notes, "in theory no class systems or unfair hierarchies exist there" (p. 188). Certainly, this framework was available to some drivers, specifically white middle- and upper-class US Americans. This "republic of drivers" (p. 1092), to borrow Seiler's (2006) term, represents the political investment in a rhetoric of "anonymity and autonomy" (p. 1092) central to articulations of the rights of US citizens to participate in the democratic public sphere. As Alderman and Inwood (2014) write, however, "geographic mobility is ... embedded within structures of power, including White supremacy" (p. 71).

As with access to the political democratic sphere, access to the open road was and continues to be unequally distributed, dependent on categories of identity including race, gender, class, and other visual markings of belonging. On the one hand, Henry Ford's assembly line system meant white working-class men came under greater surveillance as factory workers, but as drivers and consumers they could use newly affordable cars as vehicles for their autonomy, individuality, and masculine dominance (Seiler, 2008). On the other, just as Ford's Model T was redefining white working-class masculinity, it simultaneously became an aspirational symbol for those who had been promised equality through the supposedly democratized open highway. Situated in the heart of Jim Crow, this historical period positioned automobility as a means for black US Americans to finally enjoy the benefits of "self-determination and self-representation, mobility, consumption, and social encounter" (Seiler, 2008, p. 106) alongside their white peers. In 1949, Frazier wrote in an *Ebony* editorial that "the Cadillac is a worthy symbol of [Black US Americans'] aspiration to be a genuinely first-class American" (cited in Seiler, 2006, p. 1098). However, despite the rhetoric of democratized space that accompanied the development of the US highway system, its origin in the era of Jim Crow meant that practices of travel more often solidified the use of race as a structure for US American space. The supposedly open road could only be travelled within the boundaries created to maintain black subjugation. Laws and policies like Jim Crow limited physical movement through space on threat of violence.

The possibilities of the open road, attractive to US Americans across race and class lines, were open to black families only on the condition of navigating the violent potential of white supremacy in unknown territories. In this way, cars presented a paradox of space, both allowing black US Americans to escape spaces of racial aggression and requiring black families to navigate hostile spaces just to refuel, eat, or lodge overnight (Hall, 2014). As Foster (1999) notes, black travellers in the mid-twentieth century often had to sacrifice hours of their vacation time in search of accommodations, and many even planned for the contingency of sleeping in their vehicles. Travelling while black also meant, and in many cases continues to mean, carefully monitoring speed so as to avoid both speeding beyond limits and travelling slow enough to draw attention (Sugrue, 2010), or travelling at night, so that the darkness obscured skin colour from police and white vigilantes (Pearcy, 2016). All of this, plus contingencies of "packing food, fuel, and toilet paper in the event of not finding safe, black-friendly hotels, service stations, and restaurants" (Alderman and Inwood, 2014, p. 76), necessitated a level of care and planning that white travellers did not need to consider.

Audibility and agency in musical space

Sound can work to claim, disrupt, and renegotiate access to space with varying results, but any understanding of this needs historical context. Limits on the ownership of public space have been unequally distributed prior to and on a larger scale than Jim Crow laws. The legal sanctioning of noise, for example, has historically worked to reprimand those who are likewise oppressed in particular social contexts (Schafer, 1993). For example, noise violation codes focus on "the rougher voices of the lower classes" (p. 67), while other high decibel sounds, notably from things like church bells and airplanes, tend to escape legal censure. Attali (1985) likens such legal selectivity to surveillance, noting that control of cultural sounds often reflects the disciplining of racially marked bodies. Because they define ownership of space and threaten violence against those who challenge that ownership, sonic statutes are similar to restrictions on mobility. Making noise fundamentally alters the character of a space, changing it in a way that, as Goodale (2013) points out, we are "powerless against the amplified noise, and worse, unable to combat it, except through equally noisome disturbances" (Goodale, 2013, p. 223). Noise, then, threatens segregation through its capacity to transform our experience of space.

Music, in particular, invisibly defines and redefines spaces. Berish (2012) argues that the movement of racialized sounds through various spaces began before the rise of the recording industry, but it accelerated with the aid of records and radio, prompting black music to cross boundaries defined by racism. Forms such as jazz that grew from black cultural traditions and (forced) migration carried particularly heavy political meanings into spaces in which they would not have been otherwise tolerated. Facilitated by these new music technologies, the movement of black music into segregated white spaces allowed black artists to "cross the sonic color line" (Stoever, 2016, p. 247). This not only allowed black musicians to achieve levels of fame and fortune previously reserved for their white peers; it also "threatened segregation's seeming totality by . . . circulating black voices in places where Whites refused their material bodies safe passage" (p. 199). Spaces marked by segregation and the Jim Crow threat of anti-black violence were thus transformed by music into covertly desegregated spaces, but only where so-called 'black music' was allowed to be played.

This transgression of racialized space was particularly prevalent in the history and development of radio. Douglas (1999/2004) points out that radio's popularity, which rose particularly prevalently among white suburban teenagers, was marked by warnings about the ostensible moral threat of jazz music, a threat, she notes, that would resonate with "later condemnations of rock 'n' roll" and rap, and of radio's role in popularizing such music (p. 91). She argues:

> What outraged or troubled certain members of the establishment about the teenagers' love affair with radio was that White teenagers—millions of them—were listening to and falling in love with African American music and performers . . . . And here we see another critically important thread in the history of radio: its central role in providing a passageway between White and black culture. (p. 18)

Read in this light, the controversy connected with radio broadcasting was as much a moral panic over the changing definitions of racialized space as it was over the technology of radio itself. Indeed, Berish (2012) adds that, as well as ethereally placing black musicians in white spaces, beginning in the 1920s and accelerating through the mid-twentieth century, the popularity of radio heightened the touring practices of musicians and musical groups, often leading to the actual presence of black musicians in previously white spaces. Music, then, redefined not only the experience of space but also the ways spaces were racialized and the ways that racialization was maintained and disciplined.

The redefinition of racialized space through radio coincides with the redefinition of racialized space facilitated through automobility. The portability of car radios meant that drivers, particularly teenagers, could take the auditory spaces of their identities into places usually reserved for adults. Referring to those who "blasted Wolfman Jack out their open car windows while cruising the strip" (p. 219) as "squatters" (p. 253), Douglas (1999/2004) notes that spaces of business were most disturbed by teenage boys' propensity to renegotiate and reconstruct spaces through their own auditory cues. Set within the context of a growing public debate over anti-black racism in US culture (including politics and law), the renegotiation of public space that centred black performances carried with it an air of disruptive resistance. For those white US Americans who clung to de jure, and later de facto, segregation, the redefinition of public space as auditorily 'black' represented a new version of the historical challenge to physically control black bodies, a challenge that escalated through the emergence of hip-hop in the late twentieth century. Emerging, in part, because of the popularity of car stereo systems that required training to install, hip-hop used the technological and mechanical expertise of black working-class youth to actively resist the US legacy of white supremacy—particularly the disproportionate effects of austerity, broken windows policing, and over-incarceration, on black working-class and poor communities (Rose, 1994). Hip-hop's mass distribution in the 1980s and 1990s meant that not only were white suburban teenagers increasingly listening to these black sounds, but that rap music was increasingly audible in the public sphere, rising in popularity alongside the car stereo systems that aided its emergence.

Having outlined the historical moment in which automobile technology, radio broadcasting, and white supremacy initially intersected one another, I turn now to the contemporary legacy of this dangerous interaction, exemplified by the murder of Jordan Davis in 2012. Though some decried the labelling of the shooting as the 'loud music' murder, I argue that the connotations of this phrase clearly and directly reflect a broader cultural issue: namely a white shooter bent on protecting white public space from the auditory invasion of music marked as black and thus, in a white supremacist cultural framework, violent and threatening. The remainder of this chapter will discuss the murder and its surrounding discourses, forwarding the argument that popular music and automobiles have not only coincided, historically, as technologies, but also that they continually worked together to violently suppress attempts to exist, drive, and listen to music while black.

The white space of the open road

Proliferation of affordable automobiles and the US highway system was situated in a social context marked by Jim Crow. Rather than being a truly democratic development, then, the emergence of the ideology of 'the open road' instead emerged in a way that tacitly neglected the prevailing logic of segregation, black subordination, and white supremacy. For the continued maintenance of white domination in the US American legal and economic systems, a nation increasingly networked through the connections of interstate travel in actuality required that the cultural reorganization of space replicated previously established systems of racial dominance (Berish, 2012). Just like the moves against the black occupation of space in a time before the widespread availability of car transportation, continuing racial oppression in the era of the open road required practices of subjugation to be replicated and updated to determine black automobile travel. Practices of segregation included the establishment of white-only gas stations, hotels, and restaurants, as well as 'sundown towns,' where African Americans were not allowed to stay after dark under threat of violence. Places like these "worked to materially institutionalize racial inequalities and make them appear normal, when in fact they were the product of overt racism" (Alderman and Inwood, 2014, p. 69). The institutionalization of the US highway system and the concretization of spaces along the highways as open to (some) interstate travellers, materialized networked public space across the nation as white space.

Discussions of 'driving while black' generally, and of incidents like Davis's murder specifically, highlight the various ways space is constructed as white.

As a result of years of the hard-won victories of civil rights activism, overt discrimination and racial violence have officially been deemed illegal in the United States, but navigating many public spaces remains dangerous for people of colour in the United States. Nationally, white people drive more often than their black peers; yet, black drivers are twice as likely to be pulled over and, once pulled over, four times as likely to be searched (Baumgartner, Epp, and Shoub, 2018). In states like Missouri, where Michael Brown's murder at the hands of police sparked a surge in Black Lives Matter activism, black drivers are 85 per cent more likely to be pulled over than their white counterparts (Missouri Attorney General, 2018). The message, Fletcher (2018) points out, is "you don't belong." Lawyers in the Davis murder trial very clearly downplayed the role of visual indicators of race in the murder. The windows of the SUV were, as Dunn's attorney, Cory Strolla, pointed out, "the darkest legal tint you can have." The emphasis on Dunn's supposed lack of visual information regarding the teenagers' appearance—including, of course, their race—seemed designed to detract from the case's clear roots in the US American tradition of anti-black violence. Strolla's implication was that the violence against the boys could not have been racially motivated if visual information was not available to Dunn. As the attorney claimed in a different witness questioning, the only thing his client knew was that he was "talking to a car full of people," implying he had no visual information about race.

Contrary to this logic, the white space of the open road is not only maintained by visual appearance. Throughout the Davis murder trial, Dunn and his lawyers repeatedly offered Davis and his friends' use of loud music as evidence of misbelonging: in much the same way US police officers often associate visual blackness as evidence of criminality, being audible from outside the vehicle was presented as broadly sufficient, by the defence, to mark the boys as suspect. This was perhaps most pronounced in Strolla's cross examination questioning of Tevin Thompson, a friend of Davis's who was in the car during his murder. In a series of questions, Strolla asked the teenager first, "Isn't it true that the music was so loud that the windows and mirrors were vibrating in that SUV?" Secondly, he asked, "That's normal for you guys to do that, correct?" Finally, he questioned the teenager, "In fact, you've been in positions where it's been so loud it could hurt your ears?" To emphasize the issue, Strolla pressed on, "You've been in positions where you've been in another car where that car was rattling because of the bass?" At this point, the state attorney interrupted the line of questioning and the judge warned Strolla to get to the point, but the fact that such questions were presented in the first place, particularly in that order, speaks to assumptions about audio propriety for cars in public places. Not only does the line of questioning highlight, and thus imply the importance of, the teenagers' music as extending beyond the private soundscape of the car. It also foregrounds the music as something both harmful, in that "it could *hurt* [their] ears" (emphasis added), and something extending into the space of "another car" within public space.

Key to understanding the legacy of anti-black violence that informed the Davis murder, the white space of the open road is often upheld through sound. Bijsterveld, Cleophas, Krebs, and Mom (2014) note that the association between audio and cars has sometimes been accompanied by critique; in fact, they point out, early conversations about audio equipment in automobiles highlighted the idea that drivers would not be fully aware of their surroundings if their journeys were accompanied by sounds of their own choosing. By the mid-twentieth century, the idea of radios in cars was largely defined by the idea that car radios were meant to create an insular environment within the car. However, this idea is largely one embraced by white public culture. Subcultures in which "outlandish and excessive speaker systems" are used for "pumpin' up the bass" in cars, as LaBelle (2008, p. 187) points out, represent a way of using automotive living to both literally and figuratively amplify one's cultural capital. In this context, the car becomes both a status symbol and centre for cultural expression; automobile sound is used to announce the driver and passengers' presence in the public sphere, rather than intended to insulate and protect them from the outside world. The white space of the open road is then maintained through policing, whether by actual police or bystanders who take up the role of assessing which visual and audible performances are acceptable. Just as drivers of colour are more often pulled over and searched by police due to their visible blackness, so, too, did Davis's audible racialization become the centre of the trial over his murder. Even the state's attorney, John Guy, raised the importance of car sound systems in the trial, directing Davis's friend and owner of the SUV Tommie Stornes to "tell the members of the jury what type of stereo system you had in your car." Stornes's subwoofers, which are the common twelve-inch size, mounted in the standard, rear-facing position, enter into the conversation of Davis's murder only because the sound of the car was brought in here as a way of determining whether or not the teenagers should be considered citizens (wrongly gunned down) or criminals (who, in Dunn's estimation, deserved to die). Placed in the context of the white open road, this becomes a question of whether Davis and his friends operated under 'standard' (white) rules of automobility audio or whether they followed subcultural norms more often associated with drivers of colour.

Respectability, hip-hop, and the legacy of *The Green Book*

Davis's murder can be understood in the historical legacy exemplified by a travel guide known as *The Green Book*, a publication recently brought to the fore by Peter Farrelly's racially problematic 2018 film of the same name (Santi, 2019). First printed in 1936, and republished for the next thirty years, *The Negro Motorist Green Book* was compiled by Victor Hugo Green, an African American employee of the New York Postal Service. Green saw himself as an activist in the tradition of Harriet Tubman and other Underground Railroad conductors, using the book to gather travellers' recommendations for black-owned and black-friendly lodging, dining, and entertainment establishments (Hall, 2014). By mapping the existence of black spaces within the larger public space of the US highway system, *The Green Book* helped to mark and renegotiate the open road that had been articulated through the rules and boundaries of defining space within Jim Crow white supremacy. By the mid-twentieth century, Green's publication had become used by many black travellers as a means of navigating the threat of white supremacist violence. By using *The Green Book*, or similar directories such as *Travelguide* (which had the tag-line "Vacation & Recreation without Humiliation" on its cover), black travellers could safely and more easily enjoy the travel and leisure that were solidly becoming an articulation of the American Dream for middle- and upper-class US Americans and, as a consequence, the mobility that had come to characterize citizenship in the mid-twentieth-century United States. *The Green Book* stands as a symbol of entrenched ways of thinking about race, class, and space that defined the mid-century era. Specifically, the implicit assumptions about white hostility which underwrote its sales came associated with notions that, in relation to race, 'motoring safety' could be established through class-based displays of status. Middle-class black respectability was defined specifically through white standards of middle- and upper-class automobile propriety.

Particularly in the early to mid-twentieth century, middle-class African Americans were defined differently by and from their white peers: Jim Crow repression meant that black professionals were called upon to be more successful than their white peers at every turn. Whereas white sales clerks and managers were considered middle class in the 1920s, black US Americans needed to be doctors, lawyers, and newspaper editors in order to be considered middle class (Franz, 2004). The idea that African Americans should demonstrate this type of refinement not only through their professions but also through their travel weighed heavily in the promotion and distribution of *The Green Book*. Victor Green believed in and advocated the position that "racism could be conquered by convincing Whites of the material and moral progress of African Americans" (Alderman and Inwood, 2014, p. 74)—a position now frequently referred to as 'respectability politics.' At the heart of respectability politics is the idea that blackness may exist in the public sphere only when it looks and sounds like whiteness, an idea often articulated through the apparently innocuous descriptors of particular class-based aesthetics. Thus, in the era of *The Green Book*, a time when African Americans were actively and explicitly excluded from many hallmarks of citizenship, a demonstration of purchasing power articulated through automobile ownership could be interpreted as a claim to both class-based moral superiority and racial acceptability.

Understood through a lens of respectability politics, the discourses surrounding Davis's murder articulate a white logic of driving that deeply intertwines race and class. At the trial, Dunn's fiancé, Rhonda Rouer, testified that the couple pulled into the Gate gas station parking lot and parked next to Davis's friend's car. On hearing the music coming from the teenager's car, Rouer told the court Dunn remarked, "I hate that 'thug' music" (*People of the State of Florida v. Dunn, Michael David*, 2012, p. 2306). Dunn later denied using this language, saying "I would've characterized it as 'rap crap,' not 'thug' music. That's not a term I'm familiar with" (Silver, 2015, 51:02), but he used similar terminology in a letter he wrote to his grandmother while awaiting trial: "I'm really not prejudiced against race, but I have no use for certain cultures. This gangster rap, ghetto talking thug 'culture' that certain segments of society flock to is intolerable" (Dunn, 2013).

That Dunn believes he is not racist, but rather only dislikes hip-hop, a cultural form created by poor and working-class black youth as a mechanism of resistance to white supremacist violence, speaks to the same articulations of 'respectability politics' present in early discussions of *The Green Book*. The association between 'thug' music and gansta rap Dunn references speaks specifically to what McCann (2015) calls the 'mark of criminality.' Tangled up in the cultural ethos of 'tough on crime' politicians, from Reagan to Clinton, the 'mark of criminality' describes how 1980s and 1990s rap artists used the genre to call attention to the violent situations of poverty experienced in increasingly overcrowded inner-city areas, only to have their performances leveraged as evidence of their own supposedly criminal propensity. Artists like Dr Dre, NWA, and Tupac Shakur's work took up characteristics of the 'mark of criminality,' including a racialized performance of heterosexual hyper-masculinity. These discourses were leveraged both by artists, as a way of speaking back against the violence of austerity and over-policing, and by the Reagan administration, as a way of justifying those very acts of discriminatory aggression. Importantly, gangsta rap connected race and class in ways that, even in the 1980s and 1990s, prompted many middle-class black leaders to stand alongside white leaders and oppose the genre as an expression of violent, antisocial, and misogynist messages.

As the campaign against gangsta rap grew in the 1990s, the 'mark of criminality' became increasingly synonymous with rap more generally. Its opponents included Reagan Education secretary William J. Bennett's lobby group Empower America, Tipper Gore's Parents Media Resource Center, and even the National Political Congress of Black Women. Particularly for some white listeners, hip-hop was increasingly interpreted as the sound of violent criminality, something linked as much to gang violence as to the wider emancipatory potential from which hip-hop actually emerged. This pattern, which associated young black men and the hip-hop genre with violent criminality, was a constant theme in Dunn's description of the events surrounding the murder. In a phone conversation recorded for the documentary *3½ Minutes, 10 Bullets*, for example, Dunn remarked that he was surprised when he heard that the four teenagers did not have criminal records, suggesting that they must have been "flying under the radar" (in Silver, 2015, 18:55). His evidence for this assumption is that he has seen their YouTube videos and "they were bad . . . gangster rappers" (in Silver, 2015, 18:58) set within a particular "culture. This MTV culture. The gangster rap" (in Silver, 2015, 56:09). Dunn's insistence on the assumption that hip-hop blackness constituted criminality persisted, even after he went to prison himself. Tupac Shakur incorporated the term 'thug' into hip-hop, shifting its meaning away from "signifying disgust, rebellion, and nihilism to evoking coolness and power" (Jeffries, 2011, p. 89). Dunn's letters from prison, however, include many racist descriptions that use 'thug' in a less positive way, linking it to a negative view of young black men, even while, conversely, he perceives his own violent actions as righteous. In an example that bears quoting at length for its apt description of the ways hip-hop's emancipatory potential has been incorporated into the white supremacist violence of law-and-order society, Dunn writes to his daughter:

> The jail is full of blacks and they *all* act like thugs. . . . This may sound a bit radical, but if *more* people would arm themselves and kill these fucking idiots when they're threatening you, eventually they may take the hint and change their behavior. . . . Eventually, we as a society will wake up and realize that we need to arm ourselves, as the government welfare programs have produced a culture of entitlement for a certain segment of our society. These fools feel entitled to live above the law and do violence at will. (Dunn, 2013, emphases original)

Striking in this quote is Dunn's apparent lack of self-awareness. Although Dunn feels entitled to killing a teenager, he distances himself from violence and instead links criminality to blackness and hip-hop culture. In such discourse, the 'thug' moniker becomes not only a way of blaming young African Americans for their circumstances (of systemic poverty, anti-black violence, and over-incarceration) but also a means of exonerating the felon himself for murdering an innocent teenager. Wrapped up in such discourse, based at the complex intersection of race, class, and sonic subculture, is the question of who is allowed to travel through and exist within public space.

Resisting the sounds of 'polite society'

An examination of black driving under the standards of the white open road reveals not only a system of violent repression but also the framing of driving as a mechanism of black resistance. For black drivers, Alderman and Inwood (2014) write, travel offered a way to assert the right to exist in public space and gain new perspectives on institutional white supremacy. Not only did automobile ownership offer a way for African Americans to sidestep the humiliations of segregated public transit, it also allowed black travellers to gain a broader perspective of the effects of segregation in areas outside their own hometowns. One article in *The Crisis*, a magazine of the NAACP, noted that travelling near Jacksonville, Florida, in the late 1920s, the very city in which Davis was murdered, revealed only one 'whites-only' filling station which was visibly falling into disrepair due to a lack of patronage (Foster, 1999). Thus, those African Americans who could afford to purchase automobiles were encouraged by black leaders to do so immediately (Franz, 2004). With a copy of *The Green*

Book or *Travelguide* in hand, black drivers were prepared to enjoy the benefits of autonomous travel, and, by moving throughout public space in the way their white peers had always done, they made themselves visible across previously white areas in ways that were impossible previously.

In the years since *The Green Book*, black travel has become much more common, but particular visual- and audiblizations of blackness remain excluded from spaces assumed to be white. Bradley (2014) writes that true integration of black and white communities remains a persistent fear among white middle- and upper-class suburbanites. This fear, Douglas (1999/2004) and Rose (2008) remind us, also arose with the introduction of black sounds into white middle- and upper-class teenagers' cars first during the mid-century Wolfman Jack era (see Wall and Webber, this volume), and later during the boom of gangsta rap in the 1980s and 1990s. By embracing hip-hop not only within the vehicle but loudly enough that it could be heard outside the teenagers' car, Davis and his friends demonstrated a just rebellion against a public space imagined to be white as well as the expectation of black respectability. Indeed, panic over the circulation of black sounds in public spaces reserved for white people extends back to the African slavery, when African drums were banned on many plantations due to fears that the music would work as a code to facilitate slave uprisings (Rose, 1994). Across these examples, historical notions of the 'threat' of black music are defined by resistance to particular (white) sonic landscapes.

Crossing the boundary from black private sphere to the white public sphere has always carried an air of resistance and, as such, has been met with violence. Central to Dunn's defence strategy was the controversial "Stand Your Ground" law. To the letter of the law, Stand Your Ground asserts that "a person who is not engaged in an unlawful activity and who is attacked in any other place where he or she has a right to be has no duty to retreat and has the right to stand his or her ground and meet force with force" (§ 776.013(3), Fla. Stat., 2010). Stated in Dunn's defence attorney Cory Strolla's closing argument, "A danger facing Michael Dunn need not have been actual" (Strolla, 2012, p. 3240), but only must have seemed that way to him. As an extension of the Castle Doctrine, Stand Your Ground is perhaps intended to indicate that a private space such as the home has been invaded with the intention of harming the inhabitants. Applying this law to vehicles, as most US states do, aligns the private space of the home and car in a way that emphasizes a division between the private space of the vehicle and the public space of the open road. Under this defence, then, a shooter has protection under the law not only to kill a person entering their home but also entering their car. The focus on Davis and his friends' music crosses over into this conversation, since, from the perspective of the white open road, music should remain in cars marking the boundaries between public and private spaces. Instead, in Strolla's version of events, Dunn's argument for self-defence could be validated by focusing on the sound (loud music and conversation) that audibly moved between Davis's friend's SUV and Dunn's Sedan. Such logic rests on a propensity in US law to discipline black resistance, even when that resistance comes in the form of mere occupation of public space.

The idea of 'Standing Your (Sonic) Ground' enters into discussions based on 'respectability politics,' too, especially with Dunn's account of the linguistic expectations of a polite society. A popular mantra of US gun control critics is the idea that "an armed society is a polite society," in which "manners are [expected to be] good when one may have to back up his acts with his life" (Heinlein, 1942, p. 147). Put differently, advocates argue that the threat of gun violence should be sufficient to force people to adhere to *their* version of 'proper behavior' (which is itself usually articulated as white middle and upper class). Dunn's claim of 'self-defence,' in fact, centres the idea that the inability for him to command and control a verbal exchange functioned as a threat to his person. Testifying at trial, Davis's friends recounted that Dunn asked, "Can you turn the music down? I can't hear myself think." Though Thompson, seated in the front passenger seat, complied, Davis responded, "Fuck that, turn the music back up." The discussion of the events that followed this phrase is significant in two ways. First, the inclusion of cuss words in Davis's statement came to play a significant role in Dunn's defence, implying that Davis's choice to use the word "fuck" led to Dunn's escalation through its impropriety and, as a consequence, that Dunn believed Davis deserved to die. In other words, the choice to cuss was, for Dunn, not sufficient adherence to the rules of the "polite society" of the gun-saturated United States. That cussing should be understood as violating a standard of decorum was clear in the questioning of various witnesses. In questioning Davis's friend Tevin Thompson—the teenager who had initially turned down the music at Dunn's request—State Attorney John Guy asked how Davis had responded to him adjusting the volume. When Thompson testified that Davis "told me to turn the music back up," Guy followed, "Did he curse when he said that?" Later in the questioning, Dunn's attorney asked Thompson whether Dunn had "curse[d] at you," said "anything derogatory about you . . . [or] anyone in the vehicle," and, finally, whether it was possible that Dunn "said thank you and you didn't see him say it?" The issue of expressing politeness, in the form of exchanging pleasantries like "thank you" and not cussing, entered into the other teenagers' questioning as well. If Dunn believed that "an armed society is a polite society," then the teenager's choice to act impolite was, in fact, deserving of his own murder.

In raising the statement in final remarks, Dunn's lawyer Cory Strolla did not dispute that Davis said "Turn the music back up." In fact, he restated Davis's comment and added "the n-word [pronouncing] the full word with the 'r'" (Skolnik, 2014). His articulation was notable, given the history of this word as a violent weapon: a means of disparaging, humiliating, and controlling African Americans. The word itself is a violent weapon, added to the record by Strolla at Dunn's request (Dunn, 2013). By articulating the n-word within his defence of Dunn, Strolla verbally replicated hierarchical distinctions between himself (as visually white) and Davis and his friends (as visually black). The n-word, like other popular slurs under Jim Crow, was intended to position white people above black people in the social ladder, casting black men and women as childlike or dangerous depending on the situation. It is intended, in other words, not only to assert control of whites over their black peers, but to do so within a reminder that this assertion of control is legally sanctioned. Strolla's articulation of the word, then, asserts his own dominance over the teens and, as an extension, Dunn's authority over them. This addition was consistent with Dunn's recounting of the events elsewhere as well. In a prison letter to his fiancé, for example, he reassured her that he would be exonerated, based, in part, on evidence that Jordan Davis "had trouble with authority figures in school *as well*" (emphasis added) (Dunn, 2013). Within the context of the letter, the 'as well' does not point to other incidents in which Davis was in trouble. Rather, as a way of blaming Davis for his own death, Dunn positioned himself as an authority over Davis; he argued that Davis's position in the social hierarchy was inferior, and as such, the teenager's choice to argue rather than comply was evidence that he deserved to be murdered. Dunn's choice to 'Stand Your Ground,' then, is premised on the idea that he was entitled to a position of power within a 'polite society,' and that Davis's choice *not* to adhere to a 'politics of respectability' meant he deserved a death sentence.

That violent consequences that arose from Davis exercising his right to listen to music in public, speak on his own behalf, and embody the subcultural form of his choice was a continuation of history. Foster (1999) reminds us that, during the rise of the automobile and interstate travel in US American history, black drivers and their vehicles were particularly susceptible to white vigilantes who believed African Americans had no place on the open road. For black drivers during Jim Crow, too, finding oneself in a 'sundown town' after dark meant certain violence and often death (Loewen, 2005). The murder of Robert Mallard in 1948, for example, bears a striking resemblance to that of Jordan Davis in 2012. Mallard, an African American, was attacked in his car, and murdered in front of his wife and child for being "not the right kind of negro" (Seiler, 2006, p. 1099). In a context where black US Americans are marked as disruptive simply for taking up the same public space to which their white peers feel entitled, violence emerges as an extension of the white logic of the open road. In Davis's case, that was exacerbated by common perceptions about the music of hip-hop as an intersection of class and youth subculture.

Conclusion

> Guy: All right. As you were walking back to your car, did you hear anything that caught your attention?
> LeBlanc: Yes, sir.
> Guy: And what was that?
> LeBlanc: Gunshots.

As Alyssa LeBlanc, who witnessed the shooting from a nearby mall, testified, the dominant sound of the incident was not the teenagers' music; it was gunshots. The problem of unwanted sounds, Goodale (2013) reminds us, is that they are difficult to block. Often, the only way to reassert sonic dominance in a space of unwanted sound is to create an even louder sound. This is precisely what Michael Dunn chose to do, firing out the 'pop pop pop' of gunshots that overtook the sounds of Davis and his friends' music, and ended an innocent teenager's life. Speaking as part of the documentary *3½ Minutes, 10 Bullets*, the victim's father, Ron Davis, notes that "it wasn't like [Jordan] was in a bad neighborhood" (in Silver, 2015, 10:59), indicating that most people would not expect their child to face danger at a place like the Gate gas station. However, when resistant, black, working-class sounds of hip-hop enter into the white space of the open road, the disruption has historically been interpreted by white US Americans as a violent threat. In this chapter, I have argued that the technologies of cars and popular music have moved in tandem with one another to reassert logics of white supremacy in the United States. Specifically, in the murder of Jordan Davis, the white cultural logic of the open road, class, and race-based assumptions that link the resistant form of hip-hop with 'thug' criminality, and the historical precedent of quashing black resistance, have violently associated race, automobility, and music. Cars and popular music cannot be considered as separate from the logics of white supremacy that exist within the US cultural legacy of Jim Crow, where the sound of black resistance has always battled the disruptive sounds of racially motivated violence.

10

Crash! Music press coverage of performers in automobile accidents

Mark Duffett

As a constantly updated, relatively modern technology, cars are part of a globalizing, self-reproducing capitalist system (Urry, 2004) that has colonized the natural landscape with freeways, suburbs, drive-ins, and flyovers. The ubiquity of this automotive modernity has come at a cost. High-speed car crashes are, without a doubt, an absolutely horrific aspect of everyday life. Very few citizens end their days having escaped without a near miss. A number get seriously hurt in crashes or have known people who have been injured. The unlucky few lose relatives or close friends, meet their ends, or accidentally kill others. As tools of personal freedom, motor vehicles therefore reach their limits as unexpected agents of terror. My aim in this chapter is to analyse the interpretation of real automobile crashes in the music press. After consideration of the nature of music journalism, I offer some specific examples and show where music writers have reported celebrities who have had the misfortune to get hurt. Because performers' road accidents are, in effect, open to different angles, press stories can be scrutinized to reveal ways that journalists adopt frames in their missions to appeal to readers. Part of the ideological work of music journalism is therefore to interpret painful real-life incidents by using ways of thinking that are congruent to specific *genre* formations. I illustrate this by examining four interpretive topi (broad, discursive territories of myth construction) that have guided commentaries about artists who work in different musical styles and the impact of road accidents on their lives.

Popular music studies has always had a relationship with music journalism. Some of its key early contributors—writers such as Simon Frith and Dave Laing—were also prolific music journalists. However, the explicit study of music journalism has exploded in the new millennium, in parallel with a relative demise in financial rewards for jobbing music writers and, ironically, a proliferation of university courses on the subject. Catalysed by Steve Jones's seminal edited volume *Pop Music and the Press* (2002), industrial shifts have created a self-conscious, new academic subfield within the broader discipline. Research produced by the scholars in this area has diversified, but largely maintained a consistent set of messages. Three distinct phases are often presented to explain the history of the music press since the middle of the 1960s. In the first, the idiom is defined by 'personality' journalism and fanzine writing of the late 1960s and early 1970s (Forde, 2001a). There has also been some work on individual outlets (see Powers, 2013) and commentators associated with this classic rock era, notably Lester Bangs and Greil Marcus (see, for instance, Bonomo, 2012; Schulenberg, 2017). The initial period of liberating creativity was closed down, a common argument goes, by the rise of carefully branded lifestyle magazines in the 1980s and 1990s: places in which the journalist's role was primarily relegated to that of a consumer guide (Brennan, 2005; Fürsich, 2012). This second era was associated with a greater reliance on material from press officers (Forde, 2001b), rehashing of press releases (Kristensen, 2017), and more frequent discussion of non-musical topics such as the business practices of musicians (Conner and Jones, 2014). More recently, the rise of the internet has been associated with a third phase in which press outlets have directly capitalized on fan enthusiasm and social media in order to bring down the cost of written content. Reducing or eliminating payment for writers has created a crisis in which former professionals have increasingly found themselves underpaid or supplanted by more amateur content providers (McLeese, 2010; Jaakkola et al., 2015). Several scholars have explored this three-part periodization (Gudmundsson et al., 2002; Laing, 2006; Warner, 2015). Others have painted in geographic corners of the bigger picture, notably in France (Pires, 2003; Warne, 2011), and what might loosely be called Northern Europe, talking about the histories and issues specific to music journalism in their different territories (see Hellman and Jaakkola, 2012; Jaakkola, 2015; von Faust, 2016; Kristensen and Reigert, 2017). Recent work has therefore created an increasingly nuanced picture. From this perspective, the alternative music press needs consideration less as an example of generalized 'resistance' and more as a series of culturally and/or geographically distinct local spheres (see Atton, 2010; Ballico, 2015).

What academic narratives of the demise of creative journalism miss is that both auteurs and regular journalists tend to draw upon discursive resources that appeal to magazine consumers. Consequently, a parallel set of discussions has emerged in the study of music journalism to consider issues of cultural sociology and the ways in which writers find common ground with their readers. Foremost in this discussion have been questions of gender and the relative place of the writer. Scholars have repeatedly noted that both female writers, as well as female artists as subject matter, are relegated within their respective industries through the gendered construction of credibility and authenticity (see Davies, 2001; Leonard, 2007/2016; Weinstein, 2010; Hill, 2016). Berkers and Eeckelaer (2014) offer an interesting case study here by contrasting of press coverage of Pete Doherty and Amy Winehouse. They describe how various press stories about these two rather different musicians have interpreted their drug habits in very different ways, casting Doherty as a heroic individual dicing with excess, and Winehouse as a tragic victim. While Berkers and Eeckelaer's work demonstrates the prominence of gender differentiation in music writing, what it does not address clearly enough is the role of music genre in maintaining specific perceptions of gender identity. This raises the issue of how journalistic practice works, and the degree of autonomy that writers actually have in relation to the ideologies of their societies. As Fenster (2002) notes, for example, music critics and journalists sit, sometimes uneasily, somewhere between fan and expert, encompassing aspects of both identities. Related research often draws upon Bourdieu's notion of the cultural field to frame the professional culture of the journalism as a contested terrain (Lindberg et al., 2005; Varriale, 2014). Within this area of professional practice, journalists capitalize upon 'interpretive repertoires' shared with their readers (see Brown, 2007; Hill, 2016).

Interpretive repertoires can include discourses based on rock 'authenticity' (Weisethaunet and Lindberg, 2010), taste cultures (Michelsen, 2015), music histories (Shepherd, 2011), and canons (Desler, 2013). Genre is another such interpretive repertoire. It allows writers to guide their audiences to greater levels of expertise in specific areas of interest (see, for example, Strachan, 2003).

Popular music genre is arguably the key concept in music journalism. Journalists are agents in the construction and maintenance of music genres as living cultures (see Tomatis, 2014; Brackett, 2016). We can see this in action when they police genre boundaries (Brennan, 2013) and critically rescue specific music subgenres (Williams, 2010b). Writers rarely confine themselves, after all, to pure factual reportage. Quite the contrary, in fact: genre is a central element in how journalists communicate and interpret music culture—not just in the case of niche music magazines where analysts might expect genre to be paramount. From this perspective, we might consider commentaries on music stars and their car crashes as examples of genre formation.

The textual analysis from which I will furnish my case examples comes from a search of the music journalism site *Rocks Back Pages* for "car crash," a search term that throws up almost 250 entries. While some of those are metaphorical or incidental, I have chosen to focus on examples in which prominent musicians were subjects of repeated coverage that departed from factual description. What is interesting is that the reporting of these stories did not necessarily coincide with genre-specific publications. So, for example, while we might expect the blues and jazz magazine *Downbeat* to report Muddy Waters's 1969 car crash in a way that is consistent with its general subject matter, what is more enlightening is to find similar genre markers around descriptions of the same accident in less blues-orientated kinds of publication. At this point, then, it is worth discussing car crashes in popular culture and their academic interpretations, the key thing being to ask what general ways of talking about car accidents might orientate press coverage. Is there a singular myth of the car crash? What follows will suggest that in relation to popular music, the discussion of crashes can circulate around a few select spaces of interpretation. Four such terrains of mythic understanding will be considered.

The lost youth topos

There is, ontologically, no one singular general meaning of 'the car crash.' Beyond any factual interpretation of something that actually happened, it varies, in each case, depending on the idiom, form, and genre *of communication*. The term 'car crash' often gets used, for instance, as a metaphor. Folk speak in passing, describing abrasive encounters, bad jam sessions, or fraught relationships as 'car crashes.' The shock value of violent road accidents has also been of interest to fiction writers who wish to both exploit drama and engage our capacity for empathy. Automobile accidents form the subject matter of diverse musical numbers. Classic examples include "Two Hour Honeymoon" by Paul Hampton (1960), "Dead Man's Curve" by Jan and Dean (1964), "Always Crashing in the Same Car" by David Bowie (1977), "Warm Leatherette" by the Normal (1978)—which inspired an album of the same name from Grace Jones—plus "Car Crash" by the Avengers

(1992) and "Daddy's Speeding" by Suede (1994). Automobile accidents can, these songs suggest, offer a series of existential meanings: cruelty, risk, responsibility, chaos, tragedy, and survival. Crashes thus fascinate, not just because they symbolize chaos, or show the cruel capriciousness of life, or because they act as memento mori, sometimes revealing an indomitable will to survive their morbid aftermath. Car crashes entrance us in part because their causes can be so diverse and ambiguous.

Until we reach an era of driverless cars, road accidents are less a "bolt from the blue" than a potential indication of human error (Woollen and Kerr, 2002). The inclusion of alcohol, text, messaging, or even old age in the mix raises issues of social responsibility. Because crashes lend themselves to competing interpretations, when writers discuss different incidents and circumstances, their various potentials can be emphasized in different ways. This process occurs when music journalists discuss 'real' accidents. From the outset, we should therefore note that multiple frames of interpretation can be used to guide readers' understanding of the meaning of particular crashes. In other words, the factual occurrence or actuality of each event is, ontologically, a mere prelude to an explanation that makes it meaningful. I do not wish to suggest here that writers *fictionalize* crash incidents, but rather that their discussions apply frames of reference that allow them to locate the broader meanings of crashes in particular ways. Horror cinema scholar Mikita Brottman's landmark edited volume *Car Crash Culture* (2001) features James Dean, Jayne Mansfield, and Lady Diana Spencer on its cover—all figures whose untimely deaths in automobile accidents became part of their legends. Dean, in particular, seems a good place to start any analysis of how car crashes are understood in the public sphere.

Known for his intense demonstrations of teen angst on camera, James Dean's real passion was for auto racing. His fatal collision seemed to demonstrate his embodiment of the death drive and therefore enhanced his rebellious celebrity image (Holt, 2004). Not only did he call his Porsche Spyder 'Little Bastard'; his last autograph was on a speeding ticket. Such circumstantial evidence suggests that the crash actualized his macho, compensatory recklessness, but it also marked the emergence of a teen culture that took cars as symbols of conspicuous consumption. Given just an inch of adult responsibility—after all, children cannot be drivers—from one perspective Dean chose to throw it, and himself, away. Whether his car crash was an accident is, in that sense, less important that how it retro-fitted his image with a kind of melancholy romance depending, in part, on his willingness to go beyond reasonable risk and use his vehicle as a 'suicide machine' (Henderson and Joseph, 2012).

Just over a decade after Dean's Spyder hit the skids, Sam Katzman offered a suitably clichéd and knowing take on the subject with his exploitation movie *Hot Rods to Hell* (Brahm, 1967), in which a group of drag racers in a modified Chevrolet Corvette menace an ordinary family's trip on the highway, threatening to run them off the road. Such examples show that James Dean was not unusual in his youthful fascination with speed. In so far that taking risks is exciting, at least until he lost control, his action was 'sexy' in a pop culture sense (see Creed, 1998); it was also youthful, in the sense that stereotypes of youth suggest youngsters can sometimes risk nearing the edge of the abyss: age not yet having taught them that mortality is near. Dean's crash marks one point on a mythos that interprets car crashes on the basis of themes such as youth, life cut short, and individual potential wasted. Another point on this topos is arguably represented by music writing on the flamboyant pop star Marc Bolan.

Bolan was, of course, a performer who, famously, never survived his 1977 car crash. His genre, glam rock, in effect blurred the boundary between rock and pop. By this point, films such as *Privilege* (Watkins, 1967), *That'll Be the Day* (Whatham, 1973), and its sequel *Stardust* (Apted, 1974), all coming in the wake of Beatlemania, had knowingly mapped out a mythos of the typical star musician's career as a chaotic descent into intrusive self-commodification, hedonistic excess, and moral bankruptcy. Glam was a genre that self-consciously associated itself with mass commerce, superstardom, and 'crazed' fandom. Its performers made a simple rock sound, but were also self-conscious and theatrical—targeted precisely at a savvy young 'tween' marketplace. The genre thus dramatized popular music as the product of a carnivalesque business that manipulated gullible youth, in the shape of both the performers and their public. When Bolan's fatal crash was mentioned, it therefore tended to be understood not so much in the context of his flamboyant masculinity, but squarely in relation to his career. Furthermore, since Bolan was recognized as a *creative* glam rocker (perhaps less so than Bowie, but more so than most others), issues of artistry became a secondary concern.

Take this biographic sketch of Bolan as a "pop star" by Ira Robbins from 1980:

> The final stage—Bolan's decline into middle age before his recovery and fatal car crash at the age of 29—is represented poorly by recordings from those years and seems, in retrospect, superfluous to the unique accomplishments of his heyday.

Robbins's piece primarily aims to periodize Bolan's career, so it is not surprising that the singer's death is noted in relation to that issue. Nevertheless, the role Bolan's crash played in his career is specifically mentioned by other commentators. Writing for *Mojo* in 2002, for instance, Rob Chapman deployed the idea of crashing as a kind of *hypothetical* turning point in Bolan's professional journey:

> If Marc Bolan had died in a car crash in the summer of 1970 without ever having had a hit record in his life, he would still have been lauded as one of the most magical and unique figures that ever inhabited the pop landscape.

The fictionalization of the crash here functions as a way to assess the career achievement of the performer and whether he got to express his muse in a form that was satisfactorily affirmed by his audience. In contrast, Paul Morley provides a more detailed discussion of Bolan's real crash in NME from 1980, again attempting to register Marc's creativity as part of the mix and again drawing on the assumption that the moment should be located primarily in relation to the singer's career:

> And finally there was the *Marc* show: perhaps the beginning of Bolan moving away from T. Rex and a pretense to musical relevance—as a sound and style in '77 T. Rex were perilously close to revivalism. He had been signed to do another series.
>
> On 16th September he died in a car crash in London, just four weeks to the day after the death of Presley, two weeks before his 30th birthday.
>
> There was nothing tidy about Bolan's death. It was no romantic conclusion, it created no instant glamour. It brutally cut him off when he was at last beginning to compromise, seek out attention in new ways. It left behind a jagged legend. A legend wrapped around three mad years.

What is interesting about Morley's extended and poetic discussion of Bolan's crash is that it maintains the issue of career accomplishment, while at the same time placing Bolan on a James Dean topos: the tragic crash took a gently maturing star and "brutally cut him off when he was at last beginning to compromise." In that sense, Bolan's fatal accident represents a return of the repressed, freezing the glam star in his (relative) youth, heading off the moment when his career might have creatively stifled him as industrial forces of inertia threatened to end his initial creative unfolding. Even though they may be nihilistic or push things too far, those youngsters who have car crashes are, in this particular topos, ultimately framed not as jaded or experienced rebels, but as victims.

The *Mad Max* topos

As expensive, emblematic commodities, cars promise to make us all cyborgs, offering heretofore impossible experiences of speed and protection in their role as personal vehicles. Dramatized and romanticized car accidents in popular culture therefore connect with the wider notion that crashes somehow offer a perspective on automotive modernity. In this context, crashes show consumer promises are not what they seem: while offering us greater control, cars both increase our alienation and actually put us at the risk of others (see Graves-Brown, 2000; Roden, 2003). Some have argued that the automotive system has actually *normalized* mass murder, normalizing a shocking lack of outcry at over a million road fatalities globally every year (see Featherstone, 2004). The story of road safety activist Ralph Nader and his book *Unsafe at Any Speed* (1965) suggests that driver protection was not always the highest priority for automobile manufacturers. From that perspective, we might argue that cars represent the literal perils of 'damaged life' in Theodor Adorno's (1951/2005) pessimistic sense of humanity's inevitable imperfection under capitalism. The dark side of this is not only that car producers have sometimes put style over safety but also that ordinary citizens, as car buyers, may have colluded with corporations in repressing thoughts of danger, even as they have become more alienated in their vehicles (see Ferrell, 2003; Urry, 2006).

The idea that car accidents might reflect questions of class is just as certain as the fact that they can instantiate issues of gender. Hassleberg, Vaez, and Laflamme (2005), for example, have found that young, male, working-class drivers are particularly vulnerable to front-on, over-taking, and single vehicle crashes. In this context, the notion of the crash as exploitation or revenge, or somewhere between the two, is possible. Singer Jim Morrison's famous story about witnessing a group of native American workers caught up in a fatal car crash (Graham, 2009, p. 107), for example, may or may not have been true, but spoke allegorically about how the racial history of America still haunted its 'children' in the civil rights era. A final aspect here might also combine class and commodity critique. In this reading, cars *materialize conformity* as a socially stratified form of individual mass property, a material consolation against which the most nihilistic, rebellious response is perhaps destruction. Destroying a car is therefore rather like the proverbial shooting of a television (or dropping it out of a hotel window). One only needs to think of the Plasmatics' infamous cancelled Hammersmith Odeon show in 1980, where the Greater London

Council deemed it inappropriate that any group could blow up a car on stage. In this respect, it is notable that burning vehicles is symbolic of riots as well as accidents, and the spectacle of the carefully orchestrated crashes in destruction derbies—where monster trucks collide for the sake of entertainment—is a form of 'mass culture' primarily frequented by a working-class audience (Vardi, 2011). As big, gleaming, technological tools, big cars can therefore be used to express a kind of macho, cyberpunk imagination typified by George Miller's nihilistic, overdriven Australian movie series, *Mad Max* (1979, 1981, 1985, and 2015).

A *Mad Max* topos can arguably be seen in music commentary about the rock singer Robert Plant, whose recording career was punctuated by a bad car accident in 1975. Chris Charlesworth (1976) reported the next year for *Creem*:

> Plant still walks with a crutch, a wincing reminder of last August's car crash on the Greek island of Rhodes. Although the plaster has now been removed, his usual hurried shuffle has been replaced by a deliberate, careful plod. He doesn't think he'll be able to dance until the beginning of next soccer season, which is tantamount to saying that Led Zeppelin won't be able to perform live until that time also. Indestructible? Obviously not. The fractured foot has stymied Plant's usual punk arrogance. Temporarily, at any rate, he can't run with the pack and this compulsory moderation to the pace of his life seems to have brought about a certain sympathy that wasn't always apparent in his personality. He might look like the proverbial Greek god rock vocalist as he struts magnificently across stages with the stud-like hauteur of the rock idiom, but he's human just like the rest of us, broken bones and all.

In a 1979 article for the same magazine, Susan Whitall additionally explained:

> On August 4th, [1975] Plant and his wife Maureen were seriously injured in a car crash in Greece; Plant came out of it with multiple fractures of the elbow and ankle, proclaiming "I'm lucky to be alive." A drunken Greek sailor in the next bed at the hospital sang a few bars of "The Ocean" in homage. A short period of recuperation in L.A. was enlivened by rehearsals for the new album, and although Plant was still in a wheelchair, *Presence* was recorded in a scorching 18 days at Munich's Musicland Studios.

For a 2007 edition of the more neutral newspaper, the *Independent on Sunday*, Nick Coleman reviewed "For Your Life," a song Plant recorded in 1976 for his first post-crash album, *Presence*:

> You wouldn't want to dance to Led Zeppelin. But that doesn't mean that the group weren't funky after their own savage fashion. "Trampled Underfoot" is the

one everyone knows, but this is better. It is a widely ignored piece on *Presence*, Page's favourite album, a ruthless on-the-one lurch with layered guitars trying to drag Bonham's delayed backbeat out of its pile-driven hole. Plant sat down to sing it having smashed up his leg in a car crash on holiday.

All three writers interpret Plant's accident as a matter of continued survival on his part. While Coleman's narrative is more factual, the crash is still produced as an essential part of the discussion. By mentioning that Plant has 'smashed up his leg,' Coleman reveals that the singer is not 'indestructible' and the crash has caused him to embrace a temporary period of 'compulsory moderation.' More specifically, Coleman locates Plant as someone who carries on and refuses to be anything more than minimally displaced by the onslaught of life's obstacles. Plant's approach is framed as a refusal to indulge in the morbidity of his trauma. Like James Bond adjusting his cufflinks after leaping through the chaos of an exploded train in *Skyfall* (Mendez, 2012), he simply dusts himself off, with his human frailty apparently coming as a surprise. By emphasizing Plant's robust attitude, such writers evoke rock's notion of musicians embracing excess in all forms—sex, drugs, rock 'n' roll, loudness—as a masculine test of stamina. The whole narrative is organized around the notion of what Rosemary Hill (2016) has called the "the myth of the warrior": males gendered as 'authentic' rock icons by "the exclusion of 'feminine' qualities" (p. 55). Plant's automotive misadventure is located on a robust and macho *Mad Max* or perhaps James Bond topos, one in which warrior males emerge unfazed from a close brush with mortal danger. They are portrayed as shaken, but not stirred.

The heartbreaking aftermath topos

Academic commentary on road accidents, in their cultural—as opposed to practical, safety—dimension, flourished from the mid-1990s, with the release of David Cronenberg's controversial feature *Crash* (1996), a film based on J. G. Ballard's 1973 novel of the same name. Its association of car crashes and masochistic sexual fetishism caused moral outrage (see McCosker, 2005), but the story offered points of social critique in its subtexts. The first was that behind the story's shock was perhaps an unspoken disgust that disabled bodies could have sensual appeal; the second was that sex could seem monotonous, almost like (manual) work (see Sobchack, 1995; Botting and Wilson, 1998). Some researchers proposed that Ballad's aim was really to critique technology by arguing that pornography as an alienated form of intimate encounter, the car crash being an ideal metaphor to express the socially and psychically devastating metallic embrace of 'strangers in the night' as private and public worlds were suddenly and irrevocably entangled (see Harpold, 1997; Beckman, 2003). In that sense, as Day (2000) noted, *Crash* was not a tale without a sense of morality (p. 277). It is rather ironic that Lady Diana's fatal car accident in Paris came within two years of the film's release. Because her vehicle swerved when it was tailed by the paparazzi, some readings blamed the public's insatiable desire for intimate entertainment and the way it prompted reckless media intrusion (Scharrer, Weidman, and Bissel, 2003). Other researchers have argued that Cronenberg's film coincided with the technological penetration of neoliberalism—notably mass adoption of the internet—and therefore indicated a crisis of globalization that has even begun to affect the bourgeoisie (Brottman and Sharrett, 2002).

If *Crash* offered its cryptic, erotic take car collisions in order to question a world of new technology that seemed both alienating and exploitative, other interpretations have focused on car crashes as traumatic moments that engender empathy and, ultimately, a kind of sorrowful communal bonding. Questions of commerce, career accomplishment, and youth do, for example, not figure extensively in reports of country star Patsy Cline's June 1961 automobile accident—a tragedy that struck when she was age 29, at the same time that her Decca single "I Fall to Pieces" rode high in the country charts. Unlike Billboard's factual coverage of the incident at the time (*Patsy Cline hurt in near-fatal crash*, 1961), Alan Smith wrote for a December 1962 edition of NME:

> Personal tragedy is nothing to Patsy Cline, who sings of "Heartaches" on her first big hit disc in Britain. Her fast-rising career was interrupted last year by a calamity that almost left her a helpless cripple—and cost someone else his life. It happened on a lazy summer's day near Patsy's home town of Winchester, Virginia. Patsy was a passenger in her brother's car when suddenly it was involved in a shattering collision. A man in the other car, coming in the opposite direction, was killed. As on one of her biggest U.S. hits, Patsy's world could have literally "Fallen To Pieces" after that day. She awoke to find herself in hospital with severe head injuries and a broken hip. "I suppose I could have sat back and pitied myself," she reflects.

Cline's car crash is framed here almost as a kind of natural disaster: a "calamity" that has a "cost" and "almost left her a helpless cripple." Her response to the accident is similarly understood as a question of self-pity, even if she does not choose that option. In the words of Smith's story, the country singer is "overcoming" something "grave." The subtext of his discussion is that the accident, in a sense, resonates with the compensatory, stoic values of a vernacular genre that forges community support in the face of familial or personal misfortune—to borrow from the title of a 1991 song by Warren Zevon, one that offers "Heartache Spoken Here." Indeed, Smith makes the link to the concerns of Cline's music explicit by referencing the name of her single.

The romanticized African American topos

Stories that include Stevie Wonder's 1973 automobile crash occupy a very different discursive ground to those examined so far, framing their subject as a case of neither youthful misadventure, macho smash-up, or heartbreaking tragedy. Writing in the NME in 1985, for example, Gavin Martin began to describe the details of the singer's life in the wake of the crash:

> Still, it's hard not to like the man himself and his friendly sense of humour. The hair is braided, pulled back into a bunch and he carries a bit of extra weight under the chic bondage-strapped jumper. Wonder's face still bears scars from the near-fatal automobile crash that hospitalized him in the early '70s. Throughout the conversation he sips honeyed tea to stave off the effects of an English cold and revive him after a day of fundraising promotionals.... Now recognized as a one-man music machine, Wonder became twice removed from external reality—by blindness and by fame and extreme wealth. Surviving the aforementioned car crash in 1973 only heightened his introspection and spirituality, and some of the more fanciful parts of the 1976 double album *Songs In The Key Of Life*, plus virtually the whole of the aborted film soundtrack *The Secret Life Of Plants*, highlighted artistic pretentions getting the better of a gifted craftsman.

The subtext of Martin's discussion becomes clearer if we juxtapose it with Johnny Black's analysis of the same accident for *Blender* in 2003:

> Wonder had become gripped by the idea that his life was reaching a turning point emotionally, spiritually and physically, to such an extent that he felt his death might be imminent—and this was reflected in a lyric dealing with the concept of spiritual progression towards a higher plane through reincarnation.
>
> The song was released on the last day of July and, just six days later, on the way to a gig at Duke University in North Carolina, Wonder was seriously injured in a

car crash. By the time he reached the North Carolina Baptist Hospital in nearby Winston-Salem, Wonder was in a coma, with his life hanging in the balance.

"I couldn't even recognize him," recalls his long-time friend Ira Tucker Jr. "His head was swollen up about five times normal size. And nobody could get through to him."

With his vital signs perilously low, Wonder remained comatose for the best part of a week, until Tucker decided that maybe the healing powers of medicine could use a boost from a more spiritual resource. "I got right down in his ear and sang 'Higher Ground'... his hand was resting on my arm and after a while his fingers started going in time with the song. I said, 'Yeah! This dude is gonna make it.'"

What Martin and Black's extended commentaries have in common is that they discuss Wonder's accident in terms of its capacity to force physical, visual changes on the victim's body or inspire spiritual revelations. It is how Stevie *looks* and what he *feels* after the crash that matters, not what he (rationally) thinks. Beyond any connection with Stevie's visual impairment, what such stories do is frame his accident with concerns that are essentially physical or mystical. It could be argued that this is part of a longer tradition of portrayals of African American identity iterated over many decades. Stevie's personal cognition and musical creativity is understood as a matter of intuition and improvisation which, in the context of recovering from the accident, plays a contributing role. Changes wrought as a consequent of the episode, moreover, are located primarily on Stevie's physical body, an approach that emphasizes his corporeality, embodiment, and physicality—aspects of subjectivity historically associated with blackness (see McClary and Walser, 1994) and its historic association with hyper-masculinity and the use of the body in manual labour. As Tom Pechard (2016, p. xvi) recently summarized in his preface to an edited collection of writing on black music from soul to hip-hop:

> Since blacks in America were denied the status of the 'fully human' until relatively recently, that category's autonomy and authenticity is not always respected in black American music, where the notion of human subjectivity is sometimes thrown open to complication and critique. In addition, while liberal subjecthood has been identified with free will—a rationality that privileges the mind and effaces the corporeal—black people have often been identified with their bodies: as slave bodies born to work, as sexualized bodies subject to desire, and as entertaining or athletic bodies supposedly gifted with special performing powers.

Stevie's car crash is registered via his embodiment, and arguably understood through a kind of bluesy, black music lens. Music is positioned as the spiritual resource, here, that revives Wonder's endangered yet enduring body after his accident. In other words, music journalists frame Stevie Wonder's crash as an episode which reflects and catalyses the star's essential soulfulness by emphasizing his physical embodiment and spiritual grace.

Conclusion

The aim of this chapter has been to understand some examples of car crash reporting made by popular music journalists. As a result of this investigation, I have suggested four distinct 'topi' or loose fields of discussion which operate as discursive resources used to portray crashes in certain ways and align them with specific music genres: a lost youth topos emphasizing wasted potential (glam), a *Mad Max* topos highlighting robust survival (rock), a heartbreaking aftermath topos using trauma to evoke empathy (country), and a romanticized African American topos focusing on corporeal consequences and spiritual inspiration (jazz funk). One thing the textual analysis has therefore revealed is that the subtexts of different stories about car crashes have been guided by genre associations of the artist. These genre conventions operate specifically in relation to issues of social identity, for example, celebrating the robust 'warrior' masculinity of a rock singer or alluding to the intuitive spirituality of a black soul performer. Such frames effectively pre-select meanings, narrowing them down beyond the rich semiotic potential of the car crash. In this context, music journalism is a form of mediation, or, perhaps, to borrow Frederic Jameson's term, a kind of "vanishing mediator" (2008, pp. 309–43). Premising their stories on awareness of their audiences, journalists have *done cultural work*, in an ideological sense, by actively forging a link between the shared conventions of each music genre and the incident portrayed. This was even the case when an organ of publication did not specialize in the same genre as the artist, or indeed in any one particular type of music. Finally, given that my case examples of crash reporting range from 1962 to 2007, and show some similarities, perhaps we should enrich points about the changing shape of the music press with an appreciation of how frequently journalists have been informed by long-lived ideological assumptions.

Notes

Chapter 3

1. The term 'regime' is borrowed form Böhm et al. (2006) in their account of automobility as a new "regime of subjectivity" (p. 8). For other critiques of this regime see for example the edited collections by Miller (2001), and Conley and McLaren (2009).
2. For further discussion see, for example, Connell and Messerschmidt (2005); Kimmel (2013); Reeser (2010), and Segal (2009). As masculinity relates to music see, for example, Bannister (2006); Biddle (2007); King (2013); Oakes (2009); Walser (1993).
3. Repeat episodes are frequently broadcast on the British free-to-view digital television channel *Dave*, whose strapline is "the home of witty banter."
4. At a fast 4/4 tempo near to 155 bpm, the off-beat emphasis will always push the music forward as if rushing.
5. To take just one example, in the case of the programme's search for "driving heaven," a stretch of road from the Swiss to the Italian Alps was described as "mile after mile of deserted perfection" (Wilman, 2007).

Chapter 5

1. The Lapsed Clubber is a research project that started in 2015 and aims to assess ageing ravers' changing attitudes, beliefs and patterns of behaviour during their life course. Data collection and analysis is ongoing through the Lapsed Clubber Audio Map (https://www.mdmarchive.co.uk/map_home/the-lapsed-clubber-audio-map) and through interviews and focus groups with the Greater Manchester raving community.

Chapter 6

1. See Peter Finch, "A Welsh Wordscape", published in *Selected Poems* (1987).
2. See Phillips (1998) for a history of the society. An overview in English of the society's early campaigns is given in Williams (1977).

3 The first recorded eisteddfods were held in 1176, 1451, 1523, and 1567; the modern National Eisteddfod dates from 1861.
4 Iwan's career has been extensively analysed; see, for example, James (2005) and Jones (2013).
5 The only exception of which I am aware is Tony Jones of the acoustic act *Tony ac Aloma*. The duo's records were exceptionally successful at the end of the 1960s, and Jones purchased a sports car with the proceeds.
6 I hope to redress the belated and grudging acceptance by older record-buying Welsh speakers of the emergence of Welsh-language rock bands in the late 1960s and early 1970s in a future study.

Chapter 7

1 Schlager is a genre in German pop music including soft pop as well as parts of folk-inspired songs, performed by bands as well as solo artists. Famous Schlager stars are, for example, Caterina Valente, Peter Alexander, Marianne Rosenberger, Udo Jürgens, Helene Fischer, or Michael Wendler.
2 *"Ich will Spaß"* translates as "I want fun."
3 Internationally known NDW artists include, for example, Einstürzende Neubauten, DAF, Malaria!, Trio, and Nena.
4 Translated literally, *Halbstarke* means 'half strong.' The most appropriate or closest English term here is probably 'yob.'
5 A renaissance adaptation of the 1950s was generally fashionable in Germany, Great Britain, and the United States during the 1980s. For the first time there was a deliberate and transparent fall back on designs and entertainment products of a past era. Up until then, only the new was sought after, but now the old is rediscovered. The impressive cars of this epoch, its furniture, its fashion, its designs, and even its icons like James Dean, Elvis Presley, and Marilyn Monroe experienced a new appreciation by youth cultures in the West. In Germany, for example, the latter frequently adorned the front pages of youth magazine *Bravo* between 1978 and 1982. Elvis Presley could be seen fifteen times, Marilyn Monroe four times, and James Dean seven times on the front pages, which made a total of twenty-six front pages, that is more than 10 per cent. In 1980 alone the youth magazine opened twice with Elvis Presley (no. 6, no. 29), once with Marilyn Monroe (no. 23), and, again, twice with James Dean (no. 4, no. 31). Issue 20 in 1978 even made the revival its main story ("Die Superstars der 50er Jahre") with a life-sized poster of Marilyn Monroe. In the years prior, as well as those afterwards, the presence of those particular icons was far less. From the middle of the decade they disappeared

in favour of the current music, cinema, and television stars (see Hoersch, 2006, p. 460).
6 ZDF (*Zweites Deutsches Fernsehen*) is a German television channel comparable to BBC2.
7 Motorization was mainly limited to youth who were already earning their own money, which was usually not the case for A-level pupils. Thus, the *Halbstarken* culture was not a subculture of A-level pupils or young students, but rather one of apprentices and trainees.
8 The Opel equates the British Vauxhall.
9 *Ente* literally translates as "duck."
10 The term "self-irony" is used in some European countries, but not commonly used in English. It means the ability to take oneself lightly or laugh at oneself.

References

Abrams, M. (1959). *The Teenage Consumer*. London, England: London Press Exchange.

Adams, T. M., & Fuller, D. B. (2006). The words have changed but the ideology remains the same: Misogynistic lyrics in rap music. *Journal of Black Studies, 36*(6), 938–57. doi: 10.1177/0021934704274072.

Adorno, T. (2005). *Minima Moralia: Reflections on Damaged Life*. London, England: Verso (Original work published in 1951).

Al-Balbissi, A. H. (2003). Role of gender in road accidents. *Traffic Injury Prevention, 4*(1), 64–73. doi: 10.1080/15389580309857.

Alderman, D. H., & Inwood, J. (2014). Toward a pedagogy of Jim Crow: A geographic reading of *The Green Book*. In L. E. Estaville, E. J. Montalvo, & F. A. Akiwumi (Eds.), *Teaching Ethnic Geography in the 21st Century* (pp. 68–78). Washington, DC: National Council for Geographic Education.

Anthem [definition]. (2002). *Concise Oxford English Dictionary* (10th ed.). Oxford, England: Oxford University Press.

Anthem [definition]. (2006). In J. Kennedy, M. Kennedy, & T. Rutherford-Johnson (Eds.), *The Oxford Dictionary of Music* (2nd ed.). Oxford, England: Oxford University Press. Retrieved from http://www.oxfordmusiconline.com/subscriber/article/opr/t237/e455.

Arieti, S. (1976). *Creativity: The Magic Synthesis*. New York, NY: Basic Books.

Armstrong, V. (2011). *Technology and the Gendering of Music Education*. London, England: Routledge.

Arvidsson, A. (2001). From counterculture to consumer culture: Vespa and the Italian youth market, 1958–78. *Journal of Consumer Culture, 1*(1), 47–71. doi: 10.1177/146954050100100104.

Attali, J. (1985). *Noise: The Political Economy of Music*. Minneapolis: University of Minnesota Press.

Atton, C. (2010). Popular music fanzines: Genre, aesthetics, and the 'democratic conversation.' *Popular Music and Society, 33*(4), 517–31. doi: 10.1080/03007761003694316.

Auslander, P. (2008). *Liveness: Performance in a Mediatized Culture* (2nd ed.). Abingdon, England: Routledge.

Baird, R. (Producer), Curbishley, B. (Producer), & Roddam, F. (Director). (1979). *Quadrophenia* [Motion picture]. England: Universal Pictures.

Bala, I. (1999). *Certain Welsh Artists: Custodial Aesthetics in Contemporary Welsh Art*. Bridgend, Wales: Seren.

Ballard, J. G. (2014). *Crash*. London, England: Fourth Estate (Original work published in 1973).

Ballico, C. (2015). Liner notes: An exploration of local print music journalism in Perth's indie pop/rock music industry. *Perfect Beat*, 16(1), 71–86. doi: 10.1558/prbt.v16i1-2.23973.

Balsley, G. (2011). The hot-rod culture. In M. Keefe & P. Schletty (Eds.), *The Hot Rod Reader* (pp. 168–75). Minneapolis, MN: Motorbooks (Original work published in 1950).

Bannister, M. (2006). *White Boys, White Noise: Masculinities and 1980s Indie Guitar Rock*. Aldershot, England: Ashgate.

Barlow, W. (1999). *Voice Over: The Making of Black Radio*. Philadelphia, PA: Temple University Press.

Barnouw, E. (1968). *The Golden Web: A History of Broadcasting in the United States 1933–1953*. New York, NY: Oxford University Press.

Bartky, S. (1990). *Femininity and Domination: Studies in the Phenomenology of Oppression*. London, England: Routledge.

Baumgartner, F. R., Epp, D. A., & Shoub, K. (2018). *Suspect Citizens: What 20 Million Traffic Stops Tell Us about Policing and Race*. Cambridge, England: Cambridge University Press.

Bayton, M. (1997). Women and the electric guitar. In S. Whiteley (Ed.), *Sexing the Groove: Popular Music and Gender* (pp. 37–49). London, England: Routledge.

Beckman, K. (2003). Film falls apart: *Crash*, semen, and pop. *Grey Room*, 12, 94–115. doi: 10.1162/152638103322446488.

Bell, J. (2001). Boys and their toys. In J. Bell (Ed.), *Carchitecture: When the Car and the City Collide* (pp. 114–17). London, England: August.

Bennett, A. (2009). 'Heritage rock': Rock music, representation and heritage discourse. *Poetics*, 37(5), 474–89. doi: 10.1016/j.poetic.2009.09.006.

Bennett, A. (2012). 'Let me know you're out there!': Male rock vocal and audience participation. In S. D. Harrison, G. F. Welch, & A. Adler (Eds.), *Perspectives on Males and Singing* (pp. 287–95). London, England: Springer.

Berger, M. (2001). *The Automobile in American History and Culture*. Portsmouth, NH: Greenwood.

Berish, A. (2012). *Lonesome Roads and Streets of Dreams: Place, Mobility and Race in Jazz of the 1930s and '40s*. Chicago, PA: University of Chicago Press.

Berkers, P., & Eeckelaer, M. (2014). Rock and roll or rock and fall? Gendered framing of the rock and roll lifestyles of Amy Winehouse and Pete Doherty in British broadsheets. *Journal of Gender Studies*, 23(1), 3–17. doi: 10.1080/09589236.2012.754347.

Bermúdez, E. (1994). Syncretism, identity, and creativity in Afro-Colombian musical traditions. In G. H. Béhague (Ed.), *Music and Black Ethnicity: The Caribbean and South America* (pp. 225–38). Miami, FL: University of Miami North-South Centre.

Bermúdez, E. (2006). Del humor y el amor: Música de parranda y música de despecho en Colombia (I). *Cátedra de Artes*, 3, 81–108.

Best, A. (2006). *Fast Cars, Cool Rides: The Accelerating World of Youth and Their Cars*. New York: New York University Press.

Biddle, I. (2007). 'The singsong of undead labour': Gender nostalgia and the vocal fantasy of intimacy in the 'new' male singer/songwriter. In F. Jarman-Ivens & I. Biddle (Eds.), *Oh Boy! Masculinities and Popular Music* (pp. 125–44). Abingdon, England: Routledge.

Bijsterveld, K., Cleophas, E., Krebs, S., & Mom, G. (2014). *Sound and Safe: A History of Listening Behind the Wheel*. New York, NY: Oxford University Press.

Black, J. (2003, September). Stevie Wonder: higher ground. *Blender*. Retrieved from https://www.rocksbackpages.com/Library/Article/stevie-wonder-higher-ground.

Blanke, D. (2007). *Hell on Wheels: The Promise and Peril of America's Car Culture, 1900–1940*. Lawrence, KS: University Press of Kansas.

Bloke [definition]. (2002). *Concise Oxford English Dictionary* (10th ed.). Oxford, England: Oxford University Press.

Böhm, S., Paterson, M., Land, C., & Jones, C. (Eds.). (2006). *Against Automobility*. Oxford, England: Blackwell.

Bonner, F. (2003). *Ordinary Television*. London, England: Sage.

Bonner, F. (2010). *Top Gear*: Why does the world's most popular programme not deserve scrutiny? *Critical Studies in Television*, 5(1), 32–45. doi: 10.7227/CST.5.1.5.

Bonomo, J. (2012). *Conversations with Greil Marcus*. Jackson, MS: University of Mississippi Press.

Born, G. (2009). Afterword. In N. Cook, E. Clarke, D. Leech-Wilkinson & J. Rink (Eds.), *The Cambridge Companion to Recorded Music* (pp. 286–304). Cambridge, England: Cambridge University Press.

Born, G., & Devine. K. (2016). Gender, creativity and education in digital musics and sound art. *Contemporary Music Review*, 35(1), 1–20. doi: 10.1080/07494467.2016.1177255.

Botting, F., & Wilson, S. (1998). Automatic lover. *Screen*, 39(2), 186–92. doi: 10.1093/screen/39.2.186.

Bowman, R. (1997). *Soulsville, U.S.A.: The Story of Stax Records*. New York, NY: Schirmer Trade Books.

Brabourne, J. (Producer), Havelock-Allan, A. (Producer), & Collinson, P. (Director). (1968). *Up the Junction* [Motion picture]. England: Paramount Pictures.

Bracewell, M. (2002). Fade to grey: Motorways and monotony. In P. Wollen & J. Kerr (Eds.), *Autopia: Cars and Culture* (pp. 288–92). London, England: Reaktion Books.

Brackett, D. (2016). *Categorizing Sound: Genre and Twentieth Century Popular Music*. Oakland, CA: University of California Press.

Bradley, R. (2014, February 17). Fear of a black (in the) suburb. *Sounding Out!* Retrieved from https://soundstudiesblog.com/2014/02/17/fear-of-a-black-in-the-suburb/.

Braun, E., & Macdonald, S. (1978). *Revolution in Miniature: The History and Impact of Semiconductor Electronics*. Cambridge, England: Cambridge University Press.

Brennan, M. A. (2005). *Writing to Reach You: The Consumer Music Press and Music Journalism in the UK and Australia* (Doctoral dissertation). Retrieved from https://eprints.qut.edu.au/16141/.

Brennan, M. (2013). 'Nobody likes rock and roll but the public': *Down Beat*, genre boundaries and the dismissal of rock and roll by jazz critics. *Popular Music and Society*, 36(5), 559–77. doi: 10.1080/03007766.2012.718486.

Broccoli, B. (Producer), Wilson, M. (Producer), & Mendes, S. (Director). (2012). *Skyfall* [Motion picture]. United States: Columbia Pictures.

Brookesmith, P. (1983). Cars and sex and rock 'n' roll: Teenage America. *The History of Rock*, 1(5), 98–100.

Brottman, M. (Ed.). (2001). *Car Crash Culture*. New York, NY: Palgrave.

Brottman, M., & Sharrett, C. (2002). The end of the road: David Cronenberg's *Crash* and the fading of the West. *Literature/Film Quarterly*, 30(2), 126–32.

Brown, A. (2012). Drive slow: Rehearing hip hop automotivity. *Journal of Popular Music Studies*, 24(3), 265–75. doi: 10.1111/j.1533-1598.2012.01333.x.

Brown, A. R. (2007). 'Everything louder than everything else': The contemporary metal music magazine and its cultural appeal. *Journalism Studies*, 8(4), 642–55. doi: 10.1080/14616700701412209.

Bull, M. (2004). Automobility and the power of sound. *Theory, Culture & Society*, 21(4), 243–59. doi: 10.1177/0263276404046069.

Burke, J., Currie, B., Farrelly, P., Rogers, J. B., Vallelonga, N., Virtue, T., and Wessler, C. (Producers), & Farrelly, P. (Director). (2018). *Green Book* [Motion picture]. United States: Universal Pictures.

Bussy, P. (2000). *Kraftwerk: Man, Machine and Music*. London, England: SAF Publishing.

Butler, J. (1990). *Gender Trouble: Feminism and the Subversion of Identity*. London, England: Routledge.

Cantor, L. (1992). *Wheelin' on Beale: How WDIA Memphis became the Nation's First All-Black Radio Station and Created the Sound that Changed America*. New York, NY: Pharos.

Carroll, H. (2011). *Affirmative Reaction: New Formations of White Masculinity*. Durham, NC: Duke University Press.

Chapman, R. (2002, September). Marc Bolan: The Jurassic years. *Mojo*. Retrieved from https://www.rocksbackpages.com/Library/Article/marc-bolan-the-jurassic-years.

Charlesworth, C. (1976, May). Robert Plant: *Plantations*. *Creem*. Retrieved from https://www.rocksbackpages.com/Library/Article/robert-plant-plantations.

Clarkson, J. (2012, April). Clarkson on: Driving. *Top Gear Magazine*. Retrieved from http://www.topgear.com/uk/jeremy-clarkson/jeremy-clarkson-top-gear-column-april-2012-04-26.

Coates, N. (2011). 'It's what's happening, baby!' Television music and the politics of the war on poverty. In J. Deanville (Ed.), *Music in Television* (pp. 165–82). New York, NY: Routledge.

Coen, E. (Director-Producer) & Coen, J. (Director-Producer). (2017, February 5). Easy Driver [Television commercial]. Los Angeles, CA: Company Films.

Cohen, S. (1997). Men making a scene. In S. Whiteley (Ed.), *Sexing the Groove: Popular Music and Gender* (pp. 17–36). London, England: Routledge.

Coleman, N. (2007, December 2). Led Zeppelin: Why we should dig the 'rock dinosaurs' all over again. *Independent on Sunday*. Retrieved from https://www.rocksbackpages.com/Library/Article/led-zeppelin-why-we-should-dig-the-rock-dinosaurs-all-over-again.

Conley, J., & McLaren, A. T. (Eds.). (2009). *Car Troubles: Critical Studies of Automobility and Auto-Mobility*. Farnham, England: Ashgate.

Connell, J., & Gibson, C. (2001). *Sound Tracks: Popular Music, Identity and Place*. London, England: Routledge.

Connell, R. W., & Messerschmidt, J. W. (2005). Hegemonic masculinity: Rethinking the concept. *Gender Society*, 19, 829–59. doi: 10.1177/0891243205278639.

Conner, T., & Jones, S. (2014). Art to commerce: The trajectory of popular music criticism. *IASPM@Journal*, 4(2), 7–23.

Cooper, M. (Producer), & O'Casey, M. (2015). *Rock 'n' roll America* [Television series]. England: BBC Music.

Coppola, F. (Producer), Kurtz, G. (Producer), & Lucas, G. (Director). (1973). *American Graffiti* [Motion picture]. United States: Universal Pictures.

Creed, B. (1998). Anal wounds, metallic kisses. *Screen*, 39(2), 175–79. doi: 10.1093/screen/39.2.175.

Cross, A. (2004). Driving the American landscape. In P. Wollen & J. Kerr (Eds.), *Autopia: Cars and Culture* (pp. 249–58). London, England: Reaktion.

Cross, I. (2006). Music and social being. *Musicology Australia*, 28, 114–26. doi.org/10.1080/08145857.2005.10415281.

Cubitt, S. (1984). 'Maybellene': Meaning and the listening subject. *Popular Music*, 4, 207–24.

Dafis, E. H. (1974). *Hen Ffordd Gymreig o Fyw* [LP]. Wales: Sain.

Dafis, E. H. (1975). *Ffordd Newydd Eingl-Americanaidd Grêt O Fyw* [LP]. Wales: Sain.

Dahl, B. (n.d.). Jackie Brenston biography. *Allmusic*. Retrieved from http://www.allmusic.com/artist/jackie-brenston-mn0000782307.

Dant, T., & Martin, P. (2001). By car: Carrying modern society. In J. Gronow & A. Warde (Eds.), *Ordinary Consumption* (2nd ed., pp. 143–58). London, England: Routledge.

Davies, H. (2001). All rock and roll is homosocial: The representation of women in the British rock music press. *Popular Music*, 20(3), 301–19. doi: 10.1017/S0261143001001519.

Day, A. (2000). Ballard and Baudrillard: Close reading *Crash*. *English*, 49(195), 277–93. doi: 10.1093/english/49.195.277.

Decker, J. (2009). 'Try thinking of more': *Rubber Soul* and the Beatles' transformation of pop. In K. Womack (Ed.), *The Cambridge Companion to the Beatles* (pp. 75–89). Cambridge, England: Cambridge University Press.

Derber, C. (2000). *The Pursuit of Attention: Power and Ego in Everyday Life*. Oxford, England: Oxford University Press.

Desler, A. (2013). History without royalty? Queen and the strata of the popular music canon. *Popular Music*, 32(3), 385–405. doi: 10.1017/S0261143013000287.

Dickinson, K. (2001). 'Believe'?: Vocoders, digitalised identity and camp. *Popular Music*, 20(3): 333–347. doi: 10.1017/S0261143001001532.

Dockwray, R. (2005). *Deconstructing the Rock Anthem: Textual form, Participation and Collectivity* (Unpublished doctoral dissertation). University of Liverpool, Liverpool.

Döpfner, M. O. C., & Garms, T. (1984). *Neue Deutsche Welle: Kunst oder Mode? Eine sachliche Polemik für und wider die neudeutsche Popmusik*. Frankfurt am Main, Germany: Ullstein.

Douglas, S. J. (2004). *Listening in: Radio and the American Imagination, from Amos 'n' Andy and Edward R. Murrow to Wolfman Jack and Howard Stern*. Minneapolis, MN: University of Minnesota Press (Original work published 1999).

Dunn, M. (2013). *Michael Dunn's Letters from Jail: Insight into the Real Michael Dunn*. Retrieved from https://floridajustice.com/michael-dunns-letters-from-jail/.

Eastman, J. (2012a). Rebel manhood: The hegemonic masculinity of the Southern rock music revival. *Journal of Contemporary Ethnography*, 41(2), 189–219. doi: 10.1177/0891241611426430.

Eastman, J. (2012b). Southern masculinity in American rock music. In S. D. Harrison, G. F. Welch, & A. Adler (Eds.), *Perspectives on Males and Singing* (pp. 271–86). London, England: Springer.

Ebrahim, A. (2009). 40 rap stars and their performance cars. Retrieved from http://www.carthrottle.com/post/40-rapper-stars-and-their-performance-cars/.

Edensor, T. (2004). Automobility and national identity representation, geography and driving practice. *Theory, Culture & Society*, 21(4), 101–20. doi: 10.1177/0263276404046063.

Eder, M. (2013). *Elvis Music FAQ*. Milwaukee, WI: Backbeat Books.

Escott, C., & Hawkins, M. (1980). *Sun Records: The Brief History of the Legendary Record Label*. London, England: Omnibus Press.

Evans, S. (1997). *Born for Liberty: A History of Women in America*. New York, NY: Free Press.

Farrugia, R. (2012). *Beyond the Dance Floor: Female DJs, Technology and Electronic Dance Music Culture*. Bristol, England: Intellect.

Featherstone, M. (2004). Automobilities: An introduction. *Theory, Culture & Society*, 21(4), 1–24. doi: 10.1177/0263276404046058.

Fenster, M. (2002). Consumers' guide. In S. Jones (Ed.), *Pop Music and the Press* (pp. 81–92). Philadelphia, PA: Temple University Press.

Ferrell, J. (2003). Speed kills. *Critical Criminology*, 11(3), 185–98. doi: 10.1023/B:C RIT.0000005809.13127.e6.

Field, P. (2002). No particular place to go. In P. Wollen & J. Kerr (Eds.), *Autopia: Cars and Culture* (pp. 59–64). London, England: Reaktion.

Finch, P. (1987). *Selected Poems*. Bridgend: Poetry Wales Press.

Fink, J., & Holden, K. (1999). Pictures from the margins of marriage: Representations of spinsters and single mothers in the mid-Victorian novel, inter-war Hollywood melodrama and British film of the 1950s and 1960s. *Gender & History*, 11(2), 233–55. doi: 10.1111/1468-0424.00141.

Fla. State. (2010). 776.013: Justifiable use of force [Statute]. Retrieved from http://www.leg.state.fl.us/statutes/index.cfm?App_mode=Display_Statute&Search_String=&URL=0700-0799/0776/Sections/0776.013.html.

Fletcher, M. A. (2018, March 12). For black motorists, a never-ending fear of being stopped. National Geographic. Retrieved from https://www.nationalgeographic.com/magazine/2018/04/the-stop-race-police-traffic.

Fonda, P. (Producer), & Hopper, D. (Director). (1969). *Easy Rider* [Motion picture]. United States: Columbia Pictures.

Forde, E. (2001a). From polyglottism to branding: On the decline of personality journalism in the British music press. *Journalism*, 2(1), 23–43. doi: 10.1177/146488490100200108.

Forde, E. (2001b). *Music Journalists, Music Press Officers and the Consumer Music Press in the UK* (Doctoral dissertation). Retrieved from https://westminsterresearch.westminster.ac.uk/item/94116/music-journalists-music-press-officers-and-the-consumer-music-press-in-the-uk.

Forman, M. (2001). *The 'Hood Comes First: Race, Space and Place in Rap and Hip Hop*. Middletown, CT: Wesleyan University Press.

Foster, M. S. (1999). In the face of 'Jim Crow': Prosperous blacks and vacations, travel and outdoor leisure, 1890–1945. *The Journal of African American History*, 84(2), 130–49. doi: 10.2307/2649043.

Foster, M. (2003). *Nation on Wheels: The Automobile Culture in America Since 1945*. Belmont, CA: Wadsworth.

Freud, S. (1968). Poetry and fantasy. In S. Freud (Ed.), *Character and Culture*. New York, NY: Collier (Original work published in 1908).

Freud, S. (1995). Femininity. In J. Strachey (Ed.), *New Introductory Lectures on Psychoanalysis: The Standard Edition* (pp. 139–68). London, England: W. W. Norton and Company (Original work published in 1933).

Freud, S. (2001). Creative writers and day-dreaming. In J. Strachey (Ed.), *The Standard Edition of the Complete Works of Sigmund Freud* (Vol. 9, pp. 141–54). London, England: Vintage Press (Original work published in 1908).

Franz, K. (2004). The open road: Automobility and racial uplift in the interwar years. In D. Miller (Ed.), *Technology and the African American Experience* (pp. 131–53). Boston, MA: Massachusetts Institute of Technology Press.

Friedan, B. (1963). *The Feminine Mystique*. London, England: Penguin.

Frith, S. (Ed.). (2004). *Popular Music: Critical Concepts in Media and Cultural Studies* (Vol. 4). London, England: Routledge.

Frith, S., & McRobbie, A. (1978). Rock and sexuality. *Screen Education*, 29, 3–19.

Frow, J. (1991). Tourism and the semiotics of nostalgia. *October*, 57, 123–52.

Fürsich, E. (2012). Lifestyle journalism as popular journalism: Strategies for evaluating its public role. *Journalism Practice*, 6(1), 12–25. doi: 10.1080/17512786.2011.622894.

Gabriel, R., Sagara, E., & Grochowski Jones, R. (2014, October 10). Deadly force, in black and white. *ProPublica*. Retrieved from https://www.propublica.org/article/deadly-force-in-black-and-white.

Gartman, D. (1994). *Auto Opium: A Social History of American Automobile Design*. New York, NY: Routledge.

Giessen, H. W. (1992). *Zeitgeist populär—seine darstellung in deutschsprachigen postmodernen songtexten (bis 1989)*. St. Ingbert, Germany: Werner J. Röhrig Verlag.

Gilbertson, R. (Producer), Fernandez-Marengo, F. (Producer), & Evans, M. (Director). (2010). *Patagonia* [Motion picture]. England: Verve Pictures.

Gilroy, P. (2001). Driving while Black. In D. Miller (Ed.), *Car Cultures* (pp. 81–104). Oxford, England: Berg.

Gilroy, P. (2002). *Darker than Blue: On the Moral Economies of Black Atlantic Culture*. Cambridge, MA: Harvard University Press.

Gitlin, M. P. (Producer), & Scott, R. (Producer/Director). (1991). *Thelma & Louise* [Motion picture]. United States: MGM.

Goffman, E. (1959). *The Presentation of the Self in Everyday Life*. Harmondsworth, England: Penguin.

Goldblatt, D. (2013). Nonsense in public places: Songs of black vocal rhythm and blues or doo-wop. *Journal of Aesthetics and Art Criticism*, 70(1), 101–11. doi: 1010.1111/j.1540-6245.2012.01546.x.

Gomes, C. (2015). *Global Auto Report*. Toronto, Canada: Scotiabank. Retrieved from http://www.gbm.scotiabank.com/English/bns_econ/bns_auto.pdf.

Goodale, G. (2013). The sonorous envelope and political deliberation. *Quarterly Journal of Speech*, 99(2), 218–24.

Gilroy, P. (2001). Driving while Black. In D. Miller (Ed.), *Car Cultures* (pp. 81–104). Oxford, England: Berg.

Giucci, G. (2012). *The Cultural Life of the Automobile: Roads to Modernity*. Austin: University of Texas Press.

Gomery, D. (2008). *A History of Broadcasting in the United States*. Malden, MA: Blackwell.

Gracyk, T. (1996). *Rhythm and Noise: An Aesthetics of Rock*. Durham, NC: Duke University Press.

Graham, D. (2009). *Rock/Music Writings*. New York, NY: Primary Information.

Graves-Brown, P. (2000). Always crashing in the same car. In P. Graves-Brown (Ed.), *Matter, Materiality, and Modern Culture* (pp. 156–65). New York: Routledge.

Gray, D. (Producer), & Constantine, E. (Director). (2014). *Northern Soul* [Motion picture]. England: Universal Pictures.

Green, B. (Director). (2017). Carpool karaoke [Television series segment]. In G. Clements (Director), *The Late Late Show with James Corden* [Television series]. United States: CBS.

Gudmundsson, G., Lindberg, U., Michelsen, M., & Weisethaunet, H. (2002). Brit crit: Turning points in British rock criticism, 1960–1990. In S. Jones (Ed.), *Pop Music and the Press* (pp. 41–64). Philadelphia, PA: Temple University Press.

Guralnick, P. (1986). *Sweet Soul Music: Rhythm and Blues and the Southern Dream of Freedom*. New York, NY: Harper & Row.

Hall, M. R. (2014). Dramatizing the African American experience of travel in the Jim Crow South: *The Negro Motorist Green Book* in the African American literary imagination. *South Carolina Review*, 46(2), 80–94.

Harpold, T. (1997). Dry leatherette: Cronenberg's *Crash*. *Postmodern Culture*, 7(3). Retrieved from http://www.pomoculture.org/2013/09/21/dry-leatherette-cronenbergs-crash/.

Harris, M. (1988). *Art on the Road: Painted Vehicles of the Americas*. Apple Valley, MN: Pogo Press.

Hebdige, D. (1974). *The Style of the Mods*. Birmingham, England: Centre for Contemporary Cultural Studies.

Heining, D. (1998). Cars and girls – The car, masculinity and pop music. In D. Thoms, L. Holden, & T. Clayton, (Eds.), *The Motor Car and Popular Culture in the Twentieth Century* (pp. 96–119). Abingdon, England: Routledge.

Heinlein, R. A. (1942). *Beyond this Horizon*. Riverdale, NY: Baen Publishing Enterprises.

Heitmann, J. A. (2009). *The Automobile and American Life*. London, England: McFarland.

Halberstam, D. (1994). *The Fifties*. New York, NY: Fawcett.

Harvey, B. (1993). *The Fifties: A Women's Oral History*. New York, NY: Harper Collins.

Hasselberg, M., Vaez, M., & Laflamme, L. (2005). Socioeconomic aspects of the circumstances and consequences of car crashes among young adults. *Social Science & Medicine*, 60(2), 287–95. doi: 10.1016/j.socscimed.2004.05.006.

Hellman, H., & Jaakkola, M. (2012). From aesthetes to reporters: The paradigm shift in arts journalism in Finland. *Journalism*, 13(6), 783–801. doi: 10.1177/1464884911431382.

Henderson, A. F., & Joseph, A. P. (2012). Motor vehicle accident or driver suicide? Identifying cases of failed driver suicide in the trauma setting. *Injury*, 43(1), 18–21. doi: 10.1016/j.injury.2011.06.192.

Heyman, J. (Producer), & Watkins, P. (Director). (1967). *Privilege* [Motion picture]. England: Universal Pictures.

Hill, A. (2002). Acid house and Thatcherism: Noise, the mob, and the English countryside. *British Journal of Sociology*, 53(1), 89–105.

Hill, R. (2016). *Gender, Metal and the Media: Women Fans and the Gendered Experience of Music*. London, England: Palgrave.

Hill, S. (2007). *'Blerwytirhwng?': The Place of Welsh Pop Music*. Aldershot, England: Ashgate.

Hilsberg, A. (1978). Krautpunk: Rodenkirchen is burning. *Sounds*, 3, 20–24.

Hirschman, E. (2003). Men, dogs, guns, and cars: The semiotics of rugged individualism. *Journal of Advertising*, 32(1), 9–22. doi: 10.1080/00913367.2003.10601001.

Hoersch, T. (2006). *Bravo, 1956–2006*. München, Germany: Collection Rolf Heyne.

Holt, D. B. (2004). *How Brands become Icons: The Principles of Cultural Branding*. Cambridge, MA: Harvard Business Press.

Hornberger, B. (2017). NDW (New German Wave): From punk to mainstream. In M. Ahlers & C. Jacke (Eds.), *Perspectives on German Popular Music* (pp. 195–200). Abingdon, England: Routledge.

Hügel, H. O. (2007). *Lob des Mainstream. Zu Begriff und Geschichte von Unterhaltung und populärer Kultur*. Köln, Germany: Herbert von Halem Verlag.

Hyvernat, J. (Video Poster). (2014). *Markus – 'Ich will Spaß'* (Live) [Dailymotion video]. Retrieved from http://www.dailymotion.com/video/x564w:markus-ich-will-spas-live_music.

Ides, M. A. (2009). *Cruising for Community: Youth Culture and Politics in Los Angeles, 1910–1970* (Doctoral dissertation). Available from ProQuest Dissertations and Theses database. (UMI No. 304926254).

Informe anual 2010: Reseña del ejercicio. (2010). Washington, DC: Banco Mundial. Retrieved from http://siteresources.worldbank.org/EXTANNREP2010SPA/Resources/BancoMundial-Informeanual2010.pdf.

Jaakkola, M. (2015). Outsourcing views, developing news: Changes in art criticism in Finnish dailies, 1978–2008. *Journalism Studies*, 16(3), 383–402. doi: 10.1080/1461670X.2014.892727.

Jaakkola, M., Hellman, H., Koljonen, K., & Väliverronen, J. (2015). Liquid modern journalism with a difference: The changing professional ethos of cultural journalism. *Journalism Practice*, 9(6), 811–28. doi: 10.1080/17512786.2015.1051361.

Jackson, J. A. (1995). *Big Beat Heat: Alan Freed and the Early Years of Rock & Roll*. London, England: Music Sales.

Jarbou, J. (2018). Know your enemy: The Saudi women's driving campaign from flyers and faxes to YouTube and hashtags. *Feminist Media Studies*, 18(2), 321–25. doi: 10.1080/14680777.2018.1436902.

Jaimangal-Jones, D., Pritchard, A., & Morgan, N. (2010). Going the distance: Locating journey, liminality and rites of passage in dance music experiences. *Leisure Studies*, 29(3), 253–68. doi: 10.1080/02614361003749793.

James, E. W. (2005). Painting the world green: Dafydd Iwan and the Welsh protest ballad. *Folk Music Journal*, 8, 594–618.

Jameson, F. (2007). *Signatures of the Visible*. New York, NY: Routledge (Original work published in 1992).

Jameson, F. (2008). *The Ideologies of Theory*. London, England: Verso.

Jarman, F. (2013). Relax, feel good, chill out: The affective distribution of classical music. In M. Thompson & I. Biddle (Eds.), *Sound, Music, Affect: Theorizing Sonic Experience* (pp. 183–204). London, England: Bloomsbury.

Jeffries, M. (2011). *Thug Life: Race, Gender and the Meaning of Hip-Hop*. Chicago, IL: University of Chicago Press.

John, H. R. L. (2015). UK rave culture and the Thatcherite hegemony, 1988–94. *Cultural History*, 4(2), 162–86. doi: 10.3366/cult.2015.0092.

Jones, C. O. (2013). 'Songs of malice and spite'?: Wales, Prince Charles, and an anti-investiture ballad of Dafydd Iwan. *Music & Politics*, 7(2), 1–23. doi: 10.3998/mp.9460447.0007.203.

Jones, S. (Ed.). (2002). *Pop Music and the Press*. Philadelphia, PA: Temple University Press.

Karlstrom, P. J. (1980). Reflections on the automobile in American art. *Archives of American Art Journal*, 20(2), 18–25.

Katzman, S. (Producer), & Brahm, J. (Director). (1967). *Hot Rods to Hell* [Motion picture]. United States: MGM.

Kearney, M. C. (2006). *Girls Make Media*. New York, NY: Routledge.

Kemper, P. (1999). Gib Gas, ich will Spaß: Die Neue Deutsche Welle. In P. Kemper, T. Langhoff, & U. Sonnenschein (Eds.), *'Alles so schön bunt hier': Die Geschichte der Popkultur von den Fünfzigern bis heute* (pp. 187–96). Stuttgart, Germany: Reclam.

Ken [Screen name]. (2018). *Cover Me, Bette Middler: Pink Cadillac* [web log comment]. Retrieved from http://estreetshuffle.com/index.php/2018/11/26/cover-me-bette-midler-pink-cadillac/.

Kennedy, B. (Producer), & Miller, G. (Director). (1979). *Mad Max* [Motion picture]. Australia: Roadshow.

Kennedy, B. (Producer), & Miller, G. (Director). (1981). *Mad Max 2* [Motion picture]. Australia: Warner Brothers.

Kennedy, M. (1999). Where does the music come from? A comparison case-study of the compositional processes of a high school and a collegiate composer. *British Journal of Music Education*, 16(2), 157–77.

Kerouac, J. (1991). *On the Road*. London, England: Penguin Books (Original work published in 1957).

Kimmel, M. (2013). *Angry White Men: American Masculinity at the End of an Era*. New York, NY: Nation Books.

King, M. (2013). *Men, Masculinity and the Beatles*. Farnham, England: Ashgate.

Klinger, B. (1997). The road to dystopia: Landscaping the nation in *Easy Rider*. In S. Cohan & I. R. Hark (Eds.), *The Road Movie Book* (pp. 179–203) New York, NY: Routledge.

Klopprogge, A. (Composer). (1982). *Ich will Spaß* [Recorded by Markus] [7' Single]. Frankfurt, Germany: CBS.

Kohl, H. (1982, October 13). *Government Declaration 13.10.1982*. Retrieved from http://www.mediaculture-online.de/fileadmin/bibliothek/kohl_RE_1982/kohl_RE_1982.html.

Kristensen, N. N. (2017). Churnalism, cultural (inter)mediation and sourcing in cultural journalism. *Journalism Studies*, 18(10), 1–19. doi: 10.1080/1461670X.2017.1330666.

Kristensen, N. N., & Riegert, K. (2017). Why cultural journalism in the Nordic countries? In N. N. Kristensen & K. Riegert (Eds.), *Cultural Journalism in the Nordic Countries* (pp. 9–26). Göteburg, Sweden: Nordicom.

LaBelle, B. (2008). Pump up the bass: Rhythm, cars, and auditory scaffolding. *The Senses and Society*, 3(2), 187–203. doi: 10.2752/174589308X306420.

LaBelle, B. (2010). *Acoustic Territories: Sound Culture and Everyday Life*. London, England: Continuum.

Laderman, D. (1996). What a trip: The road film and American culture. *Journal of Film and Video*, 48(1), 41–57.

Laing, D. (2006). Anglo-American music journalism: Texts and contexts. In A. Bennett, B. Shank, & J. Toynbee (Eds.), *The Popular Music Studies Reader* (pp. 333–46). Abingdon, England: Routledge.

Larsson, N. (2017, October 12). Live music acts are mostly male-only—what's holding women back? *The Guardian*. Retrieved from https://www.theguardian.com/inequality/2017/oct/12/tonights-live-music-acts-will-mostly-be-male-only-whats-holding-women-back.

Lashes, L. (2014). All girls on deck: Lisa Lashes wants more female DJs. *Reprobait*. Retrieved from http://www.reprobaitmagazine.com/all-girls-on-deck-lisa-lashes-wants-more-female-djs/.

Lee, S. (2012). *The 'If You Prefer a Milder Comedian, Please Ask for One' EP*. London, England: Faber and Faber.

Leiby, J. (1978). *A History of Social Welfare and Social Work in the United States*. New York, NY: Columbia University Press.

Lemon, A. (1997). Misogyny and respect in Robert Johnson songs. In C. Danforth & A. Rissetto (Eds.), *The Robert Johnson Notebooks* [website]. Retrieved from http://xroads.virginia.edu/~music/rjhome.html.

Leonard, M. (2016). *Gender in the Music Industry: Rock, Discourse and Girl Power*. New York, NY: Routledge (Original work published in 2007).

Lévi-Strauss, C. (1966). *The Savage Mind*. London, England: Weidenfeld and Nicolson.

Lewis, D., & Goldstein, L. (1983). *The Automobile and American Culture*. Ann Arbour: University of Michigan Press.

Lezotte, C. (2013). Born to take the highway: Women, the automobile, and rock 'n' roll. *The Journal of American Culture*, 36(3), 161–76. doi: 10.1111/jacc.12022.

Lindberg, U., Gudmundsson, G., Michelsen, M., & Weisethaunet, H. (2005). *Rock Criticism from the Beginning: Amusers, Bruisers & Cool-Headed Cruisers*. New York, NY: Peter Lang.

Lipsitz, G. (1989). Land of a thousand dances: Youth, minorities and rock 'n' roll. In L. May (Ed.), *Recasting America: Culture and Politics in the Age of the Cold War* (pp. 267–85). Chicago, IL: University of Chicago Press.

Loewen, L. J. (2005). *Sundown Towns: A Hidden Dimension of Racism in America*. New York, NY: New Press.

Longerich, W. (1989). *'Da Da Da': Zur Standortbestimmung der Neuen Deutschen Welle*. Pfaffenweiler, Germany: Centaurus.

Luckso, D. N. (2008). *The Business of Speed: The Hot Rod Industry in America, 1915–1990*. Baltimore, MD: Johns Hopkins University Press.

Lumsden, K. (2010). Gendered performances in a male-dominated subculture: 'Girl racers,' car modification and the quest for masculinity. *Sociological Research Online*, 15(3), 1–11. doi: 10.5153/sro.2123.

MacDonald, R., Hargreaves, D. J., & Miell, D. (2002). *Musical Identities*. New York, NY: Oxford University Press.

Marcus, G. (1975). *Mystery Train: Images of America in Rock 'n' Roll Music*. Boston, MA: Dutton.

Market Report 2017. (2017). UK Festival Awards. Retrieved from https://www.festivalawards.com/wp-content/uploads/2018/08/UK-Festival-Market-Report-2017.pdf.

Marks, L. (2001). *Sexual Chemistry: A History of the Contraceptive Pill*. New Haven, CT: Yale University Press.

Marsh, P., & Collett, P. (1986). *Driving Passion: The Psychology of the Car*. London, England: Jonathan Cape.

Martin, G. (1985, December 21). Stevie Wonder: Ever decreasing circles. *New Musical Express*. Retrieved from https://www.rocksbackpages.com/Library/Article/stevie-wonder-ever-decreasing-circles.

Marton, K. (2001). *Hidden Power: Presidential Marriages that Shaped Our Recent History*. New York, NY: Pantheon Books.

Mayhew, E. (2004). Positioning the producer: Gender divisions in creative labour and value. In S. Whiteley, A. Bennett, & S. Hawkins (Eds.), *Music, Space and Place* (pp. 149–62). Aldershot, England: Ashgate.

MC Big Data [Screen name]. (2015, June 9). Riding dirty: The science of cars and rap lyrics. *Medium*. Retrieved from https://medium.com/cuepoint/riding-dirty-the-science-of-cars-and-rap-lyrics-21b8404a9c4d.

McCann, B. (2015). *The Mark of Criminality: Rhetoric, Race, and Gangsta Rap in the War-on-Crime Era*. Tuscaloosa: University of Alabama Press.

McClary, S. (2002). *Feminine Endings: Music, Gender and Sexuality*. Minneapolis: University of Minnesota Press.

McClary, S., & Walser, R. (1994). Theorizing the body in African American music. *Black Music Research Journal*, 14(1), 75–84.

McCosker, A. (2005). A vision of masochism in the affective pain of *Crash*. *Sexualities*, 8(1), 30–48. doi: 10.1177/1363460705049573.

McKay, G. (1996). *Senseless Acts of Beauty: Cultures of Resistance since the Sixties*. London, England: Verso.

McLeese, D. (2010). Straddling the cultural chasm: The great divide between music criticism and popular consumption. *Popular Music and Society*, 33(4), 433–47. doi: 10.1080/03007761003694118.

McLeod, K. (2006). We are the champions: Masculinities, sports and popular music. *Popular Music and Society*, 29(5), 531–47.

McLuhan, M. (1994). *Understanding Media: The Extensions of Man*. Cambridge, MA: MIT Press (Original work published in 1964).

McNeill, W. (1995). *Keeping Together in Time: Dance and Drill in Human History*. Cambridge, MA: Harvard University Press.

McRobbie, A., & Garber, J. (1991). Girls and subcultures. In T. Jefferson & S. Hall (Eds.), *Resistance through Rituals: Youth Subcultures in Post-war Britain* (pp. 209–22). London, England: Routledge.

MC Saizmundo. (2005). *Malwod a Morgrug: Dan Warchae* [CD]. Wales: Slacyr.

Mercury, F. (Composer). (1978). *Don't Stop Me Now* [Recorded by Queen]. On *Top Gear Anthems: The Best Ever Driving Songs* [CD]. London, England: Virgin.

Mercury, F. (Composer). (1979). *Don't Stop Me Now* [Piano score]. London, England: EMI Music Publishing. Retrieved from http://www.musicnotes.com.

Metzl, J. (2003). 'Mother's little helper': The crisis of psychoanalysis and the Miltown resolution. *Gender and History*, 15(2), 228–55. doi: 10.1111/1468-0424.00300.

Michaels, L. (Producer), & Spheeris, P. (Director). (1993). *Wayne's World* [Motion picture]. United States: Paramount Pictures.

Michelsen, M. (2015). Music criticism and taste cultures. In J. Shepherd & K. Devine (Eds.), *The Routledge Reader on the Sociology of Music* (pp. 211–20). New York, NY: Routledge.

Miller, D. (Ed.). (2001). *Car Cultures*. Oxford, England: Berg.

Miller, G. (Producer/Director), & Ogilvie, G. (Director). (1985). *Mad Max Beyond Thunderdome* [Motion picture]. Australia: Warner Brothers.

Miller, J. (1999). *Flowers in the Dustbin: The Rise of Rock and Roll, 1947–1977*. New York, NY: Simon & Schuster.

Missouri Attorney General. (2018). *2017 Vehicle Stops Executive Summary*. Retrieved from https://www.ago.mo.gov/home/vehicle-stops-report/2017-executive-summary.

Mitchell, D. (Producer), Voeten, P.J. (Producer) & Miller, G. (Producer/Director). (2015). *Mad Max: Fury Road* [Motion picture]. United States: Warner Brothers.

Miyake, E. (2018). *The Gendered Motorcycle*. London, England: Bloomsbury.

Moorhouse, H. F. (1986). Racing for a sign: Defining the 'Hot Rod' 1945–1960. *Journal of Popular Culture*, 20(2), 83–96.

Moorhouse, H. F. (1991). *Driving Ambitions: An Analysis of the American Hot Rod Enthusiasm*. Manchester, England: Manchester University Press.

Moore, A. (2016). *Rock: The Primary Text*. New York, NY: Routledge (Original work published in 2001).

Morley, P. (1980, September 27). The NME consumers' guide to Marc Bolan, Part 2: The rise and fall of Bolanmania. *New Musical Express*. Retrieved from https://www.rocksbackpages.com/Library/Article/the-inme-iconsumers-guide-to-marc-bolan-part-2-the-rise-and-fall-of-bolanmania.

Morley, P. (2004). *Words and Music: A History of Pop in the Shape of a City*. London, England: Bloomsbury.

Murphy, K. (Producer), & Reiner, R. (Director). (1984). *This Is Spinal Tap* [Motion picture]. United States: Embassy Pictures.

Nader, R. (1965). *Unsafe at Any Speed: The Designed-in Dangers of the American Automobile*. New York: Grossman.

Nayak, A. (2003). Last of the 'real geordies'? White masculinities and the subcultural response to deindustrialisation. *Environment and Planning D: Society and Space*, 21(1), 7–25. doi: 10.1068/d44j.

Nóvoa, A. (2012). Musicians that move: Mobilities and identities of a band on the road. *Mobilities*, 7(3), 349–68. doi: 10.1080/17450101.2012.654994.

Oakes, J. L. (2009). I'm a man: Masculinities in popular music. In D. Scott (Ed.), *The Ashgate Research Companion to Popular Music* (pp. 221–39). Farnham, England: Ashgate.

O'Brien, P. (1974). *The Woman Alone*. New York, NY: The New York Times Book Company.

O'Connell, S. (1998). *The Car in British Society: Class, Gender and Motoring, 1896–1939*. Manchester: Manchester University Press.

O'Carroll, L. (2013, July 12). Women make up only 20% of solo radio broadcasters, research reveals. *The Guardian*. Retrieved from https://www.theguardian.com/media/2013/jul/12/women-solo-radio-broadcasters-20-percent.

Ohlheiser, A. (2014, October 17). Michael Dunn sentenced to life without parole for 'loud music' killing of Jordan Davis. *Washington Post*. Retrieved from https://www.washingtonpost.com/news/post-nation/wp/2014/10/17/michael-dunn-sentenced-to-life-without-parole-for-loud-music-killing-of-jordan-davis/.

Osborne, J. (2000). *Elvis: Word for Word*. New York, NY: Gramercy Books.

Ott, B., & Herman, B. (2003). Mixed messages: Resistance and reappropriation in rave culture. *Western Journal of Communication*, 67(3), 249–70. doi: 10.1080/10570310309374771.

Partner, S. (1999). *Assembled in Japan: Electrical Goods and the Making of the Japanese Consumer*. Berkeley, CA: University of California Press.

Patsy Cline Hurt in Near-Fatal Crash. (1961, June 19). *Billboard*, 2.

Pearcy, M. (2016). *The Green Book*: Race, geography, and critical understanding. *The Councilor: A Journal of the Social Studies, 77*(2), Art. 4. Retrieved from https://thekeep.eiu.edu/the_councilor/vol77/iss2/4.

Pechard, T. (2016). *From Soul to Hip Hop*. New York, NY: Routledge.

People of the State of Florida v. Dunn, Michael David. (2012). Rhonda Rouer [Witness transcript]. Retrieved from http://lawofselfdefense.web.unc.edu/files/2014/10/Rhonda-Rouer.pdf.

Pires, M. (2003). The popular music press. In H. Dauncey & S. Cannon (Eds.), *Popular Music in France from Chanson to Techno* (pp. 77–96). Aldershot, England: Ashgate.

Powers, D. (2013). *Writing the Record: The Village Voice and the Birth of Rock Criticism*. Amherst, MA: University of Massachusetts Press.

Putnam, D. (Producer), Lieberson, S. (Producer), & Whatham, C. (Director). (1973). *That'll Be the Day* [Motion picture]. England: Anglo-EMI.

Putnam, D. (Producer), Lieberson, S. (Producer), & Apted, M. (Director). (1974). *Stardust* [Motion picture]. England: EMI Films.

Palmer, P. (2011). *Domesticity and Dirt: Housewives and Domestic Servants in the United States, 1920–45*. Philadelphia, PA: Temple University Press.

Peach, L. (1998). *Women in Culture: A Women's Studies Anthology*. Oxford, England: Blackwell.

Phillips, D. (1998). *Trwy ddulliau chwyldro… ?: Hanes cymdeithas yr iaith, 1962–1992*. Llandysul, Wales: Gomer.

Plopper, B., & Ness, M. E. (1993). Death as portrayed to adolescents through top 40 rock 'n' roll music. *Adolescence, 28*(112), 793–807.

Poole, S. (2003, August 16). Top of the pops. *The Guardian*. Retrieved from http://www.theguardian.com/books/2003/aug/16/music.

Queen Win Top Gear's Best Driving Song Ever Poll. (2005). Retrieved from http://www.queenzone.com/news/queen-win-top-gears-best-driving-song-ever-poll.aspx.

Quispel, C. (2005). Detroit: City of cars, city of music. *Built Environment, 31*(3), 226–36. doi: 10.2148/benv.2005.31.3.226.

Quitney, J. (Video Poster). (2012). *WJR: One of a Kind* [Streamed video]. Retrieved from http://www.youtube.com/watch?v=BxswozcNZnw.

Redhead, S. (1993). *Rave Off: Politics and Deviance in Contemporary Youth Culture*. Aldershot, England: Avebury.

Redshaw, S. (2008). *In the Company of Cars: Driving as a Social and Cultural Practice*. Aldershot, England: Ashgate.

Reed, R. (2014, September 22). 'Loud music' murder trial resumes after hung jury. *Rolling Stone*. Retrieved from https://www.rollingstone.com/politics/politics-news/loud-music-murder-trial-resumes-after-hung-jury-229131/.

Reeser, T. (2010). *Masculinities in Theory: An Introduction*. Oxford, England: Wiley-Blackwell.

Richards, N., & Milestone, K. (2000). What difference does it make? Women's pop cultural production and consumption in Manchester. *Sociological Research Online*, 5(1), 1–14. doi: 10.5153/sro.410.

Robbins, I. (1980, May). Marc Bolan: A wizard, a true star. *Trouser Press*. Retrieved from https://www.rocksbackpages.com/Library/Article/a-wizard-a-true-star.

Roden, D. (2003). Cyborgian subjects and the auto-destruction of metaphor. In J. Arthurs & I. Grant (Eds.), *Crash Cultures: Modernity, Mediation and the Material* (pp. 91–102). Chicago, IL: University of Chicago Press.

Rose, T. (1994). *Black Noise: Rap Music and Black Culture in Contemporary America*. Middletown, CT: Wesleyan University Press.

Rothenbuhler, E., & McCourt, T. (2002). Radio redefines itself, 1947–1962. In M. Hilmes & J. Loviglio (Eds.), *Radio Reader: Essays in the Cultural History of Radio* (pp. 367–88). New York, NY: Routledge.

Rothenbuhler, E., & McCourt, T. (2004). Burnishing the brand: Todd Storz and the total station sound. *Radio Journal*, 2(1), 3–14. doi: 10.1386/rajo.2.1.3/0.

Rusoff, L. (Producer), & Landers, L. (Director). (1958). *Hot rod gang* [Motion picture]. United States: American International Pictures.

Russolo, L. (2004). *The Art of Noise*. New York, NY: UBU Classics (Original work published 1913).

Santi, C. (2019, February 25). Spike Lee & others react to *Green Book* top Oscar win. *Ebony*. Retrieved from https://www.ebony.com/entertainment/spike-lee-react-green-book-controversial-oscar-win/.

Sargeant, J. (2002). Squealing wheels and flying fists. In P. Wollen & J. Kerr (Eds.), *Autopia: Cars and Culture* (pp. 312–14). London, England: Reaktion.

Sassoon, W. (Producer), & Cardiff, J. (Director). (1968). *The Girl on a Motorcycle* [Motion picture]. UK and France: Warner Brothers.

Scanlan, J. (2015). *Easy Riders, Rolling Stones: On the Road in America, from Delta Blues to '70s Rock*. London, England: Reaktion Books.

Schafer, R. M. (1993). *The Soundscape: Our Sonic Environment and the Tuning of the World*. Rochester, VT: Destiny Books.

Scharrer, E., Weidman, L. M., & Bissell, K. L. (2003). Pointing the finger of blame: News media coverage of popular-culture culpability. *Journalism & Communication Monographs*, 5(2), 48–98. doi: 10.1177/152263790300500201.

Scherer, J. (2016, November 18). Fla. 'loud music' murder: Firing into car full of teens playing rap music not 'self-defense,' court rules. *Washington Post*. Retrieved from https://www.washingtonpost.com/news/morning-mix/wp/2016/11/18/fla-loud-music-murder-firing-into-car-full-of-teens-playing-rap-music-not-self-defense-court-rules/?utm_term=.0bcb370bff3e.

Schiffer, M. B. (1991). *The Portable Radio in American Life*. Tucson: University of Arizona Press.

Schiller, M. (2014). 'Fun run fun on the autobahn': Kraftwerk challenging Germanness. *Popular Music and Society*, 37, 618–37.

Schinder, S. & Schwartz, A. (2008). *Icons of Rock: An Encyclopaedia of the Legends Who Changed Music Forever*. Westport, CT: Greenwood Press.

Schulenberg, U. (2017). 'Visions and versions of America': Greil Marcus's rock journalism as cultural criticism. *Rock Music Studies*, 4(1), 11–22. doi: 10.1080/19401159.2017.1291795.

Segal, L. (2009). Men after feminism: What is left to say? In J. M. Armengol & À. Carabí (Eds.), *Debating Masculinities*. Harriman, TN: Men's Studies Press.

Seiler, C. (2006). 'So that we as a race might have something authentic to travel by': African American automobility and Cold-War liberalism. *American Quarterly*, 58(4), 1091–1117.

Seiler, C. (2008). *Republic of Drivers: A Cultural History of Automobility in America*. Chicago, IL: University of Chicago Press.

Shackleford, B. A. (2004). *Going National While Staying Southern: Stock Car Racing in America, 1949–1979* (Unpublished doctoral dissertation). Georgia Institute of Technology, Atlanta, GA.

Sheller, M. (2004). Automotive emotions: Feeling the car. *Theory, Culture & Society*, 21(4), 221–42. doi: 10.1177/0263276404046068.

Shepherd, B. (2011). Rock critics as 'mouldy modernists.' *Portal: A Journal of Multidisciplinary International Studies*, 8(1), 1–10.

Sides, J. (2018, July 17). What data on 20 million traffic stops can tell us about 'driving while black.' *Washington Post*. Retrieved from https://www.washingtonpost.com/news/monkey-cage/wp/2018/07/17/what-data-on-20-million-traffic-stops-can-tell-us-about-driving-while-black/?utm_term=.914c4f1a1108.

Singleton, R. W. (2018). 'What are you gonna do tonight?' 'Wait for a phone call I suppose.' Girls, mod subculture and reactions to the film *Quadrophenia*. In P. Thurschwell (Ed.), *Quadrophenia and Mod(ern) Culture* (pp. 151–72). London, England: Palgrave Macmillan.

Silver, M. (Director). (2015, October 2). *3½ Minutes, Ten Bullets* [Streaming Video]. Retrieved from https://www.hbo.com/documentaries/3-1-2-minutes-ten-bullets.

Skolnik, M. (2014, February 6). Defense attorney just quoted Jordan Davis using the n-word and he says the full word with the 'r.' Not sure about that tactic... [Tweet]. Retrieved from https://twitter.com/MichaelSkolnik/status/431488907880833024.

Slethaug, G. E. (2017). The semiotics of the road. In G. E. Slethaug (Ed.), *Music and the Road: Music and the Popular Culture of the American Road* (pp. 19–38). London, England: Bloomsbury.

Sloboda, J. (1985). *The Musical Mind: The Cognitive Psychology of Music*. New York, NY: Oxford University Press.

Small, C. (1998). *Musicking: The Meanings of Performing and Listening*. Middletown, CT: Wesleyan University Press.

Smith, A. (1962, December 7). Patsy Cline overcame grave car crash injuries. *New Musical Express*. Retrieved from https://www.rocksbackpages.com/Library/Article/patsy-cline-overcame-grave-car-crash-injuries.

Smith, S. (2001). *Dancing in the Street: Motown and the Cultural Politics of Detroit*. Cambridge, MA: Harvard University Press.

Sobchack, V. (1995). Beating the meat / surviving the text, or how to get out of this century alive. *Body & Society*, 1(3), 205–14.

Stephens, M. (2004). Eirug Wyn: Campaigning welsh language novelist. *The Independent*, 10 May. Retrieved from https://www.independent.co.uk/news/obituaries/eirug-wyn-38451.html.

Sterling, C. H. (1984). *Electronic Media: A Guide to Trends in Broadcasting and Newer Technologies, 1920–1983*. New York, NY: Praeger.

Stigwood, R. (Producer), Carr, A. (Producer), & Kleiser, R. (Director). (1978). *Grease* [Motion picture]. United States: Paramount Pictures.

Stoever, J. L. (2016). *The Sonic Color Line: Race and the Cultural Politics of Listening*. New York: New York University Press.

Strachan, R. (2003). *Do-It-Yourself: Industry, Ideology, Aesthetics and Micro Independent Record Labels in the UK* (Unpublished doctoral dissertation). University of Liverpool, Liverpool.

Strolla, C. (2012). Charge conference and closing Arguments [Transcript]. *People of the State of Florida v. Dunn, Michael David*. Retrieved from http://lawofselfdefense.web.unc.edu/files/2014/10/chargeconfthruStrollaclose.pdf.

Sugrue, T. J. (2010). Driving while black: The car and race relations in modern America. *Automobile in American Life and Society*. Retrieved from http://www.autolife.umd.umich.edu/Race/R_Casestudy/R_Casestudy1.htm. Accessed January 15, 2019.

Sussman, A., & Hollander, T. (2015). *Cognitive Architecture: Designing for How We Respond to the Built Environment*. New York, NY: Routledge.

Tagg, P. (1987). Musicology and the semiotics of popular music. *Semiotica*, 66(1–3), 279–98.

Tilton, J. E. (1971). *International Diffusion of Technology: The Case of Semiconductors*. Washington, DC: Brookings Institution.

Thomas, J. (Producer), Lantos, R. (Producer), & Cronenberg, D. (Producer/Director). (1996). *Crash* [Motion picture]. Canada: Alliance.

Tomatis, J. (2014). 'This is our music': Italian teen pop press and genres in the 1960s. *IASPM@ Journal*, 4(2), 24–42.

Toynbee, J. (2000). *Making Popular Music: Musicians, Creativity and Institutions*. London, England: Arnold.

Urry, J. (2004). The 'system' of automobility. *Theory, Culture & Society*, 21(4), 25–39. doi: 10.1177/0263276404046059.

Urry, J. (2006). Inhabiting the car. *Sociological Review*, 54(1), 17–31. doi: 10.1111/j.1467-954X.2006.00635.x.

Vardi, I. (2011). Auto thrill shows and destruction derbies, 1922–1965: Establishing the cultural logic of the deliberate car crash in America. *Journal of Social History*, 45(1), 20–46. doi: 10.1093/jsh/shr005.

Various Artists. (1973). *41 Original Hits from the Soundtrack of American Graffiti* [Double LP]. Universal City, CA: MCA Records.

Various Artists. (2001a). *The Album* [CD]. London, England: Virgin.

Various Artists. (2001b). *The Album Vol. 2* [CD]. London, England: Virgin.

Various Artists. (2002a). *The Album Vol. 3* [CD]. London, England: Virgin.

Various Artists. (2002b). *The Album Vol. 4* [CD]. London, England: Virgin.

Various Artists. (2002c). *The Best Bands Ever* [CD]. London, England: Virgin.

Various Artists. (2004). *The Best Bands Ever: 2004* [CD]. London, England: Virgin.

Various Artists. (2005a). *Top Gear: The Ultimate Driving Experience* [CD]. London, England: Universal Music.

Various Artists. (2005b). *The Album '05* [CD]. London, England: Virgin.

Various Artists. (2005c). *The Album* [CD]. London, England: Virgin.

Various Artists. (2006). *The Anthems: The Best Bands. The Biggest Tracks* [CD]. London, England: Virgin.

Various Artists. (2007a). *Top Gear Anthems: The Best Ever Driving Songs* [CD]. London, England: Virgin.

Various Artists. (2007b). *The Anthems '07: The Best Bands. The Biggest Tracks* [CD]. London, England: Virgin.

Various Artists. (2009). *The Anthems '09: The Best Acts and the Biggest Tracks* [CD]. London, England: UMTV [Universal Music].

Various Artists. (2010). *Epic: The Bands: The Tracks: The Anthems* [CD]. London, England: Sony.

Various Artists. (2011). *Epic Vol 2: The Biggest Tracks. The Festival Anthems* [CD]. London, England: Sony.

Various Artists. (2012). *Epic: Stadium Anthems* [CD]. London, England: Sony.

Varriale, S. (2014). Bourdieu and the sociology of cultural evaluation: Lessons from the Italian popular music press. *Rassegna Italiana di Sociologia*, 55(1), 121–48. doi: 10.1423/76934.

Vintagetvs. (Video poster). (2008). *1950's WJR Detroit Off the AirRrecording* [Streaming video]. Retrieved from http://www.youtube.com/watch?v=M78aS3LOpmU.

Virilio, P. (2006). *Speed and Politics*. Los Angeles, CA: Semiotext(e).

Wade, P. (2002). *Música, raza y nación: Música tropical en Colombia*. Bogotá, Columbia: Vicepresidencia de la República.

Von Faust, B. (2016). Let there be rock: 'Western' heavy metal in Soviet press and public opinion during the Soviet Union's final decade. *Metal Music Studies*, 2(3), 377–93. doi: 10.1386/mms.2.3.377_1.

Wajcman, J. (1991). *Feminism Confronts Technology*. Philadelphia: University of Pennsylvania Press.

Wagner, P. (1999). *Pop 2000: 50 jahre popmusik und jugendkultur in Deutschland*. Hamburg, Germany: Ideal.

Wall, T. (2006). Rocking Around the Clock: Teenage Dance Fads 1955 to 1965. In J. M. Malnig (Ed.), *The Social Dance Reader* (pp. 182–98). Chicago, IL: University of Illinois Press.

Wall, T. (2013). *Studying Popular Music Culture* (2nd ed.). London, England: Sage.

Walser, R. (1993). *Running with the Devil: Power, Gender and Madness in Heavy Metal Music*. Middleton, CT: Wesleyan University Press.

Walsh, M. (2006). *At Home at the Wheel?: The Woman and Her Automobile in the 1950s*. London: British Library. Retrieved from http://www.bl.uk/eccles/pdf/baas2006.pdf.

Ward, B. (1998). *Just My Soul Responding: Rhythm and Blues, Black Consciousness and Race Relations*. London, England: UCL Press.

Ward, B. (2004). *Radio and the Struggle for Civil Rights in the South*. Gainesville: University Press of Florida.

Warne, C. (2011). Promoting punk: The cultural politics of music journalism in France, 1972–1978. *Contemporary French Civilization*, 36(1), 65–80. doi: 10.3828/cfc.2011.6.

Warner, S. (2015). In print and on screen: The changing character of popular music journalism. In A. Bennett & S. Waksman (Eds.), *The Sage Handbook of Popular Music* (p. 439). London, England: Sage.

Weigand, K. (2002). *Red Feminism: American Communism and the Making of Women's Liberation*. Baltimore, MD: John Hopkins University Press.

Weinstein, E. M. (2010). *Out of the Shadows: Breaking the Gender Barrier in Rock Journalism, from the 1950s to 2010* (Master's thesis). Available from OhioLINK Electronic Theses and Dissertations Centre (Document number: ohiou1276198656).

Weisbart, D. (Producer), & Ray, N. (Director). (1955). *Rebel Without a Cause* [Motion picture]. United States: Warner Brothers.

Weisethaunet, H., & Lindberg, U. (2010). Authenticity revisited: The rock critic and the changing real. *Popular Music and Society*, 33(4), 465–85. doi: 10.1080/03007761003694225.

Weiss, R. (Producer), & Landis, J. (Director). (1980). *The Blues Brothers* [Motion picture]. United States: Universal Pictures.

Whitall, S. (1979, February). Led Zeppelin: A psychobiograph. *Creem*, 10(9). Retrieved from https://www.rocksbackpages.com/Library/Article/led-zeppelin-a-psychobiograph.

Whiteley, S. (1992). *The Space between the Notes: Rock and the Counter-Culture*. London, England: Routledge.

Widmer, E. L. (2002). Crossroads: The automobile, rock 'n' roll and democracy. In P. Wollen & J. Kerr (Eds.), *Autopia: Cars and Culture* (pp. 65–74). London, England: Reaktion Books.

Williams, C. H. (1977). Non-violence and the development of the Welsh Language Society, 1962–c. 1974. *Welsh History Review*, 8, 426–51.

Williams, J. (2010a). 'You never been on a ride like this befo': Los Angeles, automotive listening, and Dr. Dre's G-Funk. *Popular Music History*, 4(2), 160–76. doi: 10.1558/pomh.v4i2.160.

Williams, J. (2010b). The construction of jazz rap as high art in hip hop music. *The Journal of Musicology*, 27(4), 435–59. doi: 10.1525/jm.2010.27.4.435.

Williams, J. (2014). 'Cars with the boom': Music, automobility and hip hop 'sub' cultures. In S. Gopinath & J. Stanyek (Eds.), *The Oxford Handbook to Mobile Music Studies* (Vol. 2, pp. 109–45). New York, NY: Oxford University Press.

Williams, P. (Producer), & Emlyn, E. (Director). (1994). *Gadael Lenin*. Wales: S4C.

Williams, P. (2003). *The Psychology of Distance: Wales, One Nation*. Cardiff, Wales: Welsh Academic Press.

Willis, P. (1978). *Profane Culture*. London, England: Routledge & Kegan Paul.

Wilman, A. (Producer). (2007, October 7). The one with the best road in the world [Television series episode]. In Wilman, A. (Producer). *Top Gear*. London, England: BBC.

Wilman, A. (Producer). (2013, August 4). The one with the best of British parade [Television series episode]. In Wilman, A. (Producer). *Top Gear*. London, England: BBC.

Wish You Were Here 2017: *The Contribution of Live Music to the UK Economy*. (2017). UK music. Retrieved from https://www.ukmusic.org/assets/general/Report_WYWH_17.pdf.

Witzel, M., & Bash, K. (1997). *Cruisin': Car Culture in America*. Osceola, WI: MBI Publishing.

Wolff, J. (1993). On the road again: Metaphors of travel in cultural criticism. *Cultural Studies*, 7(2), 224–39.

Wollen, P., & Kerr, J. (Eds.). (2002). *Autopia: Cars and Culture*. London, England: Reaktion Books.

Wright, E. O., & Rogers, J. (2010). *American Society: How It Really Works*. New York, NY: W. W. Norton and Company.

Yúdice, G. (2003). *El recurso de la cultura*. Barcelona, Spain: Gedisa.

Zeiger, S. (2010). *Entangling Alliances: Foreign War Brides and American Soldiers in the Twentieth Century*. New York: New York University Press.

Index

3½ Minutes, 10 Bullets   148, 153
50 Cent   9
409   42

acceleration   43, 59–62, 113
AC/DC   9
Adorno, Theodor   162
advertising   131
"Africa"   51
African Americans, *see also* biracial pop, crossover music, race, racism, segregation
   civil rights   144, 162
   'driving while black'   137–8, 143
   identity   167
   integration   141–2
   slavery   138
Ail Symudiad   108
alcohol   93–4, 132, 159
Alexander, Peter   170 n.1
alienation   162
"Always Crashing in the Same Car"   158
American dream   7–8, 40, 102
American Graffiti   6, 15–17, 19–21, 26, *see also* Wolfman Jack
anthems   51, 61–4, 68
art   46
The Art of Noise group   6
The Art of Noise manifesto   6
authenticity   78
Autobahn   11, 111
automation   10–12
automotive emotions   10
avant-garde   112
Axton, Estelle   25

"Baby Let's Play House"   7
bakelite   4
Bala, Iwan   109
"Ballad of Old Betsy, The"   43
Ballard, J. G.   164
Bangs, Lester   156

"Barbara Ann"   11
Bass   144
"Bat Out of Hell"   58
Beach Boys   2, 19, 26, 33–4, 41–2, 45, 48
Beatles   9, 42, *see also* individual song titles
   Beatlemania   160
Beethoven, Ludwig van   47
Benllech Beat Club   99
Bennett, William J.   148
Berry, Chuck   5–6, 27–8, 32, 104
Best Albums in the World   63–4
Best Anthems   63–4
Billboard   7, 11, 165
biracial pop   27, 29
Black Lives Matter   144
Bland, Bobby Blue   25
Blender   166
blues   67, 158, 168
The Blues Brothers   77
Blur   63
BodyRockers   57
"Bohemian Rhapsody"   1, 51
Bolan, Marc   160
Bond, James   164
Bonham, John   164
"Born to Be Wild"   58, 76–7, 105
branding   4
Brando, Marlon   114
Bravo   170 n.5
Brenston, Jackie   6, 28
bricolage   16, 23, 32
Brown, Michael   144
busking   128
Byd Bach   108
byd pop Cymraeg   99

"Cadillac Boogie"   28
"California Girls"   45, 47
"Cân I Gymry"   107
canonization   65

car
    clubs   17
    customization   2, 8, 15, 20, 26, 30, 41, 76
    design   3
    driverless   159
    eroticization   27, 34, 41, 43–4, 75
    female metaphor   42–3, 75
    gas   117
    gas stations   113, 153
    horns   121
    L plates   107
    as metaphor for womb   74
    as musical instrument   11
    objects inside   128
    production   20
    repair   130
    sales   11, 16, 40
    speakers   145
    as status symbols   9, 31, 72–4, 79, 102, 104, 110, 115, 134, 145
    stereo   8, 74
    symbiotic commodities argument   1–2, 71–2
    visual representation   100–1
    windows   144
    wrecks   105–6, 163
"Car Crash" (song)   158
Car Crash Culture (book)   159
car crashes   4, 18
    interpretations   155, 158–9, 162, 164–6
"Car Crazy Cutie"   44
car manufacturers and models
    AMC   1, 20
    BMW   73
    Buick   9
    Cadillac   7, 9, 32, 140
    Chevrolet   20, 75, 120, 122, 160
    Chrysler   20
    Citroen   16, 116
    Corvette   41, 75, 160
    Coupe-de-Ville   27
    Deuce Coupe   42
    Dodge   20, 120, 124, 130
    Fargo   120
    Fiat   73
    Ford   9, 16, 19, 28, 120–1, 122, 139
    General Motors   3
    Honda   43
    Hummer   9
    Impala   16
    International   120
    Jaguar   56
    Lambourghini   9
    Lincoln   7, 28
    Maserati   116
    Maybach   9
    Mercedes-Benz   9, 75, 77
    Oldsmobile   2, 6, 28
    Opel   116, 171 n.8
    Rolls Royce   9
    Skoda   9
    Stingray   42
    Studebaker   28
    Terraplane   41
    Thunderbird   42
    Vauxhall   171 n.8
    Volkswagen   6
"Cars"   2
Cars, the   10
"Car Wash"   2
Castle legal doctrine   150
Catatonia   99
celebrity   4, 31, 53, 155
Centre for Contemporary Cultural Studies (CCCS)   78, 86
charts   7, 11, 22, 27, 31, 111, 114, 165
Chemical Brothers, the   64
"Cherry Cherry Coupe"   43
Chess Records   6
child rearing   36
chivas, las   119–36
    bodywork   121–2, 133–4
    chivas rumberas   131
    objects inside   128
citizenship   147
Clarkson, Jeremy   53, 56
class   7, 16, 19–20, 31, 72, 167, *see also* social stratification
    middle class identity   146–7, 151
    Middle England   53
    working class identity   24–5, 82, 139, 142, 147, 153, 162–3
Cline, Patsy   165
Clinton, Bill   147
"Close to the Edit"   6
clothing   7–8, 18, 86, 114

clubbing 81, 119, 131–2, *see also* electronic dance music; Lapsed Clubber project; rave
Coen brothers 77
Cole, Nat King 28
collecting
records 26
communism 39
community 34, 85–91, 94, 120, 125
compilation albums 58, 62–5, 68
computer games 80
consumerism 2, 4, 8, 15, 20, 29, 33, 55, 65, 71, 156
Cool Cymru 102
Corden, James 1
Coughlin, Charles 25
counterculture 76, 84–5, 92
country music 7, 25–8, 165–6
countryside 84, 89, 92, 98, 106, 120–1, 125
Crash 164
Creamfields festival 81
creativity 46
Creem 163
criminality, *see also* juvenile delinquency
mark of criminality 147–8
The Crisis 149
Cronenberg, David 164
crossover music 24, 26–7, 29–31, *see also* biracial pop
cultural capital 145, 157
cultural fields 157
"Cwm Hiraeth" 98

"Daddy's Speeding" 159
DAF (group) 170 n.3
Dafis, Edward H. 100, 102
Dafydd, Fflur 108
"Dafydd Iwan Yn Y Glaw" 107
damaged life 162
dance 91, 119, 124, 132–3
Dark Side of the Moon 102
Datblygu 107–8
Dave (TV channel) 169
Davis, Jordan 137, 145, 147, 151–3
"Day Tripper" 9
"Dead Man's Curve" 158
Dean, James 4, 114, 159–61, 170 n.5

decades
1920s 15–18, 20–1, 139, 142, 147, 149
1930s 16–19, 21, 30, 32, 36, 41, 81
1940s 18, 19, 24, 79, 99
1950s 4–7, 9, 16, 19–26, 30, 33–7, 40, 67, 78–9, 104, 114–16, 127, 128, 129, 170
1960s 16–17, 21, 23, 25–7, 33–7, 39–42, 49, 56–7, 76, 81, 84, 86, 99, 101–2, 104–5, 107–8, 114, 118, 156, 170 n.5
1960s, ethics 118
1970s 2, 24, 26, 67, 78, 80, 86, 95, 98, 100–2, 104–8, 113, 114, 117, 126–8, 156, 166, 170 n.5
1980s 63–4, 76, 84, 89, 95, 107–8, 114, 116, 118, 128, 142, 148, 150, 156, 170 n.5
1990s 2, 53, 55, 57, 63, 81, 84, 89, 102, 131, 142, 148, 150, 156
2000s 105
Deep Purple 58
Depeche Mode 5
Depression, Great 34
Diana, *see* Spencer, Diana
Die Antwoord 3
Dior, Christian 115
disability 164–5
disco 101, 132
distance, perceptions of 97–8
DIY ethos 90, 112
Doherty, Pete 157
"Don't Stop Me Now" 51–2, 58–9, 62, 66, 69
Doors, the 75
doo-wop 4, 26
Downbeat 158
Dr Dre 2, 9, 148
"Drive" 10
drive-in theatres 5
"Drive My Car" 9–10
driving 135, 138–9, 149
drugs 83, 87–90, 93–4, 164
Dunn, Michael 137–8, 144–5, 147–53
"Dŵr" 109
Dylan, Bob 100

Earl, Harvey 3
Easy Rider 76–8
ecstasy, *see* MDMA

Einstürzende Neubauten 112, 170 n.3
eisteddfod 99, 105, 170 n.3
electronic dance music (EDM) 64, 80–1, 83, 96, *see also* clubbing; Lapsed Clubber project; rave
Eminem 9
Empower America 148
entitlement 149
environment 11, 33, 113, 117
ergonomics 11
everyday life 52, 69, 72, 93
experience economy 66

Fabares, Shelley 39
family
   inter-generational living 35
   nuclear 34–6, 115–16
   single living 36–8
fans 156–7, 160
   groupies 80
fantasy 46, 54, 61, 69
   epic drive 51–3, 56, 68
The Feminine Mystique 38
feminism 38
   patriarchy 9, 34, 44–5
festivals 65, 84, 96
Ffordd Newydd Eingl-Americanaidd Grêt O Fyw 100, 102–3
First World War 99
Fischer, Helene 170 n.3
Fitzgerald, Scott 33
Flash Cadillac and the Continental Kids 26
Fonda, Peter 77
food 5, 140
Ford, Henry 28
Freed, Alan 23
Freud, Sigmund 34, 38, 46, *see also* psychoanalysis
Friedan, Betty 38
friendship 90–1
Frith, Simon 72, 79, 80, 155
"Fun, Fun, Fun" 44
futurism 11–12

Gadael Lenin 106
Galwad Y Mynydd 98
gay culture, *see* homosexual culture

Gaynor, Gloria 8
gender 72–4, 80–2, *see also* masculinity; misogyny; sexism; sexual relations; women
   and car production 82
   and creativity 82
   inequality 82
   and music technology 81
German reconstruction 115–16
G-funk 52
Gilroy, Paul 76
The Girl on a Motorcycle 82
Glass, Phillip 12
Global Gathering festival 81
"God Only Knows" 46
Golden Earring 58
Gordy, Berry 10
Gore, Leslie 39
Gore, Tipper 148
Gorky's Zygotic Mynci 99, 102
Grease 6
Greater London Council 162
Green, Victor Hugo 146
The Green Book (book), *see Negro Motorist's Green Book; Travelguide*
The Green Book (film) 146
Guardian, the 82
gun control 151
Gunter, Arthur 7
Gurley Brown, Helen 38
Guy, John 145

halbstarke 114, 116, 170 n.4, 171 n.7
Haley, Bill 6, 26–8
Hammersmith Odeon 162
Hampton, Paul 158
"Heartaches" 165
"Heartache Spoken Here" 166
Hebdige, Dick 78
hechizo, el 129–30, 134
hedonism 40, 57–8, 77, 96, 113–15, 117, 160
"Help Me Rhonda" 45
Hen Ffordd Gymreig O Fyw 100–2
Herbie and the Heartbeats 26
heritage 136
"Hey Little Tomboy" 48
hiareth 97–8

hidden curriculum 81
Highway Star 58
highway system 3–4, 139, 143, 155
hip-hop 9, 11, 75–7, 80, 128, 137–8, 141, 147–8, 150, 167
    thug moniker 137–8, 148–9
hippies 116, 118
hitchhiking 97
Holiday Records 6
home 3, 23, 34–5, 37, 39–40, 42, 83, 89–91, 93, 95–7, 108, 150
homosexual culture 61
Hopper, Dennis 76
Hot Rod Gang 2
"Hot Rod Lincoln" 28
"Hot Rod Race" 28
hot rods 4, 17–19, 41
    lakebed racing 17–18, 20, 31
    street racing 17, 19
Hot Rods to Hell 160
Hutter, Ralph 11

"Ich will Spaß" 111–14, 116–18, 170 n.2
identity 63, 72, 83–5, 91–2, 118, 123–4, 131–2, 134, 168
"I Fall to Pieces" 165
"I Like The Way" 57
"Im Wagen vor mir" 111
independent music 51, 57, 63–5, 117
Independent on Sunday 163
individualism 66
infantilization 115, 117
interpretive repertoires 157
intimacy 86–8, 94, 101, 165
irony 117–18, 171 n.8
Iwan, Dafydd 100, 107
"I Will Survive" 8

Jameson, Frederic 109, 168
Jamiroquai 9
Jan and Dean 158
Jay-Z 9
jazz 141, 158
Jazz (album) 58
jazz funk 168
Jim Crow 138–41, 143, 146, 152, 153–4
"Johnny Angel" 39
The John Peel Show 107

Johnson, Lyndon 29
Johnson, Pete 28
Jones, Grace 158
Jones, Heather 98
Jones, Huw 109
Jones, Tony 170 n.5
joyriding 19
Jürgens, Udo 170 n.1
juvenile delinquency 2, 17–18, 160

Katzman, Sam 160
Kay, Jay 9
Kerouac, Jack 5, 33, 40
King, BB 25
kitsch 112
Kraftwerk 10–12, 111
Krautrock 10
Kylie, *see* Minogue, Kylie

La Chiva de Palo 126
Lady Diana, *see* Spencer, Diana
Laing, Dave 155
landscape 4, 98, 108–10, 122, 133, 143
Lapsed Clubber project 83, 169
Lashes, Lisa 80
The Late Late Show 1
Latin culture 8, 30, 119–36
Latin music genres
    bolero 127–8
    bullerengues 127
    carrilera 128
    corridos 127
    despecho 128
    guasca 128
    méringue 127
    papayeras 126
    parranda campesina 128
    porros 127
    salsa 127
    vallenato 126–8, 132
"Leader of the Pack" 79, 105
LeBlanc, Alyssa 153
Led Zeppellin 163
"Let Me Ride" 2
Levi-Strauss, Claude 16
Lewis, Saunders 99
Life magazine 19
lifestyle 18, 35–6, 54–5, 72

Liggins, Jimmy 28
liminality 85, 87, 89, 92, 95
listening 52, 61–2, 66, 69, 74, 90, 124, 138, 152
"Little Deuce Coupe" 2, 19, 42–3
Little Deuce Coupe (album) 42
"Little Honda" 43
"Little Red Corvette" 41, 75
live music 27, 66, 99, 100, 125–6, 128–9, 162
loudness 142, 144–5, 151, 153, 164
"Love Me Do" 10
"Low Rider" 2
low riding 30, 76

McLuhan, Marshall 8
Mad Max 162–4, 168
mainstream, musical 26, 31–2, 65, 81, 85, 112, 117
Malaria! (group) 170
Mallard, Robert 153
Malwod a Morgrug: Dan Warchae (album) 106
Manhattan Transfer 5
Marcus, Greil 24, 156
"Mari, Mari" EP 103, 105
Markus 111–12, 114, 116–18
Martha and the Vandellas 29
Martindale, Wink 7
masculinity 52, 55–6, 65, 73, 76–7, 79, 135, 139, 148, 159, 161, 163–4, 167, 169
  and banter 55, 57
  'cock rock' 80
  combustion masculinity 52, 55, 60–1
  crisis of 55
  hyper-masculinity 61, 148, 167
  lad culture 55–7
  myth of the warrior 164
mass production 32
materialism 7, 9–10, 79, 84
"Maybellene" (song) 27
MC Saizmundo 105, 108, 109
MDMA 93–4
"Me and My Chauffer Blues" (song) 2
Meatloaf 58

memento mori 159
memory 90, 109
Memphis Minnie 2
Memphis Recording Service 6
Men Behaving Badly 55
"Mercedes Benz" (song) 79
Mercury, Freddy 58, 61–2
Midler, Bette 75
Miller, George 163
Ministry of Sound label 63
Minogue, Kylie 12
misogyny 34, 44, 56
mobility 132, 139
modernity 3–4, 10–11, 15, 66–7, 155, 162
mods 78, 99
Mojo 161
Monroe, Marilyn 170 n.5
moral panic 29–30, 99, 142
Morely, Paul 12–13, 161
Morrison, Jim 162, *see also* Doors, the
motorcycles 43, 74, 77
  biker songs 105
  gangs 114
motoric beat 10
Motown 10, 29
MTV 148
music
  education 81
  history 83
  instruments 87, 112, 117, 150
  journalism 155–7, 168
Musicland studios 163
"Mynwent" 108–9
myth 7, 26, 29–30, 42, 73, 77, 93, 155, 158, 160, 164, 168, *see also* open road

National Association for the Advancement of Colored People (NAACP) 149
national identity 52, 57, 103, 109, 113, 131
  xenophobia 56
National Statistics Department (Colombia) 123
Nat King Cole Trio 28
The Negro Motorist's Green Book 146–7, 149–50
Nena 170 n.3

neoliberalism   65, 67, 81, 165
neon   5, 42, 102
Neue Deutsche Welle   111–12, 118, 170 n.3
nihilism   161
"Niwl Y Môr"   98
NME   161, 166
noise   6, 18, 56, 140–1, 153
Normal, the   2, 158
Northern Soul (film)   77
noson lawen   101
nostalgia   6, 11–12, 56, 97, 102
"Nowhere to Run"   29
Numan, Gary   2
NWA   148

"The Ocean"   163
"Olwen Dwy Olwyn"   105
Ono, Yoko   77
On the Road   33, 40, 77
'the open road'   51, 67–8, 76, 143, 145, 153–4, *see also* fantasy, epic drive
"Our Car Club"   42
Outkast   2

Parents Media Resource Center   148
participation   1, 20, 51, 62–3, 65–7, 69, 73, 79, 83, 85, 93, 95, 107, 124, 139
Patagonia (film)   106
peace movement   118
Peel, John   107
"Pentre Marw"   108
personal freedom   4–5, 33, 40, 54, 56, 68, 86, 104, 108, 110–11, 115, 117, 139–40, 162, 164, *see also* individualism; open road
Phillips, Sam   6
pilgrimage   77, 85
pill, the   9
"Pink Cadillac"   75
Pink Floyd   102
Plant, Robert   163
Plasmatics, the   162
playlists   2, 51–2, 65
politeness   151–2
politics
   great society doctrine   29
   populism   53
   reactionary   53–5
   respectability politics   147, 151
   Thatcherism   84, 91
pop   111
Pop Music and the Press   156
popular music studies   155
pornography   165
post-punk   111
post-war affluence   34
Presence   163
Presley, Elvis   3–4, 7, 24–5, 27, 80, 103, 161, 170 n.5
Prince   41, 74
privacy   40, 67, 150, 165
Privilege   160
Prodigy, the   64
psychoanalysis   36, 37, 46, *see also* Freud, Sigmund
   compulsion   46
   condensation   47
   displacement   47
   dreams   48
   fetishism   34, 82, 164
   sublimation   46
   superego   47
   symbols   47
   transformation   47
public sphere   139, 142, 145
public transport   95, 128
punk   80, 112, 116, 118

Quadrophenia   78
Queen   51, 58, 61, 69

race   8, 24, 31, 75, *see also* African Americans; crossover music; racism; radio; whiteness
racism   138–41, 143–4, 147, 149, 152, *see also* segregation; whiteness
"Radar Love"   58
radio   5, 15, 21, 29, 31, 52, 74, 124, 127–8, 141, 145
   African American   22–5, 31
   audience   22–3
   female DJs   74
   formats   5, 10, 22, 26–7, 29, 31
   history   21
   portable   21–2, 127

recorded music as content   23
stations expansion   24
stations ownership   31
radio stations
   Radio Cymru   107
   WDIA   24–6
   WINS   23
   WJR   24–5
R&B   6, 26–8, 101
rave   84, 93–4
   Castlemorton   84–5
   chillout   85
   clothing   86
   Criminal Justice Bill   85
   cultural history   84
   designated drivers   93
   drugs   87–90, 93
   journey from   92–4
   journey to   87–9
   PLUR ethos   84
Reagan, Ronald   147–8
Rebel without a Cause   76
Redbook   37–8
Religion
   Calvinism   7
   Catholic imagery   122
   Christian values   116
   Protestant work ethic   118
   spirituality   85–6, 92, 166–8
resistance   84, 90, 115, 147–51, 154, 156
Restrepo, Luciano   120
"Rhaid Yw Eu Tynnu I Lawr"   107
Richards, George A.   25
ritual   1, 8, 55, 85–8, 95
rock   65, 99, 101–3, 105, 160, 163–4, 170 n.6
   classic   58
   glam   160
   hard   75
   heavy metal   77
   indie   51, 57, 63, 65
   prog   57
   psychedelic   102
   Southern   56
Rock & Roll Hall of Fame   11
"Rock around the Clock"   26
rockers   99

"Rocket 88"   2, 28
"Rocket 88 Boogie"   28
Rock 'n' roll   19, 23, 26, 29–32, 79, 104, 110–11, 141
Rock 'n' roll America   3
Rock's Back Pages   158
Rolling Stones, the   75
Rosenberger, Marianne   170 n.1
Rouer, Rhonda   147
"Route 66"   28
Royce, Rose   2
Rubber Soul   10
Russolo, Luigi   6
Ryan, Charlie   28

S4C TV channel   107
Sain record label   100–1, 103
Salt, John   106
schlager   114, 170
Schott, Karl Heinz   111
Second World War   17, 19–20, 24, 34, 36–7, 72
The Secret Life of Plants   166
Seeger, Pete   100
segregation   138, 140–3, 145, 149
Seindorf   105
sex   164
Sex and the Single Girl   38
sexism   9, 76
   and music journalism   157
   in press coverage   157
sexual liberation   5
sexual relations   35–6, 38–40, 42, 113,
   see also gender; homosexual culture
   dating   5
   heteronormativity   65
   marriage   35–6, 38
sexual repression   3, 33, 36, 46
Shakur, Tupac   148
Shangri-Las   79, 105
Shibley, Arkie   28
"Siarabang"   103–5, 107
Sinatra, Nancy   40
Skunk Anansie   63
Skyfall   164
Smith, Patti   80
Smiths, the   63
Snoop Dogg   9

social stratification 7–8, 108, 115, 119, 134, 138–40, 142, 146–7, 153, 163, *see also* class
sones 127
Songs in the Key of Life 166
songwriting 2, 9, 48, 58–62, 74, 100, 107
soul 167
soundscape 75, 145, 150
sound studies 11
sound systems 90, 131
space
   public 9, 85, 113–16, 138–40, 142–6, 149–51, 153, 165
   safe 84, 91
spectacle 8, 18, 56, 61, 86, 98, 163
Spector, Phil 79–80
speed 4–5, 11, 20, 52, 53–4, 56, 60, 73, 104, 113, 117, 140, 162
speeding 17, 116, 140, 159
Spencer, Diana 159, 165
Spinal Tap, see *This Is Spinal Tap*
Springsteen, Bruce 75
"Stand Your Ground" legal doctrine 150–2
Stardust 160
Stax 25
Steinbeck, John 33
Steppenwolf 58, 76, 98, 105
Stevens, Mike 99–100
Stewart, Jim 25
Stig 53–4
Stoicism 166
Stornes, Tommie 145
Stortz, Todd 22
Street Sounds label 63
Strolla, Cory 144, 150–2
"Studebaker March" 28
Styrene, Poly 80
subcultures 71, 78, 83–4, 86, 114, 118, 145–6, 149, 152–3, 171 n.7
suburbs 3–4, 25, 33–4, 40, 74, 103, 141–2, 150, 155
   Levittown 3, 10
Suede (group) 159
suicide 5, 18, 160, *see also* teenicide
Sunday Times, the 54
Sundown towns 143
Super Furry Animals 102
SUV (car) 67, 137, 144–5

swearing 151–2
symbolism 120, *see also* psychoanalysis

tactical affirmation 111, 118
taste, *see* cultural capital; lifestyle
teenagers 5, 18, 23, 29, 40, 104, 115, 137, 141, 142, 144, 150, 152, 159–60, *see also* tweenagers
teenicide 18
"Terraplane Blues" 41
That'll Be the Day 160
Thelma & Louise 78
"These Boots are Made for Walkin'" 39
This Is Spinal Tap 77
Thomas, Carla 25
Thomas, Dylan 98
Thomas, Rufus 25
Thompson, Tevin 144
"Ticket to Ride" 10
time 92, 95
Tisnés, Robert 121
Tony ac Aloma 170 n.5
Top Gear 51–4, 56–7, 61–3, 68–9, 73
Toto 51
tourism 131
tradition 134, *see also* ritual
"Trampled Underfoot" 163
transformation 34
transgression 85, 88–90, 107, 115, 141, 151, *see also* criminality
Travelguide 146, 150
Travolta, John 6
T. Rex 161
tribes 88
Trio (group) 170 n.3
Troupe, Bobby 5, 28
trust 2, 87–8, 90, 93, 95
Tubman, Harriet 146
tweenagers 160
"Two Dope Boyz (in a Cadillac)" 2
"Two Hour Honeymoon" 158
"Twristiaid Yn Y Dre" 108
"Tynged Yr Iaith" 99

Underworld (group) 64
United Nations Population Fund 123
Unsafe at Any Speed 162
Up the Junction 78

urbanization 124, 128
utopianism 112, 118

V8 rocket 6
Valente, Caterina 170 n.1
vanishing mediator 168
Viking Press 5
Vincent, Gene 2
Virgin Records 63, 65
Virillio, Paul 11
Vosper, Sidney Curnow 98

War (group) 2
"Warm Leatherette" 2, 158
Waters, Muddy 158
Wayne's World 1, 61
well-being 37, 85
Welsh Language Society 99, 103, 106–7, 169
Welsh League of Youth 103
Wendler, Michael 170 n.1
whiteness 55, 75
    white supremacy 138–9, 142, 146, 149, 153–4
    white vigilantism 138, 152
"Whittier Boulevard" 7
Who, the 78
Williams, Farell 9
Williams, Kyffin 98
Wilson, Carl 45
Wilson, Richard 98
Winehouse, Amy 157

Wittgenstein, Ludwig 12
WJR: One of a Kind 25
Wolfman Jack 21, 23–4, 142, 150
women, *see also* feminism; gender
    as DJs 80–1
    as drivers 10, 44, 73, 81
    female labour 37, 73–4
    female liberation 9–10, 12–13, 34, 38, 42, 44, 49, 52, 80
    motherhood 38
    in music production 79
    objectification 44–8, 67, 77
    pregnancy 36
    Presidential Commission on the Status of Women 39
Wonder, Stevie 166–8
Wyn, Eurig 107

Y Chwyldro 107
Y Cymro newspaper 101
Y Mellt 103–5, 107
youth 108, 115, 133, 160, 171 n.7
youth culture 16–17, 21, 27, 36, 71, 80, 84–5, 90, 104, 114, 116, 159
Y Tarddiad 107

ZDF (TV channel) 171 n.6
ZDF-Hitparade 114
Zef Recordz 3
Zef style 3
Zevon, Warren 166
ZZ Top 2, 98

www.ingramcontent.com/pod-product-compliance
Lightning Source LLC
Chambersburg PA
CBHW052043300426
44117CB00012B/1946